Straight Talk
about American Education

Theodore M. Black

STRAIGHT

TALK

ABOUT

124375

AMERICAN

EDUCATION

Harcourt Brace Jovanovich, Publishers

New York and London

Requests for permission to make copies
of any part of the work should be mailed to:
Permissions, Harcourt Brace Jovanovich, Publishers,
757 Third Avenue, New York, N.Y. 10017.

Library of Congress Cataloging in Publication Data

Black, Theodore M. (Theodore Michael), 1919-
Straight talk about American education.

1. Education—United States.   I. Title.
LA209.2.B54   370′.973   81-48513
ISBN 0-15-185584-6   AACR2

Printed in the United States of America

First edition

B C D E

This book is lovingly dedicated
to
BARBARA, my patient and understanding wife,
and to
BEV, DOT, WALT and MIKE, our children,
who grew quietly and nicely
from kids to young adults
during those dozen years
when I was in Albany or Washington
or somewhere else,
working for everyone's children
and writing this book
about what I learned . . .

Hey, Gang!
Dad's back!

Contents

Acknowledgments

There are many people who deserve to be thanked by name, as contributors to the preparation of this book as well as to the education of its author. Space limitations prevent my doing so; I must restrict myself to naming but a few. I ask all others for their forgiveness; I am grateful to them.

Those who had nothing to do with writing this book but lots to do with my being able to write it include three fellows named Joe: Assemblyman Joe Margiotta of Nassau County, New York, who enabled me to become a Regent; Chancellor Joe McGovern, who taught me by example and patient advice how to be a leader; and Commissioner Joe Nyquist, who supervised my basic training in the nuts and bolts of education. To them, I add those Regents who served with me, not only for their confidence in twice unanimously electing me their Chancellor, but for adding (each in his or her own way) to my knowledge of the art and science of learning—and of people.

Regents Counsel Bob Stone cheerfully answered hundreds of my questions about constitutional law and court decisions. Faithful, capable Bill Carr, Regents' Secretary and my good right arm, gave of his personal time to help with my research, as did his competent aides, Ruth Weinberg and Judy Winslow. My secretary, Anne McCrory, has kept things sorted out and moving nicely. My wife, Barbara, has provided me with frank and helpful citizen-parent reactions to my ideas. My editor, Peter Jovanovich, has added polish and strength. To all of them, and to my publisher, Bill Jovanovich, who shared my experience on the Board of Regents, I am deeply grateful.

Sands Point, New York   Theodore M. Black
1982

Preface

WHAT kind of book is this? It is not a memoir. It is not a textbook. It is not a reference work. Nor is it a handbook for professional educators, many of whom, in the privacy of their own thoughts as citizens and parents, will concur with more of what is in this book than they will admit publicly.

This book gives my personal observations of more than a decade of daily involvement in almost every facet of American education, first as a member and for five years as Chancellor of New York State's Board of Regents. This unique body, founded in 1784, has greater authority over all education—elementary, secondary, collegiate, graduate, and all professional save law—than any other such governing board in the United States.

I have attempted to salt my observations with a pinch of logic, a dash of common sense and good humor, a further seasoning of occasional reflections upon history, and a final flavoring of my own values and viewpoints. The result, I hope, is a set of reasonable conclusions about what's right—and what's wrong—with the way we're teaching our young people, and some suggestions as to how we might do it better.

When I announced my retirement from the Chancellorship of the Board of Regents of the State of New York, I said: "Above all, I want to write. Having been asked to do a book about education, I have agreed—on condition that it not be one of those weighty tomes, encrusted with distracting footnotes and written in obscure, contrived educationese that few people can or even want to understand, destined to feed the silverfish on some high shelf until it crumbles to dust. My book will be as readable as I can make it. In it, I will attempt to show where we are in education, how we got there, where we should be headed, and how we can reach our destination. Leaving the Board of Regents will not only give me time to write my book but the freedom to 'tell it as it is' without pussyfooting or pulling punches."

Here is the book.

Straight Talk
about American Education

1.

Will We Ever Find Our Holy Grail?

No — but We Must Never Stop Searching for It

EVERY STUDENT of medieval history and English literature knows that the Holy Grail was the cup from which Jesus Christ and his apostles drank at the Last Supper.

Legend has it that Joseph of Arimathea, one of the earliest Christians, took the Grail to England, where it was lost. King Arthur selected his three most impeccable knights—Bors, Galahad, and Perceval—to locate the Grail, which they did, only to watch it rise to heaven. According to legend, no one has seen the Holy Grail since.

Fact or fiction, or a bit of both, the story of the quest for the Holy Grail is rich with symbolism. It is an allegory of man's eternal search for perfection.

Perfection, we know, can never be attained by mere humans. But that is no reason—no reason at all—for humans not to attempt to gain perfection. Though we will never be perfect, and we know it, we know also that *by seeking perfection we gain excellence*. And excellence *is* within human grasp.

What's right or what's wrong with American education today is the story of how we set our sights upon perfection and tried to pursue the reachable goal of excellence. It is the story of our times . . . what they and we have done to and with the best educational system ever conceived and built. It is a story with many lessons for today and tomorrow.

3

The Age of the Slob

In June 1972, the New York State Board of Regents was debating a staff proposal to eliminate the 107-year-old Regents' examinations, uniform statewide tests at the secondary level in various disciplines. Although then the most junior Regent, I felt strongly enough about what I considered a frontal attack upon the pursuit of excellence to speak in support of the Regents' exams.

I will not quote myself to excess in this book, but what I said at Albany on June 23, 1972, expresses in concrete terms, addressed to a specific issue, a response to the challenges then being mounted against the maintenance of standards of quality in academic performance—that is, against excellence in education:

"Through the medium of the Regents' exams, we have for more than a century provided objective yardsticks to measure educational accomplishment, free from the dangers of individually subjective misjudgment and indoctrination.

"But by far the most important contribution of the Regents' exams is that through them we offer to each student taking certain subjects in our secondary schools a set of uniform standards of academic achievement, a set of new challenges, a set of interim goals which we on this Board must fervently hope will help to develop in these young people a lifelong urge to seek excellence in all of their endeavors.

"Where there is no evaluation of performance, there can be no meaningful goals—and where there are no goals, there can be no values. The concept of excellence is thus too often doomed to be smothered in a soggy blanket of mediocrity.

"Excellence has not had an easy time of it lately.

"At least in part because of our negligence and permissiveness, we find ourselves living in what I am compelled to label the Age of the Slob . . . a time when a slothful, disinterested shoddiness in the performance of one's tasks . . . seems to be the order of the day.

"One fears that the pursuit of excellence is well on its way to join the quest for the Holy Grail as a matter of only historical and literary interest. One wonders whether we ought, in all honesty, to change the motto of our State from 'Excelsior'—'Go higher, do better'—to whatever the Latin phrase may be for 'Who cares?' or 'Whatever turns you on.'

"Charged as we are with the educational development and to that extent the intellectual growth of the young people of the State of New York, this is hardly the moment for us on this Board to lower yet another flag or surrender yet another outpost in our continuing struggle in defense of excellence. Perhaps we are fighting a rear-guard action, but we owe it to the present and future citizens of New York to hold out. Who knows? The tide may turn."

Perhaps the tide *did* turn that day. By a vote of twelve to three, the Board decided to retain the Regents' examinations. Since then, they have added other statewide tests with the same objective in mind: the achievement of educational excellence.

But the struggle for excellence has not been easy—and it is far from over.

Who Doesn't Want Educational Excellence?

That sounds like a stupid question and, put in those terms, it commands a single answer. *Nobody* opposes excellence.

That's quite true, but the problem is that a good many folks involved in education accord priority to other things, some of which block the road to excellence and others of which actually depress educational quality—always in the name of some good cause or high-sounding theory.

Those who impact negatively upon our educational processes (for whatever reasons or however innocently) will howl like banshees when accused, but accused they must be, because they are guilty of a capital crime against the quality of life in America: the slow killing of our once-great educational system.

It is the primary purpose of this book to identify those who help the cause of better education and those who don't, to explain why and how they either focus upon excellence or divert us from it, and to suggest ways to restore American education to its former glory . . . and beyond.

The essential requirement is this: Whether we are planning a policy, procedure, or program or whether we are evaluating one already in existence, we must—I repeat, must—determine not only how it will or does achieve its stated ends but also *how it impacts upon educational excellence.* Our first question must be this: Does it promote excellence or retard it? All other considerations are secondary.

We will never find our Holy Grail—the cup of educational perfection—but we must never stop searching for it.

2.

The State of Education Today

Have We Snatched Defeat from the Jaws of Victory?

TO FIND OUT where we're going, and how to get there, we must first establish where we are.

Author-philosopher Jacques Barzun, writing in the *New York Review of Books* (November 1981), calls attention to the current problems of our schools and colleges:

"The once proud and efficient public school system of the United States—especially its unique free high school for all—has turned into a wasteland where violence and vice share the time with ignorance and idleness, besides serving as a battleground for vested interests, social, political and economic.

"The new product of that debased system, the functional illiterate, is numbered in millions, while various forms of deceit have become accepted as inevitable—'social promotion' or passing incompetents to the next grade to save face; 'graduating' from 'high school' with eighth-grade reading ability; 'equivalence of credits' or photography as good as physics; 'certificates of achievement' for those who fail the 'minimum competency' test; and most lately, 'bilingual education,' by which the rudiments are supposedly taught in over ninety languages other than English. The old plan and purpose of teaching the young what they truly need to know survives only in the private sector, itself hard-pressed and shrinking in size.

"Meanwhile, colleges and universities have undergone a comparable devastation. . . . The flood of students [after World War II] caused many once modest local colleges and deplorable teachers' colleges to suddenly dub themselves universities and attempt what they were not fit for. State university systems threw out branches in cities already well provided with private, municipal, or denominational institutions; . . . The purpose and manner of higher education were left behind."

Rugged words, these—adding up to a searing indictment of our whole educational system.

My friend Chester E. (Checker) Finn, Jr., of Vanderbilt University, a former teacher and author of several books on education, pinpoints our present situation as he sees it in "A Call for Quality Education," written for *Time*'s American Renewal series in March 1981:

"American education today is the object of nationwide discontent, the source of malaise tinged with frustration, dashed hopes and unrealized expectations. Parents are dismayed by reports of pushers hustling drugs in high school washrooms. They are angry when children are failed by teachers who never took the trouble to correct their papers. Literacy is in decline in one state after another. Students seek admission to college but cannot write a coherent letter of application. Others leave vocational schools unable to read a metric scale. Young people are graduated from high school unfamiliar with the rudiments of American history and unacquainted with concepts fundamental to the common heritage of Western man. School administrators and teachers founder in coils of federal red tape. In our schools, values are rarely stressed. Standards are in decline. The measurement of achievement is neglected—or denounced.

"To say that American education is in trouble is a time-worn commonplace. But unless and until we can agree that the future of America, the betterment of society and the security and survival of generations to come are directly and inseparably related to what and how well we teach our children—and how well they learn—we will continue to pursue a course fraught with peril."

Amen. Our problems are very real, and we have no one to blame but ourselves. We've allowed them to develop; we've even contributed to them. That being so, we should be able and willing and ready to understand and admit what we're doing wrong, to take whatever steps are necessary (however painful and unpopular they may be) to correct the situation, and to do so without delay. As Finn reminds us: "The United States cannot risk passing through another decade with its elementary and secondary education system in disrepair," to which I will add our higher-education institutions, only slightly more trouble-free than our schools and the source of some of our schools' difficulties.

America's schools and colleges were not always in such worrisome shape. What happened?

Writing in *Commentary* (March 1981), Dr. Joseph Adelson, professor of psychology at the University of Michigan, offers a perceptive answer. He first analyzes the euphoria which characterized America's schools during the post-World War II years of growth: "Education came to be seen as a sort of universal solvent for the problems of the polity. The utopian tendencies in the American mind were to some large degree invested in the schools, in the notion of perfectibility through learning. . . . I think it is fair to say that through most of the 1950s the authority of the schools rested upon a sense of inner confidence—they believed in themselves because we believed in them. . . ."

Adelson notes that the tremendous growth of the school-age population, coupled with the accelerated consolidation of public-school districts (shrinking the total of 127,000 in 1932 to about 16,000 by December 1980), increased the size of school systems and forced a change "from traditional modes of authority—that is, direct and personal—to legal and contractual modes, in which the emphasis is placed upon conformity to rules and legal codes." The result was diminished educational authority. Says Adelson, ". . . forces and ideologies both extrinsic and alien to the schools and to education—in this case, the courts and the adversarial spirit—have begun to penetrate the practice of education in America, not only with regard to discipline, but in other realms of education as well."

We will return to Dr. Adelson's specific comments upon the intervention of courts and bureaucracies into education as we deal with that influence later. At this point, however, it is important for us to hear his conclusions about the schools' "great fall" from their former place in American life:

". . . more than any other institution in American society, the schools have become an arena for the struggle between the values of traditionalism and of modernity. Among the values of traditionalism are: merit, accomplishment, competition and success; self-restraint, self-discipline and the postponement of gratification; the stability of the family; and a belief in certain moral universals. The modernist ethos scorns the pursuit of success; is egalitarian and redistributionist in emphasis; tolerates or encourages sensual gratification; values self-expression as against self-restraint; accepts alternative or deviant forms of the family; and emphasizes ethical relativism. . . . In a morally unified and harmonious era, the schools can serve the public intention readily. In an era marked by multiplicity of aims, or by competing aims, the schools tend to become ambivalent, or confused, or inhibited—often all three at once."

That struggle continues and the schools continue to suffer, as do their clients, the children. While modernists contend that their ideas for education have not yet been fully tested, and that post hoc, ergo propter hoc (after that, therefore because of that) is not a fair way to judge, the fact remains that as and where modernism has nudged out traditionalism as the governing philosophy of education, *the quality of education has suffered.* And why should we have expected otherwise? The modernist credo is nothing less than an invitation to mediocrity, in the name of equality.

What's Wrong?

What's wrong with American education today? A familiar question because it has been asked so often for so long. For the 1980s, Checker Finn's diagnosis provides a start. It would take an entire book just to spell out all of our problems, without essaying answers. Any attempt to compile a catalog of education's troubles runs a serious risk of being incomplete, as new crises arise while we grapple with those confronting us.

Nevertheless, we must begin somewhere, somehow. I will try to point up here, at the outset, what I consider some of the most serious *general* impediments to educational excellence; in later pages I will cite specifics and offer solutions. Those who may disagree should be ready with solutions of their own, for the impediments are there and will not go away. As Eldridge Cleaver once remarked: "If you're not part of the solution, you're part of the problem."

The Decline of Basic Competencies

In the learning process, the ability to *read* intelligently, to *write* and *speak* intelligibly, and to *figure* are fundamentals without which the grasp of other disciplines is extremely difficult. Reading and 'Riting and 'Rithmetic, the much-maligned three R's (which I have rechristened for our sophisticated age as Comprehension, Communication, and Calculation, the three C's), are essential to education in all subjects and at all levels. *We have neglected these fundamentals.*

To correct this error, the currently popular "back-to-basics" movement asks that we devote more time and effort to the development of skills in reading, writing, and mathematics—which in turn should guarantee that students improve their understanding of other vital subjects, such as the sciences, literature, history, and the arts. Back-to-basics does *not* mean that we downgrade these other subjects; it means that we enable pupils to deal with them more intelligently. Each child has only so many hours and so many weeks in school each year. To stress the fundamentals properly, we must scrap the time-wasting, gimmicky electives— the "frills"—that sneaked into the curriculum during the trendy sixties and seventies. That is the message of the back-to-basics folks, and I suggest that we listen—knowing, as we do, that what we've allowed to happen in the last two decades hasn't worked.

The Endless Chain

In one sense, education is like an endless chain. When one link is dangerously weakened, the strength and usefulness of the whole chain is threatened. When children are not sufficiently trained in the three essential disciplines during the elementary years, they will have difficulty handling secondary-school work. Whether they move on to careers or to college, this lack will be troublesome to them and to those who rely upon them. The competitive disadvantage of an undereducated young person entering the job market is painfully obvious. At college, more and more time and money and teacher talent are being spent upon *remediation*—bringing incoming students up to the point at which they can master college-level subjects, a job which the schools should have done, but didn't. Time spent on remediation is time taken from other courses, and the individual's college work suffers. Remediation cannot compensate for all the shortcomings which developed in the early years and were compounded by lax practices in college; many college graduates still will not have an adequate grasp of the basics. *And some of these will go on to teach.*

At that point, the chain has completed a full circle. One-time pupils whose training in the fundamental disciplines was neglected or poorly conducted in their elementary years (or anywhere along the road) now must tackle the job of instructing another generation of youngsters in what they themselves never mastered. The twenty-one-year-olds who are handed education degrees in the 1980s are the bright-eyed kids who entered first grade in the sixties when educational faddism was at its worst.

No Effort + No Accountability = No Results

Where once the schools and colleges placed a premium upon effort and encouraged it by rewards and penalties, both now adopt a carefree attitude toward academic discipline. As we will see later, grading and promotion policy has become too loose and flexible. A student quickly discerns that not much effort is needed to get by; if everyone but the very worst will pass and be promoted and receive a diploma, why knock yourself out?

Competition was once an effective promoter of maximum effort. I considered a 96 unsatisfactory if my high-school classmate, Bill Robinson, got a 98; we were both unhappy if the smartest kid in the class, John

Sherwood, got 100 (that was the usual order of finish). Today, liberal psychologists maintain that qualitative comparisons may be unfair or even traumatic for those who don't finish on top. For numerical or alphabetic grades, many colleges substituted "pass/fail" in the sixties and seventies, and many schools adopted "satisfactory," "unsatisfactory," or such novel categories as "needs help." The kind of help many students need most is some teacher-supplied incentive, competitive or otherwise, to encourage them to do what they are capable of doing.

One stumbling block, which I will also deal with later, is that *pupil effort must be accompanied by teacher effort.* If a student is assigned homework or after-school projects to expand his knowledge of a subject, the assigning teacher must evaluate the student's work or the assignment will mean less than nothing to the student. Teacher disinterest, real or presumed, can be a wet blanket dropped over student motivation.

Are today's teachers putting out as much effort as yesterday's? As a general rule, and always allowing for exceptionally dedicated individuals, I am afraid they are not.

In recent years, teachers as a group have concluded that their interests would be better served if entrusted to a labor union than by a continued reliance upon their traditional status in society and upon state and local regulations. The shift from professionalism to unionism made good sense to teachers. Technicians were paid more than teachers; in 1980 the average plumber earned 10 percent more than the average teacher.

Although I do not begrudge teachers their union affiliation, the substitution of union-contract work rules for the traditional acceptance of assigned duties has resulted in *decreased* teacher productivity. As a consequence, the efforts required of students tend to stress those exercises on which the teacher expends minimal effort. For example, essay-type questions which require time-consuming reading and grading by the teacher have often been abandoned in favor of multiple-choice and true-false check-the-box questions which can be machine-graded. Extra help for struggling students is also limited. I will deal with the teacher-student relationship later; suffice it to say here that *the quality of education has suffered because less effort is asked of and expended by teachers and pupils alike.*

Testing's Troubles

Compounding the problem is the modernist rejection of the idea of accountability for the quality of educational services. I will talk further about testing, but in considering the state of education today it is worth mentioning now.

When the quality of education improves, those responsible for it are happy to have evidence of that improvement to display. When quality slides, the reverse is true. Recent ominous declines in scores on standardized tests like the Scholastic Aptitude Tests (SATs) and the College Entrance Examinations have produced not only complaints from parents and taxpayers about poor results but also gripes from the educational community about the tests themselves, and even the idea of testing. Exams that would be flaunted like banners if their results showed a rise in scholarship levels are denounced when they fall off; demands mount for the banning of standardized testing. We are told the tests are "unfair." How so? Because the kids whose scores were substandard should not be stigmatized for "the failures of their teachers" . . . because school boards and faculties should not be faulted for poor results, in light of uncontrollable factors impeding the educational process . . . because certain groups of youngsters come from disadvantaged families and therefore should not be criticized if they fail.

It always seems to be the tests themselves which are condemned, not the root causes of the substandard achievement they reveal. Everyone flails about, furiously damning the tests and attempting to fix the blame for unsatisfactory results on anyone and anything other than themselves and their methods, while what they should be doing is analyzing test results—digging out, identifying, and eliminating the very real deterrents to academic excellence which might not have been discovered without the tests.

Nobody enjoys being tested and found wanting. An end to testing would serve as a "Linus blanket" for the teaching profession's weaker practitioners, by removing the only objective measuring rod whereby educational achievement may be evaluated.

John V. Fels, of Phoenix, Arizona, a former school board member, took an irreverent approach to the question in a letter to the *Wall Street Journal* (October 7, 1981). Commenting upon a reader's statement that "to evaluate teachers simply on the basis of students' test scores . . . seriously misunderstands what good teaching is," Fels remarked:

"To get the real flavor of this, try imagining a major league manager saying, 'Evaluating a hitter on the basis of his batting average or a pitcher on his won-lost record and earned-run average seriously misunderstands what good baseball is.' . . .

"If educators (and school board members who think like educators) were running Ford Motor Co. they would still be making Edsels, avowing triumphantly that the assembly line people were engaged in a meaningful and relevant work experience and that suggestions the Edsel was a lemon represented a demonstration of that most heinous of crimes, insensitivity."

Student achievement is certainly not the only criterion by which teachers should be evaluated, but it is an important one—and one that cannot be disregarded.

When teachers reduce their own efforts and demand less effort from their pupils, and when the schools are no longer held accountable for their performance, the outcome is preordained: *a loss of educational quality.*

Have We Asked the Schools to Do Too Much?

In a sense, our schools are the victims of their own success. Universal public confidence in education after World War II led us to ask the schools to resolve all the problems of society at the preadult level.

Finn points out that we expect the schools "... to forge good citizens, to feed hungry youngsters, to compensate for disadvantages in individual family backgrounds and overcome centuries-old prejudices, to instill values that perhaps not all hold sacred, to discipline the unruly and buttress the psyches of the unstable, to inculcate an appreciation of the arts, to transmit our common culture while preserving each of its diverse elements, to confer equality on youngsters with physical or mental handicaps and to exalt the life of the mind in the eyes of adolescents whose outside activities are anything but exalted and whose bodies are ablaze with nonintellectual urgings.

"All these things and more we ask of our schools. We should not be surprised that they cannot do all of them and we should be grateful that they do so much."

Adelson's analysis adds another dimension to the overburden we've placed upon our schools, that of the philosophical and practical divergence between parents and their children's educators:

"In the postwar period, the schools were to do everything at once. They were to help us beat the Russians into space; they were then to liberate poor and minority youngsters from the heritage of slavery and oppression; they were shortly thereafter to help middle-class children free themselves from their bourgeois constraints; and then someone noticed that the SAT scores had plummeted, and so they were to fix that, too.

"It is now fairly clear that the schools took on too much, and by doing so without sufficient caution or demurral, they were implicitly promising more than they could fulfill. Furthermore, what the schools had accepted for their agenda was not necessarily responsive to the interests and values of the ordinary families they were serving.

"... the schools were being persuaded by our governing elites—the universities, the foundations and the mass media—to accept the claims of the modernist spirit. In pressing these claims upon the schools—as always, in the name of progress—these elites were in fact helping to separate school from family."

Adelson's words remind us that the real elitism of our time is not insistence upon excellence (which is regularly panned as elitist by liberal pundits) but rather the assumption by the Establishment (the more liberally oriented leaders of our society) that their own intellectual superiority and "progressive" orientation entitles them to displace the judgment and the standards of the American public by substituting their own sets of values, often quite different from and at odds with traditional criteria for quality in education.

There is a further point in Adelson's remarks. Parents were once expected to lend a hand in the education of their children, not only by backing up the schools in disciplinary matters but by enforcing proper after-school study habits and, when asked, giving their kids guidance on their academic subjects. All that came to an end under the modernist dispensation; parents were invited to keep out of the educational process, thank you, because school professionals could handle things quite nicely without "outside interference." Parental criticism, however calmly and logically expressed, was dismissed as "meddling."

Education's success had gone to education's head. Success often breeds arrogance, and arrogance usually breeds foolish overconfidence. Those schools which discouraged parent cooperation and disregarded parent concerns found themselves losing their most loyal and effective supporters. Adelson remarks: "That the assault on traditional education was a struggle about values did not escape the attention of the ordinary citizen, who quickly came to believe that his children's schools were becoming trendy in curriculum, gimmicky in methods, lax about standards and confused about purposes. He came to feel that the schools were abandoning his interests, were devoted to ideals he found alien, and were doing a poor job of teaching besides. Accordingly, he began to withdraw both emotional and financial support from the schools."

Today, when education needs all the friends it can muster, its once-solid base of support in the public-school sector has been seriously eroded; in Adelson's words, "One sees little of that profound allegiance to the idea of public schooling that marked an earlier generation."

To contend that the public schools are as good as they ever were is not the answer; too many parents simply refuse to believe it, and the facts generally support their skepticism. Nor is it helpful to denounce the alternative independent schools as elitist or divisive or snobbish; again, the facts attest to the good quality of education in the nonpublic sector.

If the public schools and their principal proponents keep on stonewalling, refusing to concede that they are in trouble and need help, they will continue to slide in public esteem. If, on the other hand, they concede their errors and renounce them, taking positive steps to restore standards, principles, and practices which have been allowed to atrophy, they will recapture public confidence and support.

It is as simple as that.

"Publish or Perish" Hasn't Helped

Every professional educator knows what "publish or perish" means. Personal advancement in academia has been largely a matter of credentials; one can move ahead only if one has acquired the proper degrees, which vary in status and acceptability. For example, the doctorate in philosophy (Ph.D.) is much more sought after than the doctorate in education (Ed.D.), apparently because the Ph.D. is older and has always been highest rated for those in education; it stresses research, while the Ed.D. emphasizes instruction. Schoolteachers spend their nights and summers acquiring masters' degrees which entitle them to higher pay after a set period of field experience. College faculty members go for the doctor's degree, which requires a scholarly thesis—and from there on, moving ahead in the ranks from instructor to assistant professor to associate professor to full professor requires that an ambitious pedagogue's writings be displayed in print as often as possible (presumably indicating someone else's assessment of his excellence). Hence, "publish or perish."

But what does an aspiring professor of education write about? He or she must come up with something new and different. A paper, article, or book which simply reiterates an existing principle or endorses a technique already in use is not likely to make a big splash in the educational pool. Innovation becomes a must. It has been said that innovation for its own sake is more prevalent in education than in any other field of endeavor.

If, however, things are working well, what changes can one suggest? A country sage once advised, "If it ain't broke, don't fix it." That wise counsel has been widely ignored in education, and our schools are not the better for it.

When I was in school some "bigdome" at Albany (nobody local would acknowledge the fiasco) decreed that we would no longer be taught the graceful, free-flowing Palmer method of penmanship. Everybody would henceforth learn manuscript; everyone's work would look as if it had been done on a typewriter. The idea was abandoned after a couple of years, but my own handwriting (now a labored succotash of printing and Palmer) became almost illegible.

As we discuss in a later chapter, a battle continues to rage over two rival systems of teaching reading: traditional phonics and the experimental "look-say" word-recognition approach. We had been doing reasonably well with phonics until someone decided we might do better with look-say. Now reading comprehension scores have declined. Pressed to mandate a return to phonics, the New York Regents came up with a wet-tissue compromise: use whichever method the child's own approach to reading seems to suggest.

In high school, one of my youngsters spent a whole year in English class "learning" (the quotes are deliberate) from an unusual new workbook that apparently had to be shipped back and forth between the school and some Midwestern company for evaluation. The harassed instructor confessed to me that he couldn't teach the subject because the company seldom if ever returned the corrected workbooks on time. Another grandiose new idea flopped, leaving lots of youngsters with a wasted year behind them, never to be recaptured.

Here is Dr. Adelson again: "The story of education in this [postwar] period is a story of experiments—an abundance, a cornucopia of reforms and breakthroughs, each introduced breathlessly, each kept afloat by publicity, and each sinking out of sight, soon to be replaced by more publicity, and more disappointment—the New Math. Head Start. Computer instruction. Programmed learning. Closed-circuit TV. Community control. Contract teaching. Open classrooms. Sensitivity training."

Innovation was not born after World War II; it was simply intensified. And as results began to show signs of tarnish, the experimentation became more frenzied. Of course, nobody thought of reverting to a previous, tested, successful way of doing the job. Oh, no—that would be unacceptably reactionary. What was really needed (we were told) was progress—something new, something different.

I am no opponent of improvement. One cannot favor excellence and oppose improvement. In business, I am constantly testing alternative ways of doing things, and additional things to do. But when something is working well, doing the job I want it to do, I won't mess with it; I won't try to fix it, if it "ain't broke." If the schools followed that advice, they would avoid many costly failures which leave countless young citizens less well educated than they have a right to be.

Equality versus Quality: A Dangerous Choice

In the following chapters, we will look at the most serious challenges to educational excellence in America today: crises in discipline, in standards, in motivation, in competition, in methods, in many aspects of the art of learning. But there is one dangerous new trend that threatens to wreak havoc upon our educational system—a new thrust which can kill America's traditional enthusiasm for constantly improving the nation's schools and colleges, simply by making improvements costly, difficult, or illegal.

I refer to the contemporary insistence upon *equality,* even at the expense of quality.

Despite the rosy-hued assurances of our ever-more-powerful modern egalitarians, *quality and equality are seldom if ever compatible in education.*

Equality in public schooling can be attained only if two conditions prevail: (1) sufficient resources exist to bring every school up to the qualitative level of the best schools, and (2) the best schools are prevented from becoming better, which, to me, is an unacceptable restraint upon their desire to improve the quality of their children's schooling.

We do not have the resources available today to raise the quality of every public school to that of the top public schools. There simply is not enough revenue, even if we were to rob other essential government services to expand the education budget. That being so, the only way to achieve equality in such a situation is to *reduce* the best schools' level of excellence by deliberately diverting resources away from them while penalizing, restraining, or forbidding the people they serve from compensating for those lost resources out of their own pockets.

If preventing a school from improving the quality of its services is bad, forcing it to *lower* the quality of its services is a crime against education. But that is exactly what is being proposed today. It is the direction that the New York State Board of Regents has taken (over my lonely "no" vote); it is what the courts of New York State, among others, are contemplating—as analyzed in more detail later. I can think of no more shattering blow to educational excellence—no policy, no action more likely to destroy the impetus which has made our American system great: the urge to excel.

All I ask as you read on is that you keep in mind the fact that while excellence may be *your* goal for *your* children's and *your* grandchildren's schooling, as it is mine, it isn't everyone's. Those who have abandoned our quest for excellence to embrace the new egalitarianism have mounted a very real threat to our educational system and the nation which depends upon it. And the only force with enough strength to stop them is public opinion, yours and mine, expressed clearly and emphatically to our elected officials who will be making the crucial decisions, including appointments to the courts.

Each child passes through our educational system but once. Each child has a birthright: the best possible schooling we can provide. Judge for yourself whether we are living up to our obligations to the children—and if not, how we can do better.

3.

Discipline or Disruption?

It Should Be an Easy Choice —
but It Isn't

IF THERE is one statement about education on which everyone agrees—students, faculty, administrators, parents, and the general public—it must be this: We all know that bad behavior causes disruption in schools. But not all of us know that some of the things we do in education with the purest of motives also tend to promote disruption.

Disruption Defined

In the 1970 research report of the National Association of Secondary School Principals titled *Disruption in Urban Public Secondary Schools,* my colleague on the New York Board of Regents, Stephen K. Bailey, wrote: ". . . school disruption is any event which significantly interrupts the education of students. Most common among these would be student boycotts, walkouts, or strikes; property damage including arson and vandalism; rioting and fighting; picketing and unauthorized parading; the presence on campus of unruly, unauthorized, nonschool persons; and lastly, that catch-all phrase—abnormal unruliness among students."

Lack of Discipline:
Number 1 Problem in Public Schools

In its 1980 poll of citizens, asking their attitudes toward the nation's public schools, the Gallup organization reconfirmed previous surveys in which Americans put "lack of discipline" at the top of their list of con-

18

cerns. Twenty-six percent were most worried about this problem; next came dope and drug abuse at 14 percent. Crime and vandalism (4 percent) and drinking and alcoholism (2 percent) were less troubling, although all of these are related.

In the same survey, Gallup asked students thirteen to eighteen to rank the problems they perceived in their own schools. Almost 30 percent complained of lax discipline, 24 percent listed dope and drugs, and 8½ percent were troubled about crime and vandalism. Asked to name "very big" or "fairly big" problems in their schools, 63 percent listed absenteeism, marijuana use, and "students creating disturbances in class"; 51 percent deplored thefts of personal property, and 46 percent complained of vandalism. Drinking (37 percent), fighting (32 percent), use of hard drugs (26 percent), and bringing weapons to school (19 percent) completed the list.

In a 1978 report titled *Violent Schools—Safe Schools,* a federal body, the National Institute of Education (NIE), indicated some disturbing statistics: 22 percent of secondary students were afraid to use certain lavatories, 20 percent were afraid of being hurt or "bothered" by other students, and 4 percent (representing about 800,000 pupils) actually stayed away from school out of fear. The NIE study indicated, contrary to some popular misconceptions, that the majority of offenses against discipline are committed not by outside intruders but by enrolled students.

Teachers as Victims

Assaults—pupil against pupil and pupils against teachers and other school personnel—are driving educators to change their careers. A survey of 12,000 teachers taken in May 1980 by the New York State United Teachers (NYSUT), an AFL-CIO affiliate, ranked "disruptive children" as the most distressing condition in their school environment. And the situation worsens.

Consider the case of Deby Salama. Mrs. Salama, a fourth-grade teacher in New York City, suffered severe injury when a ten-year-old student smashed a heavy chair across her back. The same boy had earlier bloodied another child's face with a screwdriver. Was the young offender suspended or otherwise disciplined? No. Said the school's principal: ". . . we did not think it would be beneficial to him."

In a Manhattan junior high, a teacher reported that a fifteen-year-old had set up a drug display in his classroom, peddling drugs to other students. When the teacher challenged the boy, the latter pulled a knife and warned: "You fool with my business and I'll kill you." Presented with this situation, the school's principal was quoted as responding: "I don't wish to discuss the matter. I have important matters to deal with."

In 1979, sixty suburban school districts on Long Island, New York, reimbursed teachers for vandalism of their cars and other property, usually committed in retaliation for disciplinary actions against students. Garden City, New York, allows payment of up to $200 for damage to a single car; a neighboring town pays up to $500 per year to a teacher for all types of damage, "although teachers there claim that their annual losses through vandalism are at least four times that amount," according to *Newsday,* which reported in 1981 that the problem persisted in the area.

Decline of Authority

In his analysis of crime in American public schools which appeared in *The Public Interest* (Winter 1980), Professor Jackson Toby of Rutgers University wrote:

"A generation ago, it was possible for principals to rule schools autocratically, to suspend or expel students without much regard for procedural niceties. Injustices occurred; children were 'pushed out' of schools because they were disliked by school officials. But this arbitrariness enabled school administrators to control the situation when real misbehavior occurred. Assaults on teachers were punished so swiftly that they were almost unthinkable. Even disrespectful language was unusual. Today school officials are required to observe due process in handling student discipline. Hearings are necessary. Witnesses must confirm suspicions. Appeals are provided for. Greater democratization of schools means that unruly students get better protection against school officials, and most students get less protection from their classmates."

During the troubled Vietnam years, many educators who were unaccustomed to disruption knuckled under to the disrupters. In New York, in 1970, the State Education Department issued a gaudy booklet decorated with those peace and sex symbols made popular by agitators of the time. It was entitled *Guidelines for Student Rights and Responsibilities,* but its heavy stress was on rights. The text dwelt largely on an exposition of what students can do, and what school authorities cannot do, and in so doing court cases and commissioner's decisions were cited by the dozen. As a Regent, I should have objected at the time, but I blew the chance. I was conned by the argument that the more rights students are given, the less disruptive they become. How wrong I was! What I forgot—what a lot of us forgot—is that the greatest student right, taking precedence over all others, is the right to a good education, free from distractions and interruptions and any other acts which interfere with the learning process.

Is Anyone Doing Anything About Disruption?

In May 1980, California's Attorney General filed a suit against Los Angeles city, county, and school officials, charging that they had failed to ensure the safety of the 600,000 students in the nation's second-largest school district. He stated: "It is cruel and unusual punishment to compel students to attend public schools where there is an excessive level of violence."

In 1979, New Jersey's Governor signed into law a bill mandating the immediate suspension of a student who assaults a teacher or a school employee, and providing an expulsion hearing within twenty-one days of a student's suspension.

In Prince Georges County, Maryland, burglar alarms costing $600,-000 have captured "several hundred" intruders, while a paid staff of investigators has checked into thousands of complaints; the *Saturday Evening Post* reported in 1978 that these measures "reduced lawlessness by at least 64% in the last five years."

By the way, have you checked your own high school's security system lately? Maybe there isn't one. Maybe you don't need one. There are districts where disruption and crime are almost unknown. Recently, I inspected a brand-new high school in a Long Island suburban district whose security system seemed worthy of Alcatraz in its heyday: uniformed guards, a closed-circuit TV monitoring the halls, and a complex and expensive alarm system. Morris High School in New York City's South Bronx at one time sealed all doors except the main entrance (which was manned by a guard to identify those who wished to enter) and set up hall patrols with five guards communicating by walkie-talkies. Classrooms were locked after classes began, study halls were shut down to prevent fights, lockers were removed because "kids used to store drugs in them and light fires." Troublemakers were segregated in trailers outside the main school building.

In the Groveport-Madison school district, Ohio, "problem children" were isolated in restricted classrooms and required to complete class work. (How about *that?*) Moreover, they were obliged to write a plan on how to change their behavior, and could not join their classmates for lunch or extracurricular activities. The minimum "sentence" was set at three days. Elk Grove, California, developed a round-the-clock program of "vandal watchers," living rent-free in mobile homes on school property. Broward County, Florida, schools sealed their locker rooms at the start and end of the school day, and removed locks from lavatories. In San Antonio, Texas, lights were turned off after school hours because "a lighted school is to kids what a lighted candle is to moths—it attracts them."

I'm not sure that all the antidisruption measures cited here will work. While parents must certainly be involved in remedies for disruptive action, it does little good to punish parents for their children's acts of vandalism if there are no responsible parents, or if the parents cannot afford to pay, or if fines mean nothing to permissive parents who can afford them.

Compassion Isn't Always the Right Answer

I am a compassionate man. I love babies and birds and small animals. The number and variety of charities to which I have given—many inherited from my mother, one of the most compassionate humans God ever created—has occasionally strained the credulity of the IRS.

If Americans are compassionate, and they are, New Yorkers must bubble with the milk of human kindness, because their good will manages to attract and generate more freeloaders, junkies, thugs, and punks than most other parts of the country. Yet, do-gooders have zeroed in upon New York *schools* as centers of child abuse. A survey in 1979, conducted at my behest as Chancellor of the State of New York, disclosed that relatively few complaints were made by parents about the use of physical force by New York teachers and administrators, and that the complaints were easily handled by local districts or courts. Still, groups of citizens, buoyed by the support of the State Parent-Teacher Association (PTA), came on strong in 1979 with a demand for a state law to make corporal punishment of pupils by teachers a *legal* offense. This was done at a time when physical force was being employed primarily by *students against teachers*.

The proposal was so embarrassingly wrong that it had to be studded with exceptions. Physical force could be used by teachers in self-defense, or if a student threatened destruction of school property or physical harm to another student. Physical force itself was not evil and thus to be prohibited; it was physical *punishment* that was forbidden. Force as a *deterrent* could be legally used. But the availability of physical force as punishment is itself a great deterrent. I've never used it on my own kids, and never had to—undoubtedly because they knew I could use it if I chose.

When I stated that our real problem was student assaults upon teachers, not the reverse, a woman in California wrote me that the end of "violence" by teachers against students would mean the end of student attacks on their teachers. Great Scott! New York City outlawed corporal punishment in its schools in 1928. If the argument stated by my California correspondent is valid, attacks on NYC teachers should have disappeared in the ensuing half-century. But there are more than ever before: 1,200 reported cases in New York City in 1978 alone.

This is hardly the time to clog our courts with cases based upon alleged physical punishment in schools. What has always been and should continue to be settled by school authorities should not become public spectacles which keep children and teachers out of their classrooms and in the courtrooms. The cause of education would not be aided thereby, and for many teachers, this further dilution of their disciplinary authority could cause them to join the thousands of educators who have already ended their careers prematurely.

Child abuse, a serious crime, occurs generally in *family* situations, but we have become so conditioned to relying upon the schools to correct our social ills that some of us now attempt to shift the *blame* to the schools.

Some Other Compassionate Idiocies

Those who believe that restoration of discipline in schools is simply a matter of applied common sense should contemplate the roadblocks thrown up by an alliance of educational "liberals," editorial writers, and "progressive" theorists. Take the U.S. Supreme Court's *Gault* decision, for example. As Jackson Toby explains in *The Public Interest,* the Court ruled in *Gault* in 1967 that juvenile offenders cannot be sent away for rehabilitation unless they have committed a crime "for which imprisonment was appropriate." This was translated by some legislatures (New York's and New Jersey's among them) into a prohibition against reform school for "status offenses," behavior that would not be criminal if done by adults. Because adults do not normally play hooky from school or raise hell in classrooms, juvenile courts can no longer send habitually truant or disruptive youngsters away.

If you add to this the tendency to forbid expulsion from school—as opposed to temporary suspension—for disruptive acts, we have a sure-fire method of keeping young troublemakers right where they cause the most trouble: in school. Professor Toby, who is Director of the Rutgers Institute for Criminological Research, comments: ". . . humane considerations suggest that after a student has committed violent acts against students or teachers in a school, they ought not to have to encounter him in the corridors day after day. (In point of fact, it is at least as common for victims—both teachers and students—to transfer out voluntarily as it is for perpetrators to be compelled to transfer.)"

The icing on this astonishing cake is supplied by suppression of disciplinary records. Toby cites a case study of "Rogers" Junior High:

"Since it is not legally possible to expel students considered disruptive, it is customary at Rogers as in other schools, to transfer students to other schools. By board regulation, the school is not permitted to inform the receiving school of the reason for the transfer or to provide any disciplinary records.

" 'This can present some real problems,' one Rogers dean commented. 'We had a kid last year who slashed another kid's throat with a razor blade, and we finally had to transfer him into one of the intermediate schools, but we couldn't tell them officially what he had done or even that they should keep an eye on him because he was potentially violent.' "

If such transfers of records are absolutely necessary for the protection of students and teachers in the receiving school, as they are, why are they suppressed by official order? Presumably, suppression is intended to provide the youngster with a clean bill of health in his new school environment, but, as I see it, that consideration, however well intentioned, is far outweighed by concerns for the safety and well-being of those into whose midst he is dropped.

Ultimate Idiocy: Punishment Quotas

Albert Shanker, President of the American Federation of Teachers (AFT), surely no rock-ribbed reactionary, sounded yet one more alarm in 1980. Watch out, he warned, for a federally imposed quota system for school discipline.

Shanker reported that the U.S. Department of Education's Office of Civil Rights (OCR) planned to require that schools receiving government funds keep records of disciplinary actions, showing in each case the child's race, ethnic background, and handicap (if any). Local boards would have to be able to prove that they are not punishing racial minorities or females or the handicapped in greater numbers than their proportion of the school population. Shanker predicted: "Under the disciplinary quota system, once certain numbers of students are punished, once the right proportion is reached, all additional violence will go unpunished.... Students soon find out that once the magic number is reached, they can get away with murder."

Unreal? No. In March 1981, Ted Elsberg, President of the Council of Supervisors and Administrators of New York City, reported that "several high school principals were cited by their superintendents for allegedly excessive suspensions of an ethnic group, suspensions that were out of proportion to the number of such pupils in the schools," as a result of pressures brought by the OCR. Urging that we not label the firm and fair exercise of discipline as "discrimination," Elsberg added: "For too many years, the leadership of the school system bent to every social pull and pressure until standards of decent behavior were surrendered to a 'do your own thing' anarchy. . . . We cannot and must not accept disruptive or violent behavior, no matter what its label or origin."

But if school authorities fear that they could face legal charges of discrimination, which could cost their district all of its federal funds should they take justifiable disciplinary action against certain students, Shanker predicts that they would throw in the towel.

It is difficult to think of a more effective way to undermine, possibly to destroy, discipline in our public schools. (U.S. Secretary of Education Terrel H. Bell did education a great favor by scrapping this ridiculous policy in 1981.)

Integration as a Cause of Disruption

For more than a generation, the racial desegregation of our schools has been a national commitment, one shared by most Americans. But the achievement of that goal, however just, has its price. Is the attainment of racial integration in U.S. schools worth the price we are paying for it? This question (usually argued in terms of busing) has divided the nation since 1954, when the U.S. Supreme Court's *Brown v. Board of Education of Topeka* decision set the course of school-integration policy.

School integration is discussed—and discussed sympathetically and rationally, I believe—later in the book. Yet it must be said that the price we pay for racial desegregation is pertinent. *Racial integration of schools has contributed to disruption in those schools.* In 1970, Regent Steve Bailey, whose devotion to civil rights is unquestioned, said, in summarizing his study of disruption in urban secondary schools:

"Disruption is positively related to integration. Schools which are almost all white or all black are less likely to be disrupted.

"It may be an unpleasant subject, but no honest observers of the urban high school scene could by-pass the phenomenon of black revenge . . . [for] the long and ugly centuries of disgrace in which they and their kind were oppressed purely on the basis of color. . . . We found that much of the physical fighting, the extortion, the bullying in and around schools had a clear racial basis. This was particularly apparent where the student mix was predominantly but not wholly black.

"It is our considered judgment that disruptions caused by these kinds of issues [cross-cultural clashes] will occur most frequently in moderate-income, middle-class schools into which are bused significant numbers of low-income students, and not in either the predominantly or all-white or all-black school settings."

Dr. Bailey does not believe that disruption in schools justifies ending our efforts to desegregate schools. On the contrary, he feels "this option is unavailable. Among other drawbacks, it is unconstitutional." The achievement of school integration on a national scale is, in his view, worth whatever price we must pay for it. He goes on:

"Integrated schools with higher percentages of black students are less likely to be disrupted if such schools also have high percentages of black staffs. Conversely, schools with high percentages of blacks but with predominantly white staffs are more likely to be disrupted.

". . . it is a wise policy to promote or recruit a black teacher and/or administrator rather than a white one in a predominantly black school."

This suggestion by Dr. Bailey for improving discipline in integrated schools runs counter to pressures by zealots in the Department of Education who are determined to integrate school staffs. It is not enough, they say, to integrate student bodies; the faculty and administration must also achieve a proportionate mix of blacks and whites. Let discipline be damned!

"Mainstreaming" as a Cause of Disruption

There exists a relatively new drive to mainstream handicapped youngsters by moving them from special schools designed to meet their special needs into (or back into) regular public-school classrooms. This has already aroused an emotional fervor unmatched by anything except racial busing.

As in the case of integration, one byproduct of mainstreaming is disruption. Most of the clamor against mainstreaming, at least in its early stages, has been directed against the tremendous new dollar burdens imposed upon local taxpayers to meet federal and state mandates requiring the buying and use of facilities for physical handicaps: visual, hearing, and motor defects, as well as wheelchair confinement.

But when the child's handicap is emotional, possibly autistic, he may be (and often is) a disruptive presence in the classroom. Children quickly become accustomed to their physically handicapped peers, but neither teachers nor students can avoid being distracted and diverted from their educational pursuits by those disturbed kids who "act out" their problems by committing acts of violence. David H. Galerstein, assistant principal of a junior high school in Floral Park, New York, points out that children with contagious diseases can be barred from school, but not so with violent and disruptive children, whose right to be in school is now regarded as being as great as (or greater than) the right of normal children to an uninterrupted education.

Cataloging the long-drawn-out formal procedure required to transfer a disturbed and disturbing child from a public to a special school, Mr. Galerstein reminds us:

"In the interim, schools are required to retain these children in regular classes. Thus, the other pupils must continue to be subject to the lesson-upsetting antics of those who are 'acting out' and the crimes of the violent ones. . . . It is these disturbed children—regardless of skin color or other irrelevant factors—who cause middle-class families to remove their children from public schools.

"The present policy of 'mainstreaming' such children as much as possible undoubtedly helps some. But it is done at the cost of returning to the regular schools and classes those still disturbed who will again engage in the anti-social behavior that necessitated their removal in the first place."

As is sometimes the case with racial integration of the schools, a well-intentioned purpose is ill-served. A good motive can also generate disruption, hindering the educational progress of all the kids.

Teacher Strikes = Disruption

Withholding of teachers' services, by whatever name it is called, is disruption of the education of youngsters by teachers who were hired to serve them. If good teaching is beneficial to the students and the community, then it follows that the absence of that teaching, for whatever reason, is hurtful. Most Americans correctly instruct their children to respect and obey their teachers, not because we believe teachers are demigods, but because we know that respect and obedience in school enable the learning process to proceed without costly distractions.

What conclusions do youngsters draw by observing illegal strikes and defiance of court orders by their teachers? The lesson is obvious: one can with impunity disobey laws or rules or regulations. Strikes depreciate the authority of both teachers and administrators, as angry parents and taxpayers denounce one side or the other. It is bad enough that community support for public education is seriously undermined. The real damage is done in the minds of impressionable young people who see and judge the actions of their elders.

Don't close your eyes and hope that the number, and resultant effects, of teacher strikes will disappear as school enrollment declines. The American Federation of Teachers reported a new national high of 242 strikes in 1979–80, of which twenty-nine were by AFT unions, affecting 58,000 teachers and more than one million students.

Subtract One Dad, Add Disruption

A study by the National Association of Elementary Schools in 1980 showed that each year the number of American kids who live in one-parent families increases by one million; there were 12 million such youngsters in 1980. The report pointed out that one-parent children, who so often lack the elements of family authority and discipline, are three times as likely to be suspended from elementary school or expelled from secondary school as are their classmates.

It has been suggested that welfare laws make it tempting for fathers to live apart from their families so that the latter may qualify for higher benefits. Those who write such laws are ignorant of the permanent damage they can cause; the disastrous effect on children and their schools is not worth whatever dollar savings might be involved. Whatever we can do to keep families together is helpful in promoting better school discipline.

Transients Can Be Troublesome

Anyone who has watched how some grown men behave when they are away from home at a convention, or who has observed the conduct of soldiers in towns they temporarily occupy, knows that transience—the condition of being in a place or situation only for a brief time—rarely breeds responsibility.

Those who know they will soon be leaving a place seldom form lasting friendships, nor are they likely to develop an affinity for, much less a loyalty to, the institutions where they are transitory tenants. It is easy to understand why disruption is a problem in schools where the student population is constantly shifting. Some principals of city schools will tell you that amazing proportions, often 30 to 40 percent, of the youngsters registered in September will not be in their seats next June. They will have moved with their families to other schools or other districts, and their places will have been taken by a new batch of transients who have moved in and will in turn move on.

Educating children under such circumstances is tough enough. Trying simultaneously to impress them with a rationale for behaving themselves during their brief stay is even tougher.

Booze, Drugs, and Disruption

You will not usually find me among those who blame all the troubles of the schools upon "society." That's a copout. Nor will I be found among those who think that all society's problems can be solved by the schools.

That's a delusion. Yet in the case of alcoholism and drug addiction, these evils *do* originate outside the schools. Education is the victim—the education of those hooked on drink or drugs, and the education of those whose learning is interrupted by the behavior of their stewed or stoned classmates. The schools didn't cause this kind of disruption; the schools can't cure it.

As stated earlier, the kids themselves tell us that in their own schools the major disciplinary problems include marijuana smoking, drinking, and the use of hard drugs. In those urban schools whose authorities have lost control, liquor and drugs are available even inside school buildings.

The schools are trying. Many states mandate instruction about drugs and alcohol (and tobacco). Many principals have driven drug dealers off school grounds; many school authorities do call police to arrest offenders. Yet students who have been interviewed say that these risks are minor compared with the thrills of smoking marijuana and drinking beer.

We *can't* give up. If we just shrug our shoulders and turn back to the TV, more generations of young Americans will ruin their lives. Indeed, television and the movies are in part to blame for disruption and disorder in our schools. I'm not talking about all those hours kids waste being glued to the tube; I'm speaking here of the glorification of violence and disruption by the visual media.

It is the television news that is most troublesome. Conflict makes news; violent physical conflict makes TV news. The Vietnam War, the ghetto riots, the furious confrontations at colleges and political conventions in the sixties were all expertly and thoroughly covered by the TV news cameras. A generation of campus firebrands learned quickly: to get your message across to the largest possible audience, don't waste time making statements. *Cause trouble.* Disrupt normal college activities. Picket with sloganeering placards. Provoke battles with campus or local police. And be sure to tip off the TV news people beforehand—they'll get there.

In 1976, the Regents held a hearing in New York City to get citizen opinions on their quadrennial master plan for higher education. As Chancellor, I was informed upon arrival at the hall that the police had been tipped off by a TV station: there would be a demonstration. About midmorning, it materialized. We were listening to a statement by the President of City College when a din was heard in the entrance hallway. Soon a shouting, chanting mob—preceded by floodlights, TV cameras, and a gorgeous blond TV-news reporter—poured into the room. Ignoring my suggestion that they be seated and listen, the demonstrators streamed down the aisles and began a noisy drumfire of interruptions and four-letter imprecations directed at the speaker and the Regents, protesting tuition increases at City University.

One of my colleagues suggested I direct the police to remove the interlopers. I was tempted—believe me—but a confrontation with the law was precisely what the disrupters (and the TV people, waiting patiently) wanted. So I declared what was probably the longest lunch break in Regents' history. Eventually the cameras, followed by the demonstrators, drifted out of the hall. We went back to our business, which, it turned out, had nothing to do with their protests. Did the TV people tip the police about the demonstration as a civic duty, or on the chance that the cops' presence might produce some head-busting to titillate viewers of the six o'clock news? Who knows? One thing we know is that if you can organize conflict and disorder, you can create filmable "news," carrying your message to millions of otherwise inattentive watchers.

Halloween: Institutionalized Extortion

Given our acute national distress over youthful misbehavior, violence, and vandalism, why do we continue to tolerate, indeed to encourage, the annual mid-fall madness called Halloween? Why do we spend 364 days a year discussing and framing stratagems and rules to discourage juvenile disruption during school hours and vandalism after hours, but then, on October 31, allow our kids to roam the neighborhood terrorizing smaller children, bugging home owners, and damaging or destroying property?

I suppose one answer is that we are victims of historical inertia. We let our children do these things because we did them, and because our fathers regaled us with tales of outhouses overturned and silk hats flour-bombed when they were young. But those days are gone. Outhouses and silk hats have disappeared. Barbaric pursuits such as dueling and fraternity hazing are dead or dying. Now, it is time for Halloween to go, too.

Indeed, it seemed not so long ago that Halloween was about to fade away, and it probably would have, had not some dimwitted do-gooder come up with the idea of having schools provide younger children with empty milk cartons, into which householders would be obliged to drop coins for the United Nations Children's Fund (UNICEF), lest they be subjected to a Halloween trick.

What does this action tell our kids? Instead of teaching them the Golden Rule (behave toward others as you would have them behave toward you) and that true charity is giving without thought of reward, "Trick or treat for UNICEF" teaches them that the end justifies the means, and that extortion can be an acceptable form of civilized behavior.

We demand stern punishment for child abusers and child molest-

ers. We wisely legislate against fireworks which might injure young cele-
brants on Independence Day. We keep guns and knives and other potentially lethal weapons out of their hands; we don't let them drive cars
until they've reached the upper teens. We ban asbestos from school
buildings and lead from house paint, so the kids won't be poisoned. We
contrive bottle caps for drugs that young children cannot open. We
mandate that students learn about the dangers of tobacco, alcohol, and
drugs to their health. We hire school doctors and nurses and psychologists and nutritionists to safeguard their physical and mental well-being.

We protect our children at every turn, save for Halloween, when we
dress them up in ridiculous masks and costumes representing ghosts,
goblins, witches, and monsters, and push them out into the cold black-
ness of a late October night to scare the wits out of each other, to be
frightened by older children, to be clobbered by debris, to risk being run
down by anxious motorists hurrying home on dark, leaf-covered, often
slippery roads, to collect bags of loot which will cause bellyaches or tooth
cavities or worse, and finally to stagger back into the sanctuary of home.
Is it worth it? I say no.

In 1979, a fifteen-year-old Valley Stream, New York, boy was hit in
both eyes by eggs thrown by other youths; microsurgery and sixteen
stitches were required to save the ruptured globe of one eye and repair
lacerations of the other. In Lakeview, New York, an eight-year-old
shared his treats with his grandmother, who bit into a candy bar and
discovered that several straight pins were buried in it; a year later, in
another town, a watchful mother spotted a straight pin in a candy to
which her two-and-one-half-year-old tot had been "treated." The danger of drugs, glass, metal, pins, and even razor blades in Halloween can-
dies and fruits has led hospitals, including Piedmont Hospital in Atlanta, Georgia, to provide X-ray screening of goodies. Some cities,
including Atlanta and Miami, have urged parents to curtail their
youngsters' Halloween ventures because of the real dangers involved.

The question comes naturally to mind: Who in the world wants to
continue this Halloween nonsense? Nobody, really, except possibly those
doting mommies and daddies who think the little ones look cute in their
costumes. Some people make money on Halloween, but not much. The
principal perpetrator, you may be surprised to know, is Miss Kindly, the
elementary schoolteacher who would not hurt a soul. Each year, Miss
Kindly knows that she will repeat the same October theme as last year
in her classroom. On October 1, up go the orange paper jack-o'-lanterns,
up go the cardboard witches and ghosts, keeping the youngsters' crayons
(and imaginations) at fever pitch for a full month until the big day,
which thus has been given the seal of approval by the children's daily
source of authority: their school and their teacher.

The remedy is obvious—get the schools out of the Halloween business. Stop the repetitive cycle of brainwashing before it begins in the earliest years, and Halloween will eventually be nothing more than a curious historical footnote about the customs of pre-2000 America.

But let's not leave Miss Kindly, who cares about teaching our children, without an October theme. How about devoting October to the feats of our explorers? Columbus Day on October 12 can serve as a focal point. Instead of dressing kids up as creatures who never were, why not dress them as Columbus, Père Jacques Marquette, Lewis and Clark, General John C. Frémont, Nellie Bly, Amelia Earhart, Admiral Richard Byrd, and Neil A. Armstrong? There is no month, nor even (as far as I know) an Explorers' Day, devoted to these daring heroes of our history. Why not use October?

If that doesn't catch Miss Kindly's fancy, then make October the month devoted to government. Political campaigns reach their climax in October. We hear of students who can tell us of the indignities suffered by Indians, blacks, and Chicanos over the years, but who don't know how many Senators represent them in Congress, who they are or how they stand on the issues of the day, including indignities to minorities. We all might learn something from a month in which we zero in on government.

If this is not enough to put an end to Halloween as a school-promoted, parent-permitted annual exercise, I suggest a sure-fire tactic: write a "concerned citizen" letter to the nearest branch of the American Civil Liberties Union, complaining that teachers in your local public schools spend a whole month promoting a *religious* holiday—which is what Halloween is all about. It originated with the ancient Druids, then was accepted in Europe and America as the Eve of All Saints—All Hallows—Day, a religious feast still widely observed throughout Christendom. If that doesn't get some anti-Halloween action from your local school board before you can say "separation of church and state," the ACLU is not as sharp as it used to be.

Seriously speaking, Halloween is no longer a joke, if it ever was. At a time when disruption in American schools is a major source of concern to parents, teachers, administrators, and students alike, we can no longer afford to tolerate what has become a dangerous and pointless annual tribute to unruliness. Let Halloween die quietly. And permanently.

Is Disruption Dead on the College Campuses?

Lest we forget, the current tide of disruption began back in the 1960s on the college campuses, not in the elementary and secondary schools where its residue is so troublesome today. College vandalism seems to have died down, but is it really dead? Probably not. It simply takes a different form.

The end of the Vietnam War, the achievement of assorted social and environmental goals, the termination of the military draft, the economic recession, which has sharpened competition for after-college jobs—all these have tended to cool the campuses. College students seem alert to the fact that their dollars spent on higher education are in danger of being wasted if education is interrupted by a noisy minority which disrupts normal campus activities. It appears that the sensible majority (resisting goadings from the media about their "apathy," which doesn't make news) will hold the lid down on their disruptive classmates, at least for a while. But there are new sources of disruption to take the place of the old.

One is the rise of crime on college campuses. In New York, the president of the State University at Oswego gave permission for campus police to carry guns at night, because of the high incidence of rapes and knife attacks, but the Oswego student association opposed the move on the ground that it "threatened the tranquillity of the campus"! And along with violent crime, the cost of vandalism in the colleges is rising annually, as respect for property rights, one of the most cherished of human rights, declines.

Measuring the Cost of Disruption

In some respects, the cost of disruption can be measured; in others, it cannot. In dollar terms, one 1978 report listed the annual cost of school vandalism alone at $200 million—just about $1 for every man, woman, and child in the United States; this figure is a compilation of damage reports from school districts all over America. All this money, and the money we spend on guards, alarm and surveillance systems, and other security devices, could otherwise buy a lot of good education for our youngsters. How much? Half a billion dollars is within the ball park. Because it is spent by the schools, all this cost of security is put down as "money for education," although not a penny goes for teaching and learning. Next time someone complains about "all the money we're spending on the schools," tell them about the cost of disruption. This must also be measured in *time:* minutes, hours, days lost forever when the teaching and learning process is interrupted. And we must measure the costs of disruption in terms of the *quality* of education. While we will never know the total answer, we do know that some of our best veteran teachers and some of our most promising young instructors are dropping out of teaching because of the stress caused by young disrupters.

What Happened to Our Social Contract?

Civilized societies adopt constitutions and laws to serve the aspirations and needs of their citizens in a variety of ways. I need not redefine the purposes and the terms of our American social contract here; the preamble and the text of our Constitution does so far better than I can. It is a contract between the citizen and the society to which he or she belongs. To the extent that we as individuals agree with and respect and obey our society's Constitution and the laws devolving from it, our contract remains strong. But our American social contract is fraying at the edges.

In the last two decades, respect for American institutions has declined sharply, according to reliable opinion surveys. We think far less than we once did of our legislators, our courts, our armed forces, our government services, our business and industries, our religious institutions, our schools and colleges—even of *ourselves* as citizens.

Many books have been written about the reasons for this downturn in Americans' attitudes toward the principal foundation blocks of our society. I shall not try to write another—at least, not here and now. I can say that we all receive daily doses of social confessions by guilt-ridden voices of the Establishment who tell women, blacks, Indians, Hispanics, and others that they and their predecessors were always treated abominably by dominant white Anglo-Saxon males, and that they are owed some form of compensation for centuries of oppression. A tremendously unpopular, badly botched military action in Vietnam, coupled with the unmasking of venality at the American summit in the Watergate scandal, reinforced the notion that our society was rotten and contemptible. Those who were all too willing to accept that premise had an easy jump to their own solution: laws and rules made by a rotten society need not be obeyed.

The New Subculture

We have thus created a whole new subculture, one which does not consider itself at all bound by the regular rules of society. The existence of this subculture is perhaps most evident in the breakdown of law enforcement. A system of criminal justice depends upon its deterrent effect if it is to be of value to society. But members of the new subculture seem to be immune to deterrence and entirely without a sense of guilt or remorse.

Does this widespread disregard for law outside the schools breed contempt for rules within them? Of course. It also breeds a feeling that *school is essentially imprisonment,* with teachers and administrators the jailers. Lacking in intellectual motivation, youths of the subculture create work of various kinds: they push narcotics and commit other crimes. When they drop out of school, or raise enough hell to be suspended or expelled, this is exactly what they want—*out*. And why not? They have come to believe that school makes no difference anyway; society will try to rip you off as it always has, so you might as well get out and learn to cope.

Should Attendance Be Compulsory?

The existence of this antieducation element in schooling in the new subculture raises a serious question: Should school attendance continue to be compulsory up to sixteen years of age? Consider this: not all students are members of the subculture. In fact, a majority are motivated to study and learn. Do we give these youngsters a real chance to achieve scholastically when we pack them into crowded classrooms with chronic disrupters who don't want to learn, won't study, and would rather be somewhere else? I submit that we do not give serious learners a fair shake.

A first step to correcting abuses is to realize that *attendance, by itself, does not guarantee learning.* A second step is to understand that the segregation of disrupters into "special schools" may help the rest of the students learn, but simply creates prisons for the rule breakers, in which no education at all is conducted. A good third step would be to visualize different kinds of motivation for those who might choose to leave school if they were allowed to do so—motivation toward constructive careers which bring not only monetary rewards but new self-respect as members of society.

What You and I Can Do About All This

If you are a parent of a school-ager (I am), be sure that you are not part of the school's problem. If Junior is disciplined for some in-school infraction, don't react as if your family and ancestors have been insulted; don't rush to the school to confront the cruel, callous martinet who has unjustly punished your child. The teacher may be right. And Junior might just profit educationally from an occasional, forceful reminder that he's in school to study, not to "horse around."

You might even conduct a mental review of your own home discipline. Does Junior understand that the world does not operate on the basis of his momentary wants, that things do not always happen as he would like them to happen? Does he know, from experience as well as being told, that rewards will be withheld, restrictions imposed, or punishment meted out if he doesn't conform to the family's rules? Does he know those rules? If you make a promise or issue a threat, do you live up to it if results so dictate? Do you set a good example for him? Does he know that you care about what he does, and is, and can be? Does he know that you love him? Have you told him? If your answer to any of these questions is "no," it's time for you to have a long talk with yourself, and then another long talk with Junior. Years from now, he'll thank you for it.

Whether you are a parent or not, get involved.

You don't have to join the Parent-Teacher Association or the Home & School Association to be helpful at school, although better results will sometimes be achieved if demanded by a group of voters rather than by one. The problem, insofar as discipline is concerned, is that PTA people too often tend to be bleeding-hearts who frown upon any discipline more severe than a slap on the wrist (and even that should be outlawed, according to the New York PTA). If you join the PTA, watch carefully; if you see it heading toward more permissiveness, more laxity, squeal like a stuck pig. But if the bleeding-hearts win out, quit—and don't quit quietly. Sound off. You'll attract a like-minded group of your own.

Find out whether the schools need your help as a "disciplinary auxiliary"—a hall monitor, playground order-keeper, or the like. Teacher-contract limitations being what they are these days, the school authorities may welcome your volunteer service; they may even pay you, if they need you badly enough. We have paraprofessional teachers; why not paraprofessional monitors? It makes sense.

Ask to see your local school district's manual of rules and regulations governing behavior and discipline at the various levels of schooling. If the authorities demur (they probably won't), insist upon seeing the documents, which are public papers viewable by citizens under freedom-of-information laws in most places. Determine which rules seem sound and which seem excessively lax; look for the ones that aren't there, but should be. Ask questions about meanings and enforcement. Some districts still suffer the countereducational burdens of relaxed behavior codes and disciplinary rules imposed upon them by local pressures during the Vietnam era. Don't be surprised if school authorities welcome you as an ally in their drive to regain control over their (and your) schools.

Once you and those who think as you do have decided what should be in the rules (and isn't) and what's in the rules (but shouldn't be), learn whether the objectionable rules or omissions are the result of local decisions or outside mandates. If the locality sets these policies and makes these rules, ask all the candidates for the Board of Education at the next election to state their precise views on these specific questions. The League of Women Voters or some other organization usually holds an open forum for Board candidates. Be there; ask the right questions. If a candidate is absent, write to him or her for answers. If you get none, ask again—through the columns of your local newspapers. You have a right to know where the candidates stand. If there is no response, or if a candidate hedges unreasonably, don't vote for him or her. And be sure the candidate knows you're unhappy.

Attend meetings of your Board of Education. If the Board allows public participation (there is a difference between a meeting and a hearing, not always observed), make your points about discipline and behavior. Lend your support or state your opposition to proposals which may become policies. Be specific, be accurate, be informed, be forceful, be articulate. You may win the day, which could otherwise be lost.

If you should find that unacceptable policies and rules about behavior and discipline are imposed upon the locality by higher authority, go after your state and federal lawmakers. But first be careful that you are on solid ground. Local school people sometimes tend to avoid responsibility for unpopular acts or regulations by attempting to disguise their origin; be sure that it belongs in your state capital or Washington, D.C., before you shift your fire in those directions. How can you be sure? Ask to see the federal or state law or decision or rule involved.

Insist that your legislators analyze carefully the contents of every proposal affecting the schools, to detect by-effects detrimental to discipline or educational quality. Ask for copies of the bills, and analyze them yourself. If you spot any weaknesses, point them out to your lawmakers; they can't possibly read everything, and they can easily miss fine points that you may catch. Help them to do what you want them to do.

All this sounds like a big order. But think about this: The quality of education in your schools may depend upon what you and those who think as you do can achieve. And because your position makes good sense, you'll pick up allies all along the way. Among these will be the law-abiding majority of students; they will welcome your efforts to pinpoint disrupters as pariahs, not heroes, by tying the availability of student extracurricular activity funds to the absence of requirements for repairing the damages of vandalism, a stratagem that has been successful in quite a few schools.

Summing Up

I believe that every American child has a right to the best education his or her parents and their community can provide. Because each child passes through the educational system only once, any interruption of the child's learning experience or concentration upon studies is a *permanent* loss to the child. It is, therefore, a denial of the child's right to a good education.

I believe that succumbing to disorder and disruption in the schools and colleges will not bring order and tranquillity, but will lead to more disorder and disruption—and to a greater denial of the educational rights of students. I believe that our modern tendency to overstress the rights of the accused or convicted offender has contributed to the rise in crime. Similarly, our overemphasis upon the rights of students at the expense of the authority of teachers and administrators has contributed to the rise in school disorder. This has denied the rights of students who do not misbehave.

I believe that schools and colleges should not be held responsible for, or be expected to cure, social ills which originate in society and infect students no less than adults. The role of schools and colleges is to inform students of the negative aspects of their behavior and to prevent disruption of education; their role is also to advise parents as to how they may best cope with their children's problems in the home environment, which is the parents' responsibility.

I believe that wider circulation should be given to the facts about the extent and cost of disruption, vandalism, and crime on our nation's campuses, all toward emphasizing that resources diverted to combat these evils could be better used to educate young people and should not be debited against the costs of education, as they too often are.

Disruption will not disappear from the schools and colleges by itself. The bad habits of decades must be tagged, then unlearned and discarded. And who is going to see to this? *We are.* Each one of us, individually or together with like-minded neighbors and colleagues, will see to it by standing up and making it plain to all those who oversee education—governors, legislators, judges, and members of state and local school boards—that *the vast majority of Americans want discipline restored to our educational institutions, and restored now.*

4.

Educational Pluralism

The Future of the Republic
Depends upon It

DURING my service on the New York State Board of Regents, I was sometimes accused of harboring an affinity for the nonpublic independent schools and colleges.

I plead guilty . . . guilty of believing that it is vitally important for *both* independent and public educational institutions to survive and prosper.

And there are reasons why.

The Gestapo's Message — to Berlin and to Me

On September 12, 1944, the U.S. Third Armored Division slammed through the barbed-wire and dragon's-teeth of Hitler's Siegfried Line, the first Allied unit to enter Germany in strength. And a dog-tired twenty-four-year-old captain of military intelligence became, on that day, the initiator of the de-Nazification of the Third Reich. As commander of the Division's Counter-Intelligence Corps (CIC) detachment, whose regular job was to protect the unit from espionage, sabotage, and subversion, I now had a new responsibility, to be shared by other CIC agents who followed: dismantling the Nazi Party apparatus and Himmler's SS police organization wherever we found them.

In the Rhineland, the local Nazi and SS officials had fled to the East with the retreating German Army, but they left behind evidence that would later help to condemn Hitlerism before the world.

Special Agent Bruno Stramel, my chief clerk, interpreter, driver, and good companion, discovered and translated some classified papers left in an abandoned SS office in the city of Stolberg—copies of reports filed in the mid-1930s by undercover agents of the Secret State Police (Gestapo) who had infiltrated the Rhineland's churches and religious schools. Bruno is gone now, but I can recall the Gestapo's findings. Germany's churches and independent schools were considered a major barrier to the total acceptance of Hitlerism, and were to be eliminated at the earliest moment so that the "enlightenment" of the German people about the glories of National Socialism could be complete. (Incidentally, companion documents revealed that the reported 80+ percent "yes" vote in the 1934 plebiscite on Hitler's popularity was a fraud; Hitler won a bare majority.)

The Gestapo reports had a message for SS headquarters in Berlin, but they had a different message for me:

Monopoly in education is dangerous to liberty, which is why tyrants insist upon it. Monopoly in education is wholly unacceptable in a democratic society, because it contains the seeds of that society's destruction.

Monopoly in education can become *thought control,* denying the individual teacher's and student's right to read and listen and think and debate and make decisions and speak out. The views of those who hold the monopoly are exalted, while nonconforming views are suppressed or ignored. Thus education ceases to be education and becomes indoctrination.

Monopoly in education is wrong, no matter what element of society wields its power—but it is at its worst when it is a *state* monopoly backed by the force of government, because it then becomes an instrument for the imposition of a totalitarian regime upon a free people.

The experience of twentieth-century Germany—one of the most technologically advanced nations of Western civilization, in which the liberal arts flourished—tells us that *no* country, not even the mighty United States of America with its two hundred-year history of freedom, would be immune to the terminal virus of dictatorship if its educational system were allowed to become a government-run monolith.

It makes little difference whether the seizure of schools and colleges or of the army and police occurs first: *A tyrant's grip on a nation cannot be absolute as long as educational freedom is tolerated in the slightest degree.* There can be total control of a people only if the state controls education . . . *all* education.

Hitler understood the principle. In a speech after taking power in 1933 he said: "When an opponent declares, 'I will not come over to your side,' I calmly say, 'Your child belongs to us already. . . . You will pass on. Your descendants, however, now stand in the new camp. In a short time, they will know nothing else but this new community.' "

"They will know nothing else . . ." By 1945, every German seventeen years of age or younger knew nothing else but Hitler. As the advancing American troops moved deeper into Germany, we found that our most determined adversaries were the young Nazis, some in their pre- and early teens, who had been mustered into the crumbling *Wehrmacht* to take the places of older men who had died, surrendered, or deserted in what all but the young people and the most hardened SS fanatics knew to be a lost cause. Hitler's monopolistic "enlightenment"—political indoctrination disguised as education—had spread its poison effectively.

Is it so difficult, then, to understand why this wartime experience, reinforced by later study, convinced me to work with all the strength I possess to prevent any monopoly—particularly a *government* monopoly—from capturing America's schools and colleges, by default or otherwise?

Competition: Key to Quality

If that is not enough, keep in mind that I am a businessman. Like any businessman, I am acutely aware that the key to quality is *competition,* not only in business but in every walk of life. With competitors breathing down your neck, you must *be* good and *stay* good. Your product and your service must be as good as or better than the next man's—or your customers will exercise their option to buy from him and not from you. On the other hand, if you have no competition, or if your competitors must operate at a disadvantage, your incentive to do the very best job you can will not be so strong. If your customers have nowhere else to go, why knock yourself out to please them? They can take what you offer, or go without. Comparative quality of goods and services assumes less importance in the absence of competition.

So it is with education. Where there is no competition—no practical alternative within the reach of the average citizen—there is little impetus to improve the quality of services delivered by schools and colleges enjoying a monopoly position.

A veteran gambler was once asked why he continued to play in a game he knew was crooked. He replied, "It's the only game in town." The parallel with education is in terms of quality, not honesty, but the gambler's point is well made.

The necessity for competition in educational services is clearly reflected in the principle of *educational pluralism,* which may be defined as the healthy and competitive coexistence, side by side, of public and independent educational systems at all levels of academic endeavor.

Educational pluralism in practice offers us two priceless guarantees: First, the quality which comes only as a result of competition; second, the intellectual freedom which can only be served by an assured marketplace for the competition of ideas.

Any Monopoly Is Bad

Lest it be thought that the advocates of educational pluralism are all solidly committed to the survival of the independent sector without regard to the fate of the public institutions, we should remind ourselves that plural means "more than one." To be sure, a *government* monopoly in education is the most dangerous kind, because it is supported by the state's monopoly of force. But other educational monopolies would be unacceptable as well; we could not tolerate, for example, a system wherein all schools and colleges were controlled by one religious denomination or sect. Pluralism means what its roots imply: *diversity.* Anyone who calls himself a pluralist must be dedicated to the well-being and survival of both public and nonpublic education equally.

Educational pluralism deserves the wholehearted and active support of every American, because our future depends upon it. Everyone pays lip service to the concept. But do their actions reflect their words? Not always. Let's look at a bit of history.

Education's Troubles in the Colonies

In the British king's American colonies, and even into the early days of the Republic, education itself (not to mention the idea of pluralism in education) encountered difficulties.

Sir William Berkeley, colonial Governor of Virginia, offers a revealing example. He wrote to London in 1671: "I thank God there are no free schools or printing [in Virginia]; and I hope we shall not have these hundred years [*sic*]: for learning has brought disobedience and heresy and sects into the world, and printing has divulged them and libels against the best government. God keep us from both!"

Education and publication are parts of the same function: the diffusion of knowledge. Colonial authorities were hesitant to promote that diffusion in either form.

When Lord Howard became Virginia's Governor in 1683, he brought royal instructions to "allow no person to use a printing press on any occasion whatsoever." Ten years later, it was only with great difficulty that the Reverend James Blair was able to found the College of

William and Mary at Williamsburg. That isolated though memorable victory for intellectual freedom and progress was not followed by the legitimization of printing in the colony until 1733, the year after George Washington's birth, and then only the laws of 1733 were allowed to be reproduced.

There were two principal reasons for official hostility to education and its handmaiden, publication.

First, accepted theory of the times held that if the masses of people were kept ignorant, they would remain subservient to their educated rulers—and the British in America were already feeling the first stirrings of popular unrest.

Second, education in early America was almost entirely the job of the churches, in the formal sense. Public schools as we know them did not exist. In every one of the original thirteen colonies save Rhode Island, there was one "established" church, that is, one denomination to the clergy and membership of which the state extended rights and privileges (usually including the right to operate church schools) which were not available to others. Even when there was official toleration of worship by nonestablished sects, their schools were discouraged.

The domination of religious influence in our nation's early years resulted in educational pluralism in the form of interdenominational rivalries. With different religions being established in various colonies, educational competition became an intercolonial matter. Stories are told, for example, of the efforts by King's College in New York (run by the Church of England) and the College of New Jersey (Presbyterian-operated) to win the brilliant young Alexander Hamilton as a student; the outcome (expressed in the present-day names of these institutions) was Columbia 1, Princeton 0.

Development of the Public System

Although Massachusetts, in 1647, required towns with at least fifty families to build and fund elementary schools (which were run by the established Congregational Church), the public-school movement as we know it did not begin to flower in America until the 1800s, when Horace Mann and others pushed successfully for the creation of state school systems to give direction and aid to communities. Compulsory education through specific grades or ages began after 1850. Although the first high schools had opened earlier, the conversion of one-room schoolhouses to separate teaching by grades took place in the second half of the nineteenth century.

Similarly, most colleges and universities were operated under private auspices until 1862, when federal land grants encouraged the development of public higher education. The sharp increase in demand for college training after World War II, spurred by the "G.I. Bill of Rights" (Servicemen's Readjustment Act) tuition awards to veterans, expanded the number and size of public institutions. Today the State University of New York (in 1948 a collection of small specialized colleges until Governor Nelson Rockefeller made SUNY his personal priority in 1959) is the country's largest, followed closely by California State University and the City University of New York, all part of the public sector. As of 1979, U.S. government sources estimated that 7,699,000 young people were enrolled in public colleges as against 2,280,000 in the independents.

In elementary-secondary education, the public schools long ago outstripped their independent counterparts. Federal figures indicate that as of the 1980–81 school year, there were 40,950,000 youngsters in 82,266 public schools, served by 2,163,000 classroom teachers, at an annual cost of $2,406 per student; 1980–81 statistics list 5,028,865 students in 21,000 nonpublic schools being taught by 281,150 teachers, at an estimated yearly cost of $1,100–1,200 per student. For those who enjoy juggling percentages, these data tell us that of all our children, 11+ percent attend nonpublic schools, which number 20 percent of all schools, and that they are served by 11+ percent of the nation's teachers, at a cost which is, per student, 46–50 percent of the cost of educating a youngster in public school. Quibble about exact figures if it pleases you, but there can be no question as to which member of the education family is the bigger and which is the smaller.

There is absolutely nothing wrong with this relationship, unbalanced though it is. It is the result of free choices made by free people acting as they think best under existing circumstances. It is educational pluralism in action, as each member keeps the other on its toes in healthy competition. Relative sizes are not important and may vary without disturbing the whole, unless one member becomes so overpoweringly dominant that the other is threatened with extinction. Oddly enough, that's what all the fuss seems to be about. Politicians, editorial writers, powerful leaders of the academic community sound dire warnings: If we do anything to help the independents, public education will be destroyed. Give the smaller partner anything, and he'll wipe out the bigger one. Or so they say. I find it hard to believe.

Who's in Charge?

The first principle of education is that *parents are responsible for the education of their children.* No, not government—parents. This postulate is accepted by the United Nations, the United States, and most free nations of the world.

The second principle of education is that *all children must be educated.* A democratic form of government (whether direct or on the republican model, as is the United States) cannot survive without an educated citizenry. "Only the educated are free," wrote Epictetus in the first century. Jefferson warned, "If a nation expects to be ignorant and free, in a state of civilization, it expects what never was and never will be." And American freedom was the concern of Harvard's James Bryant Conant when he said, "The primary concern of American education today . . . is to cultivate in the largest possible number of our future citizens an appreciation of both the responsibilities and the benefits which come to them because they are Americans and are free."

The third principle combines the first and second: *parents have the right to decide how and by whom their children will be taught.* The last serious attempt to deny that right by a frontal attack was turned back in 1925, when the U.S. Supreme Court's decision in *Pierce v. Society of Sisters* affirmed that a student can satisfy compulsory attendance requirements at a nonpublic school. That ruling is the cornerstone of educational pluralism in America today.

From these three fundamentals, a fourth principle—this one an action principle—has emerged. We call it the "child benefit" principle upon which numerous legislatures and courts have acted for years, and it can be stated this way: Inasmuch as society requires, for the good of the whole, that all children receive a formal education, and inasmuch as parents have the right to fulfill that requirement in either public or independent schools, what is done in the name of education should benefit every child, regardless of the kind of school he or she attends. Only in that way can the mutual interests of the commonweal and the individual be best served.

All Americans understand these principles and agree with them, right? Wrong.

The Running Battle Against Nonpublic Education

Earlier on, I noted, through the words of Dr. Joseph Adelson in *Commentary,* the ongoing struggle between traditionalists and modernists for control of the public schools, observing that traditionalism values "merit, accomplishment, competition . . . success . . . self-discipline . . . and a belief in certain moral universals," while modernism "scorns the pursuit of success; is egalitarian and redistributionist . . . and emphasizes ethical relativism."

Given that clear delineation of the differences between these two forces, we quickly perceive that the modernists, who have been successful in capturing many public-school systems, must be arch foes of the independents. To be sure, some nonpublic schools cater to parents who feel that their public schools are not modernist enough, but the vast majority of the independents (especially those conducted under religious auspices) offer sanctuary to families who desire more discipline, more emphasis on merit and accomplishment, and more stressing of shared values than their local public schools are willing or able to offer.

The availability of alternatives in the form of nonpublic schools drives the modernists up the wall. I noted earlier how the imposition of modernist theory upon a public-school system tends to separate the schools from their client families, by substituting for accepted values and practices a whole new set of emphases and approaches which some parents dislike, distrust, and consider detrimental to the development of their children into well-educated citizens. The existence of alternatives to the public schools offers these parents a way out and they take it.

Because the modernists (like the rest of us) believe in the correctness of their own ideas, they want those ideas applied to *all* children. This makes it doubly distressing for them to watch the growing flow of escapees from those public schools on which modernist theory has been imposed. I have seen no surveys which prove that more kids leave modernist-dominated public schools than leave those which continue to follow traditionalist practices, but every sounding of parent opinion confirms that the *reasons* why they take their children out of public schools are those which modernism seems to foster, or at least to produce: lower scholastic achievement, greater disciplinary difficulty (including alcohol and drug abuse), and the absence of any school-promoted code of accepted values and standards.

The modernists fully understand that there are only two ways to stop the exodus of students from their public schools. One is unacceptable: surrender, and hand the schools back to traditionalism. The second is to remove alternatives. Short of a Supreme Court reversal of the *Pierce* decision, the only way to weaken and eventually to destroy the independent schools (and after them, the independent colleges) is to manipulate government power and money so that nonpublic education is placed at an impossible disadvantage. That is the course of action which the educational modernists and their liberal colleagues have chosen, and to which they have recruited others who (although they may not object to nonpublic education per se) fear for the future of the public schools if the independents offer attractive alternatives.

The Unholy Alliance

To fight the war against educational pluralism (while calling it a war to *save* pluralism by protecting public education from the independents), a coalition with considerable clout has been formed among natural and not-so-natural allies.

In the van of this army are the pundits and editorialists, bylined or anonymous, of those newspapers, magazines, and radio and television stations which invariably take up the cudgels on the "liberal" side of every question. Powerful support, most effective as a lobbying effort using the carrot-and-stick ploy on legislators, comes from the organized teacher groups: the National Education Association (NEA) and the American Federation of Teachers (AFT), bitter rivals in the struggle for power in Washington and the state capitals but united against nonpublic education. In this cause, they are partners with their traditional adversaries, the public-school boards of education, superintendents, and administrators (all equipped with their own lobbyists at state and federal levels), as well as most state boards of education and chief state school offiers who, at state level, seldom have responsibility for nonpublic education. Civil-rights groups like the National Association for the Advancement of Colored People (NAACP), suspicious of private schools as havens for those fleeing racial integration, and the American Civil Liberties Union (ACLU), hostile to the nonpublics on issues of church-and-state, add their voices to the clamor against the independents.

And on the fringe are the bigots, those who know that Roman Catholic schools enroll almost two-thirds of the students outside the public sector, and who are—although they would never spoil their public image by admitting it—still obsessed with the old Know-Nothing fear of papism in America.

Oh—you were sure that religious bigotry was dead in this enlightened age of ours? It isn't, and you need not take my word about the ongoing strength of anti-Catholic feeling in this country. Listen to some observers. Yale Professor Peter Viereck: "Catholic-baiting is the anti-Semitism of the liberals." Richard Hofstadter, in *The Paranoid Style in American Politics:* "Anti-Catholicism has always been the pornography of the Puritan." Professor John Higham of Johns Hopkins: "The most luxuriant, tenacious tradition of paranoic agitation in American history has been anti-Catholicism." And Harvard Professor Arthur M. Schlesinger, Sr.: "I regard prejudice against [the Catholic] Church as the deepest bias in the history of the American people."

Currently, the most virulent examples of anti-Catholicism are found in the crude pamphleteering of certain fundamentalists who call themselves Christians but sound like Klansmen. Examples are abundant, but one should suffice here. No less a personage than Henry C. Clausen, Sovereign Grand Commander of the Ancient and Accepted Scottish Rite of Freemasonry, 33rd Degree, Southern Jurisdiction, USA, is shown as the author of a 1981 (1981, not 1921) pamphlet titled "How to Pauperize Your Schools," contending that aid to nonpublic schools would be "a disaster that foreshadows the death of an American ideal" and "the undermining of our fundamental freedoms as a nation," because church schools threaten "our democratic unity." The intellectual level of the pamphlet is established by its drawings of torture devices used during the Spanish Inquisition.

We certainly cannot blame the liberals for such attacks, but I have yet to hear of any liberal standing up to protest them. Prejudices among liberals (and there are always exceptions) are more subtly expressed, more neatly rationalized, by opposition to any measures which might improve religious-sponsored education, those who choose it for their children, or the children themselves.

You Name It: They Don't Like It

In various combinations, plus or minus this or that component element, the anti-independent coalition has bucked every effort on the part of government to assist the independent schools and their clients. Whether it be bus transportation, or secular textbooks, or health services, or field trips, or shared facilities, or the costs of complying with state testing requirements, or whatever—the coalition has opposed it at school-board level, in the legislatures and the Congress, and finally in the courts, where they have had their greatest successes.

Lately, their big push has been against tuition tax credits and educational vouchers.

Simply described, tuition tax credits are prescribed amounts deductible from the income-tax obligation of a family for each child whose school or college education requires a tuition payment. Vouchers are credit slips, of a given value, which families may submit to either public or private schools in payment for their youngsters' education; the schools are compensated by government for the vouchers they receive. For reasons of fiscal feasibility and political acceptability, tax credits could become less costly tax deductions, their awards could be reduced, and there could be an income ceiling on eligibility. Similar variants might be found in the basic voucher proposal. Both concepts are more complex than I have indicated here, but the gist of each is as I have stated.

Not all advocates of tuition tax credits favor vouchers, or vice versa, but both have one common element which is the basic purpose of each: *both make it less onerous for families to choose the kind of education they want for their children.* As property taxes for support of the local public schools (taxes which everyone must pay directly or indirectly) continue to rise, and as the cost of sending youngsters to nonpublic schools rises as well, a family's capacity to choose between the public and private sectors for their own children is lessened, especially if the family has a limited income. Tuition tax credits attempt to protect that freedom of choice without disturbing the principle of universal taxation to support public education; vouchers would expand the choice considerably, but by using tax funds to support the public schools only to the extent that parents select them.

For those who are devoted to the concept of freedom of choice in education, as I am, both tuition tax credits and vouchers deserve serious consideration and a chance to prove their validity.

Dispelling the Fog

When I worked in 1940 for Big Jim Farley and Ed Flynn in the publicity division of the Democratic National Committee, my boss, Charlie Michelson (the man who pinned horns and a tail on Herbert Hoover in 1932) wrote a column entitled "Dispelling the Fog," in which he periodically demolished the latest Republican arguments. Let's dispel some fog.

Of course, the trouble with writing a book on a topic of ongoing interest and action is that between the writing and the publication of the work, things happen. When you read these lines, tuition tax credits (as proposed by New York Senator Daniel Patrick Moynihan and Oregon Senator Robert Packwood) could be a part of the U.S. Internal Revenue Code, or the Congress could have killed or postponed them, in whole or in part. The voucher plan proposed by Professor Jack Coons could have been adopted, turned down, or ignored by the voters of California.

In such an "iffy" situation, there is little value in a detailed analysis of the specifics of current tax credit and voucher proposals, and I shall not essay such an analysis. But inasmuch as some thick fog has been generated by the *Nebelwerfer* (in the German Army, smoke-throwers) of the anti-independent coalition, some fog-dispelling is in order—in the course of which we will learn what the anti-independents *really* think about educational pluralism.

One theme running through the anti-independent literature is that tax credits constitute "federal spending"; I have also seen credits characterized as "giving money to private schools." Neither designation is correct. Taxation and spending are two different things, as our national debate over which should be cut first and most has emphasized. Look at it this way: When government allows you to keep more of what you earn—by reducing tax rates, increasing exemptions and credits, or adding to deductions—do you think that government is "giving" you money, or "spending" money on you? Of course not. Government is simply letting you keep more of what was yours in the first place. "Spending," "giving," "rebates" (of taxes not paid?) and "subsidies" (all being used to describe tax credits) are out of place in the debate.

In an attempt to paint tax credits as a help-the-rich deal, the coalition contends that they will go "mainly" to those parents who don't need them because they can afford to send their youngsters to nonpublic schools now. But if that is so, what happens to the coalition's contradictory argument that tax credits will break the back of public education by luring into the nonpublic schools thousands of public-school kids whose parents could *not* previously afford tuition?

On this point, the anti-independents claim that tuition tax credits are "incentives" for families to transfer their children from public schools into private schools. Here they miss the point entirely, demonstrating their lack of understanding of public education's very real problems. Tax credits are not the incentive for transfer to the nonpublic sector. *The incentive is the reason or combination of reasons which convince parents that their children will learn better and become better citizens by attending an independent school rather than the public school in which they are or could be enrolled.* Tax credits merely help parents, who already have the incentive, to exercise that option.

Get Out the Crying Towel

An important element of the anti-independent coalition's campaign against tax credits and vouchers is their cost to the taxpayer. Predictions of vastly increased "spending" on uncontrolled "open-ended entitlement" credits which are bound to become still more expensive as time goes on are all very scary.

Having been a member of the educational community for eleven years on New York's Board of Regents, I must confess amusement at the sight of teacher unions, school administrators' organizations, and boards of education at all levels shedding crocodile tears for the poor, beleaguered taxpayer, when all of these outfits have annually, for years, besieged the halls of Congress and the state legislatures demanding ever more funding for education. Only when it is *nonpublic* education that might be aided do these people play Horatio at the Bridge for the taxpayer.

We've already pointed up the difference between spending and tax credits; the question of how much money the government will not take in because of the credits is debatable. We know that the government will pay out nothing, except to those who have little or no tax liability—the low-income people who, according to the critics of credits, will not benefit from them.

Tax credits are indeed "entitlement" programs, in that their overall cost in forgone revenue cannot be exactly predicted because it depends upon the number of kids qualifying for and using credits. But we don't hear the coalition complaining about such other entitlement programs as Social Security, Medicare, Medicaid, and Aid to Dependent Children (ADC), each of which produces unpredictable claims on public funds. As for the possible escalation of dollar requirements, since when have we turned down a worthwhile effort because it might become more costly as the years passed? Can you name *one* program of any significance which is no more expensive today than it was in its first year? Neither can I—and neither can the coalition.

Having been one of their number for eleven years, I don't believe that the traditional tax-eaters of the educational community will fool anyone in their disguise as watchdogs of the Treasury.

The Core of the Matter

It is only when we learn the nature of the *social* arguments advanced against tax credits and vouchers that we realize the ultimate goal of those who oppose them—and that goal is *not* educational pluralism.

Right up front, of course, is the rich-versus-poor syndrome. An AFT broadside in April 1981 called credits "Aid For Those Who Need It Least," repeating the fallacy that "in most cases" credits would go to those families "who already are willing to pay the cost of private education and thus least need financial help." Do you get the picture? The nonpublic schools are havens for the affluent. Right?

Wrong. The fact that a family sends its children to a nonpublic school does not necessarily mean that the family is well-to-do. Thousands of middle- and lower-income parents dig down until it hurts, to send their youngsters to independent schools; this is particularly true of denominational schools and those in inner-city areas. Even at that, subsidies from church and private sources are needed to help cover the cost of educating kids whose parents cannot afford to pay the whole freight.

In the same ad, the AFT indirectly concedes that tax credits would indeed help less than affluent families, when it complains that 1,250,000 more youngsters would swell the nonpublic schools' enrollment by 25 percent as a result of tuition tax credits. If a $250–$500 tax credit could produce such a mighty migration, that migration must be a movement of middle- or lower-income kids. To a well-to-do family, $250–$500 does not make that much difference. The help-the-rich argument is spurious.

The "Bad Schools" Bugaboo

The anti-independent forces have been quick to raise the specter of tax credits or vouchers being used by parents to cover their children's tuition in "schools with negative values"—by which they mean schools that teach points of view other than those presumably held by most people, schools run by "extremist groups of the left and the right, irresponsible cults, and organizations that promote discrimination and racism."

Has the veneer of liberalism begun to peel?

Who is to determine that a given nonpublic school is "good" or "bad," "positive" or "negative"? Will the Congress create a Committee on Un-American Schools? Do the anti-independents believe that bad schools (if they can be identified) should be shut down by the government? If so, they should say so, and turn in their liberal credentials. This qualitative discrimination against certain kinds of institutions is exactly what the Nazis practiced in 1933–45.

If a school encourages or indulges in practices that are illegal, that school and those who run it must take the consequences. What is worrisome is the notion that a school's *values* (as defined by government or any self-appointed group) should disqualify it or its clients from receiving benefits extended to others. Yet the message from the coalition is that if this cannot be done, *no* schools, *no* children, should qualify for government help.

It seems to me that if a school can meet all the standards established by society for institutions which conduct full and full-time educational programs, then that school and those who select it should not be discriminated against, regardless of the particular *values* the school professes. Legislation can rule out schools which are inadequate in terms of their quality: the quality of their educational offerings; the qualifications of their faculty; their plant, facilities, and equipment; their health, safety, and security arrangements, and all the mandates that their state's educational standards impose upon them. But legislation must not penalize schools (or families) for the *values* they esteem. And the existence of schools which foster unpopular ("negative") values should not be a barrier to the extension of child-benefit assistance to nonpublic school children as a class.

If you believe in democracy . . . practice it.

The Power of the State over Private Education

This is an appropriate point for me to specify my views on the question of government power over nonpublic education.

Although New York's Board of Regents has always included independent schools and colleges under its aegis (the Regents antedate the public systems at both levels), and has evolved a set of standards and regulations arrived at with the participation and consent of the independents, not every state enjoys the same pleasant relationship. There is a strong movement, especially in the Midwest, to deny state governments any regulatory powers over nonpublic schools, particularly religious schools.

Frankly, I do not believe that self-regulation is an adequate guarantee of quality in education. I do not believe that anyone should have the final say as to the excellence of his own product.

If we are to enjoy educational pluralism, we must be assured of high quality in all of the educational systems which make up the pluralistic whole. If we permit children to receive their formal education in schools which, by default, we allow to be inferior and of poor quality, we do a disservice to the national interest as well as to the children themselves.

For these reasons, I favor the principle of public (i.e., state) oversight of *both* public and private sectors.

As Regents' Chancellor, I supported inclusion of the nonpublic schools of New York in all of our state uniform testing programs—not only the periodic performance tests in reading and math at third-, sixth-, and ninth-grade levels, but also the recently developed competency tests as requirements for high-school diplomas. I favored stricter standards for certification and recertification of high schools, including nonpublic high schools. I backed Commissioner Joe Nyquist's program for re-evaluation of all doctoral programs in the independent colleges as well as State University (it was State U., not the independents, which fought unsuccessfully the Regents' right to evaluate).

I see no compelling reason why nonpublic schoolteachers should be exempted from whatever qualitative requirements or competency tests may eventually be adopted for school faculties in New York State or elsewhere.

Finally, I do not believe that any form of government aid, on the child-benefit principle or otherwise, should be extended in the form of grants, loans, tax credits, or vouchers if the school does not maintain satisfactory standards of excellence, as defined by a qualified, neutral judge such as the State Board of Education. It should also be the accrediting unit for federal assistance.

Is Discrimination a Factor?

The foes of independent schools love to drop broad hints that the non-publics, which can admit or reject individual applicants, discriminate on the basis of race or ethnic origin. Denominational schools are, of course, permitted to favor those of their own creed, but even that is looked down upon, as "divisive."

I do not believe that people should be included in or excluded from anything on the basis of irrelevant factors (e.g., for schools: race, creed, or color, except for denominational-school preferences). I value a person on individual merit. Thus, exclusionary admissions policy in a school is (in my view) inappropriate if it excludes by category and not by individual evaluation. If a school does *not* exclude students for reasons of race, creed, or color, but still has no students of certain races, creeds, or colors, that school should not be penalized because of decisions made by parents, nor should the school be required to go out and beat the bushes for kinds of youngsters they don't have, or don't have in sufficient numbers to satisfy some bureaucratic quota.

Freedom of association is an old American principle that has more of a traditional and common-sense than a formal or constitutional standing. It is human nature to prefer associating with people for whom we have an affinity; we associate with them because we want to, not because we are forbidden *not* to associate with them. If that is to be changed, if private facilities are to be forced by the government (as if they were public) to admit everyone and anyone who wants to "join" or participate, that is a policy decision which should be referred specifically and directly to the American people and their elected representatives, not to administrators and courts.

Personally, I opt for unfettered freedom of association.

Many liberals now object to long-standing laws and policies against abortion and contraception and pornography and the like, arguing that individuals and groups should not use the power of the law to impose their private opinions upon the rest of society. Most of those laws and policies reflect the preponderance of public opinion over the years, but (say the liberals) that is not the issue; private rights are protected even from majority viewpoints.

Very well. If that be the case, government should not use laws to force *its* preferences upon private organizations as to whom they should admit, nor should individuals or groups be penalized for not abiding by government guidelines for private organization membership. Here majority opinion is probably on the side of free association; it is the doctrinaire egalitarians in high government posts who insist upon obedience to their personal notions, imposed by administrative or judicial fiat.

At the risk of repeating myself, I believe that the educational resources of the public should extend to all children, no matter what school they attend, as long as their school meets accepted *educational* standards.

But do the independent schools reject or neglect minority youngsters? No, says this 1981 U.S. Department of Education report:

"Private schools play an increasingly important role in the education of minority and disadvantaged children. In 1978–79, 249,000 Black Americans and 248,000 Hispanic Americans attended Catholic schools.

This represented 16.5% of the enrollment in those schools. During 1975–76, Catholic schools in the ten largest inner-city areas showed a minority enrollment of 113,302, or 45% of the total Catholic school enrollment in those areas. In 1978–79, minority enrollment in Lutheran schools increased 7.3% to a total of 13%. During the past year, while enrollment in Independent schools increased 2%, minority enrollment in these schools rose 9%. Minority students currently account for 8.6% of Independent school enrollment."

Writing in *Policy Review* (Winter 1981), E. G. West comments:

"The question is whether wealthier children in independent schools are more racially isolated than wealthier children in public schools. In the suburban areas of New York there is, on average, not more than 2 percent minority enrollment in public schools and the proportion of low-income children attending is also tiny. But forty-four private schools in New York City that are members of the National Association of Independent Schools were found, in a recent survey, to have *a minority enrollment of twice the national average.* And in half of the Western states, there are more members of minority groups in private schools than in public schools."

Catholic schools enroll 64.5 percent of the nation's private school students. In April 1981, the *New York Times,* reporting a conference of the National Catholic Educational Association, noted:

"In Manhattan, non-Catholic students now make up 17 percent of the [Catholic-school] enrollment, and the proportion of non-Catholics in the seven Catholic elementary schools in Harlem ranges from 60 to 80 percent. Non-Catholics are a majority in the Catholic elementary schools of Newark [N.J.], and at least 10 percent of the students in the Catholic schools of Brooklyn [N.Y.] and Hartford [Conn.] are not Catholics.

"Most non-Catholic students are urban black Protestants, but white Protestants in outlying areas are increasingly turning to Catholic education, as parents—professing disenchantment with discipline and morals in public schools—seek alternatives."

As a general rule, possibly with some regional exceptions, the independents are admitting more and more minority students, who apply for admission in greater and greater numbers. This troubles the liberal-modernists who fear that their stranglehold on much of public education cannot survive any significant movement of children from the public sector (where they have established their hegemony) to the non-public sector (where liberalism-modernism is not a requirement).

So they have conceived and used their allies in the U.S. government to enforce a plan to remodel the private schools in the image of the public schools.

Everything Must Fit into One Mold

Here's the new drill, and for once it is not the Department of Education's Office of Civil Rights zealots who are pressing it. This time it's the Department of Justice. The latest liberal gimmick, applied to private clubs and associations as well as private schools and colleges, is simply stated: If any private organization hopes to share in any government benefits at all, or if its members hope to enjoy such benefits, *the organization must be conducted as if it were a public facility.*

For example, if a club does not admit (or seems not to admit) individuals because of their race, color, or ethnic heritage, that club's members cannot deduct their expenses at the club in any way, even if those expenses were incurred for good business reasons.

Second example: If a nonpublic school was "established or expanded" while nearby public schools were in the process of integrating their student bodies, that school would automatically be presumed guilty of racial discrimination if it did not enroll a government-prescribed quota of minority pupils—*even if no minority kids had applied.* Such schools could lose their tax exemptions and their right to receive tax-deductible contributions, which other nonpublic schools could retain if they agree to cast themselves in the public image.

My own views on racial quotas are expressed elsewhere quite clearly: I don't like them. But quotas are not the essential question here, which I ask once again: Is it now to become a fixed principle of U.S. policy (by administrative fiat without input from the American public or their representatives) that private organizations, in order to qualify for those affirmative considerations traditionally extended to them by government, must henceforth behave exactly like public organizations? Put in another way, will the power of the public purse be used to force everyone into the same mold?

Much of this chapter has been devoted to the principle of *pluralism* as a defense against totalitarianism. Educational pluralism in America is now threatened on two fronts: a frontal attack continues to deny nonpublic schools the benefit of any state assistance to them, or to the parents and children who choose and use them, while from the rear they are threatened with the loss of those governmental considerations which they already have, unless they become just like the public schools.

Don't let the "racial justice" or "equal opportunity" arguments fool you on this one. They are window dressing; if they don't work, some other attractive principle will be advanced as a valid reason to make the private schools duplicates of the public schools. And that is what it's all about—by whatever means, to weaken or eliminate the independent schools *as alternatives to the public schools.* The goal? An educational Tweedledum and Tweedledee.

Are They Bragging or Complaining?

It is difficult to know whether the anti-independents are bragging or complaining when they state that the public schools will (or is it "must"?) take all children, including those with learning disabilities, handicaps, language, or disciplinary problems, while private schools can exclude "anyone they want."

Is that so? It is only within the last few years that U.S. and state legislation has mandated acceptance of children with special disabilities into the public schools—and mainstreaming has been bitterly fought by some public schools, even into the courts. Far from excluding handicapped and troubled children from the private sector, many good independent schools make a special effort to address their needs on an individual basis.

As for disciplinary cases, it was standard practice some years ago for students whose conduct was unacceptable in public schools to be thrown out or pulled out and (if the family's finances permitted) sent to military school, where discipline is a way of life. There are independent schools today which specialize in the retraining of the disruptive youngster. Although our liberals have made it difficult for the public schools to rid themselves of the violent, disruptive, and criminal elements (as I discussed earlier), it is still possible, though not easy. And there is no reason why we cannot change the rules to make enforcement easier, as Albert Shanker has suggested.

The foes of nonpublic education are somewhat schizoid about the public schools. In one breath, they talk of "the tradition of universal free public education, which has long served as a core of American democracy"—and they are right. But in the next breath, they grouse that the public schools have to admit all children "regardless of their strengths and weaknesses," as if that were a burden they would like to throw off.

Public education is free for all, and should be. It is the responsibility of all, and should be. Nonpublic education offers *alternatives* for those who want something for their children that their local public schools cannot or do not provide. That something may be daily instruction in religious and moral values, special concentration upon physical, mental, or psychological disabilities, advanced training in Russian or equestrianism or shorthand or etiquette or athletics or military science, or strict disciplinary control. The private schools exist because they offer, *in addition to the prescribed general curriculum,* something else for those families who need it, want it, and cannot obtain it in the public sector.

The American people should not be denied this option.

How to Lose Friends and Alienate Voters

Every citizen is responsible for the maintenance of the public school system in his local district and his state. This responsibility exists whether he has children in the public schools, in nonpublic schools, or no children in any school. Anyone who believes in educational pluralism supports the principle, as I do.

But to "support" public education does not bind one to approve everything that goes on or doesn't go on in the local schools or to vote for everything the schools ask in terms of budgets, bond issues, or disposal of excessed buildings, or for specific board candidates. Paying school taxes is one thing; rubber-stamping the policies and procedures of school boards and administrators is quite another.

The coalition gripes that people who send their kids to nonpublic schools should pay the whole freight for them, despite the fact that those schools fill a public function (general education) and lessen the load of the property taxpayer who would otherwise have to pay for the schooling of these youngsters.

The coalition also claims that tuition tax credits would wean away "middle- and upper-class parents, who have traditionally been the most ardent supporters of increased funding for public education," which in turn would "erode voter support" for budgets and bond issues.

Parents don't transfer their kids from public to private schools just because they would qualify for a few hundred government dollars. They do so for positive or negative reasons, or a bit of both; the private school may offer something that the public school cannot, or things may be going on in the public schools that the parents don't like. Those with the latter motivation are already disenchanted with their local public schools and probably would not turn out to support more spending, but those who just want for their children something affirmative, something extra, are not necessarily hostile. As a matter of fact, some independent systems (for example, the Catholic schools at the parish level) usually do not have a post-eighth-grade element; parents know they may be sending their youngsters into the public junior-high and high schools, and therefore are personally concerned about the quality of those schools.

For those reasons, I cautioned my friends of the Nassau-Suffolk [counties] School Boards Association (New York) not so long ago against badmouthing of the independent schools and against opposition to any type of government assistance for them. I pointed out then (as I do again, now) that such hostility goes a long way to turn friends or at least neutrals into enemies who, given their right to vote on public-school funding, will (if sufficiently alienated) turn out in droves to vote "no." Don't the public schools have enough trouble with lessened public confidence these days?

The rules of elementary common sense apply: When you are about to ask someone to give you money, it is sheer folly to question his motivation or criticize his judgment in handling his own affairs.

The "One Big Pot" Theory

Part and parcel of what I believe to be the unwarranted hostility of many public-school champions to the matter of government aid for nonpublic schools is what I call the "one big pot" theory: the idea that there are only so many dollars (in one big pot) for all of education, and that giving one of those dollars to the independent schools or their students means one less dollar for the public schools and their students.

The theory has been discredited so often that I am surprised to know it still lives. Those of us who have been personally involved in devising government-support-for-education principles and plans at state and federal levels know that no legislature is likely to adopt any suggestion that does not help to meet the learning needs of all children, subject to required differences in delivery systems and recognizing the priority status of the state-run schools. If there is anyone who thinks that the Elementary and Secondary Education Act of 1965 (ESEA) could have passed the Congress if it had excluded nonpublic school kids from its aid provisions, that person wasn't around in 1965, or wasn't paying attention.

Proponents of the "one big pot" theory have things backward. It is not the number of dollars in the pot that determines or should determine how educational needs will be served; it is those needs which should determine how many dollars will be in the pot. No budgetary authority worthy of the name starts with a dollar amount and fits requirements into it; that is about as intelligent as jamming a size 7¼ head into a 6½ hat. *Needs* are determined first, and assigned priorities; then the cost of meeting those needs is assessed. If the demands of other state functions compete with those of education, decisions must be made on the basis of both general and intraeducational priorities. But the basis remains *need*, not what's in the Treasury.

The Key

When one has run through all the technical arguments, the *real* reason for liberal-modernist opposition to tax credits, vouchers, and other efforts to assist the nonpublic schools is simply that *the liberal-modernists do not believe in pluralism.* They do not give a hoot in hell whether the independents live or die, because *they consider diversity to be bad and uniformity* (read: *conformity*) *to be the ideal.* Their viewpoint is summarized revealingly by the American Federation of Teachers' statement: ". . . such [aid to independents] legislation would, if enacted, encourage the development of primary and secondary schools fostering segregation on the basis of religious, social, racial and ethnic differences . . ."

If you want everyone to be fashioned from one mold, you will agree. I do not.

Independent Schools and the Constitution

Whenever Congress or a state legislature is about to consider a measure that would benefit children in nonpublic schools, a howl goes up from the liberal-modernists: "You can't *do* that! Independent schools always include denominational schools, and government can't help them at all, because to do so would violate the principle of separation of church and state."

On this issue, opponents of aid to nonpublic schools become instant Supreme Court Justices. Most other legislation is allowed to be voted up or down; if it passes and is challenged on constitutional grounds, the courts can *then* rule on it . . . but not if the issue is state aid to independent school children. That is presumed from the start to be automatically unconstitutional and thus pointless to enact. This presumption has become so strong that newspaper articles parrot it; even the *New York Times* has been guilty. In April 1979, it reported: "The Federal constitution specifically forbids state aid to parochial schools," which it does not.

The problem is that certainty and clarity are not characteristic of the U.S. Supreme Court's decisions in school-aid cases. Just the opposite is true.

I have said publicly on more than one occasion that church-state school cases are not a constitutional field but a swamp. If you'd rather I didn't rely on quotes from myself, Professor Philip B. Kurland of the University of Chicago has written that "the Court is thoroughly unprincipled in the area" of public aid to church-related schools (meaning, as Senator Pat Moynihan has pointed out, that their decisions reveal no coherent principle). Former Assistant U.S. Attorney General Antonin Scalia has said, "It is impossible . . . to describe with any completeness the utter confusion of Supreme Court pronouncements in the church-state area. . . ."

Here's one example: Chief Justice Warren Burger (in the 1971 *Tilton v. Richardson* decision) justified government help for church-related colleges but not for church-related schools because "there is substance to the contention that college students are less impressionable and less susceptible to religious indoctrination." Try to explain that distinction . . . why eighteen-year-old Tommy, a high-school senior, is so much more impressionable than his nineteen-year-old brother Timmy, a college freshman.

The thought is silly, and off the point. If the Constitution bars state aid to church-related schools *because they are church-related,* how, as a matter of principle, can the state aid church-related colleges? Of course the Constitution does not bar the state from doing either, but the encrusted errors of prior Courts inevitably lead to weak rationalizations like Chief Justice Burger's.

Consider also Justice Harry Blackmun's losing battle with consistency in the 1977 *Wolman v. Walter* decision, which reaffirmed the government's right to provide nonpublic school students with books but denied that they could be given "instructional materials and equipment," including maps. As Senator Moynihan observed acidly, "The Court has yet to rule on atlases, which are books of maps." The Justices long approved the use of public-school buses to transport pupils to and from parochial schools (where religion is part of the regular curriculum), but have frowned upon the use of the same buses to take the same kids on field trips to secular places of interest.

The Supreme Court's Very Own "Catch-22"

A "Catch-22," named for Joseph Heller's delightful book with that title, is a combination of principles or rules which are mutually incompatible, and unworkable because of each other.

The Supreme Court has constructed a nifty Catch-22 in their requirements for the constitutionality of state aid to nonpublic schools. First, they insist that the aid must be used only for secular, not religious, purposes. Second, they require that administration of state aid must not involve "excessive entanglement" of state agencies with the administration of the church schools. The Catch-22 is that state procedures sufficient to ensure that government aid is not used for religious purposes are, per se, "excessive entanglement." Try to beat *that* combination.

Prejudice on the High Court?

Religious prejudice—hostility toward others because of their religious beliefs—is bad enough when it becomes lodged in the mind and the heart. It is worse when it prevents free citizens from enjoying equal opportunities in employment, in housing, or in education; antidiscrimination laws were passed to eliminate these negative effects of prejudice. But religious prejudice is at its very worst when it influences government policy at the highest irreversible levels, affecting the lives of millions of people. (If you don't agree, just ask the survivors of Hitler's official policy of genocide, which killed 6 million European Jews during the Holocaust of 1933–45.)

The late Justice William O. Douglas, who set a record for the longest service on the Supreme Court, may not himself have harbored any prejudice against Roman Catholics, and I do not charge him with so doing. But Justice Douglas's own opinions reveal that on issues of government aid to nonpublic schools (by no means all of which are Catholic-related) his "no" votes were bolstered by references to a text which Professor Douglas Laycock of the University of Chicago Law School has called "an elaborate hate tract." The book, a 1962 publication whose neutral title, *Roman Catholicism,* may have put Justice Douglas off his guard, is the work of Loraine Boettner, whose philosophy on Catholicism is expressed quite plainly: "Our American freedoms are being threatened today by two totalitarian systems, communism and Roman Catholicism. And of the two in our country Romanism is growing faster than is communism and is the more dangerous since it covers its real nature with a cloak of religion."

That Mr. Boettner's book influenced Justice Douglas's opinions is certain; a footnote in his concurring opinion in the *Lemon* case (1971) quotes Boettner as follows:

"In the parochial schools Roman Catholic indoctrination is included in every subject. History, literature, geography, civics and science are given a Roman Catholic slant. The whole education of the child is filled with propaganda. That, of course, is the very purpose of such schools, the very reason for going to all the work and expense of maintaining a dual school system. Their purpose is not so much to educate, but to indoctrinate and train, not to teach scripture truths and Americanism, but to make loyal Roman Catholics. The children are regimented, and are told what to wear, what to do, and what to think."

I share the views of Senator Moynihan, who told an audience: "Ponder the implications of Mr. Boettner's charge that Catholic schools do not teach 'scripture truths'! One cannot easily imagine such 'evidence' being used against the interest of another major religious or ethnic group in our nation without raising puzzled eyebrows, if not indeed holy hell."

It is sad when religious bias is allowed to play any role at all in formulating final decisions about what government can or cannot do, particularly when the education of so many youngsters (of a variety of religious beliefs) is at stake. Yet that seems to be what has happened in this case. Justice Douglas may not have been fully aware of the implications of his reliance upon Boettner's hate tract (his open use of Boettner would so indicate), but if a jurist of his stature—he was almost a demigod to liberals—can make such a misstep, one cannot help but wonder whether others in high places have been similarly and more subtly affected.

Two Suggestions

Returning to the present confusion about aid to church-related schools, is there a way out of the constitutional thicket? Two Justices have arrived at separate answers.

Justice John Paul Stevens, dissenting in *Committee for Public Education v. Regan,* has construed a novel solution which some of my local lawyer friends (in their kinder moments) have called injudicious as well as unjudicial. It is Stevens's view "that the entire enterprise of trying to justify various types of subsidies to non-public schools should be abandoned. . . . I would resurrect the 'high and impregnable' wall between church and state constructed by the Framers of the First Amendment." In other words, Justice Stevens suggests that the door be slammed shut on any and all forms of government-church collaboration, forever—that present and future Supreme Courts simply accept his view of the First Amendment and write *finis* to the question.

Not being an attorney, I will not comment on the idea of eliminating in one stroke a whole segment of constitutional law, beyond pondering the possibility that it might lead to a system of predetermined positions on *all* issues, in which case the law clerks could look up the approved solution and cast nine "yes" or "no" votes, depending upon how the question is put in each case. We wouldn't need a Supreme Court, would we?

Justice Stevens's view is wrong on two counts. First, he envisions a post-Revolutionary nation whose leaders and citizens wanted a complete divorce of God from government, and that is a nation that never was. Second, he suggests that the "high and impregnable" wall of separation, built by the First Amendment, has been undermined and chipped away by Supreme Court decisions since 1790, when that is the opposite of what has been happening.

There can be no question as to the direction which church-state decisions involving education have taken in recent years. While the course has been zigzag, the separation has been made more strict. Who would have suggested in 1790 (or a century later, in 1890, or fifty years thereafter, in 1940) that a nondenominational, noncompulsory prayer, recited in a public facility, violated the First Amendment? It was not until 1962 that the Supreme Court said it in *Engel v. Vitale,* the "school-prayer" case, outlawing a practice which was as old as public education itself. The "wall" is building, not eroding.

Like Justice Stevens, Justice Byron White wants a return to the principles of the First Amendment. Unlike Justice Stevens, he knows what the First Amendment was and is intended to mean. In his brief *New York v. Cathedral Academy* dissent, quoted here in its entirety, he points the way: "Because the Court continues to misconstrue the First Amendment in a manner that discriminates against religion and is contrary to the fundamental educational needs of the country, I dissent here as I have in *Lemon . . . Nyquist . . . Levitt . . . Meek . . .* and *Wolman."* (Those were cases wherein, contrary to Justice Stevens's impression, new buttresses were being added to his "wall").

I believe it would be helpful to our understanding of the issue to return briefly to early America, and to examine what "establishment" and "free exercise" meant to our first citizens.

Back to the First Amendment

The United States Constitution drafted at the Philadelphia Convention in 1787 to replace the weak Articles of Confederation did not include a summary of the rights of citizens and states, or of the restrictions placed upon the new federal government. As agreed at Philadelphia, that was to come later; it took the form of the first ten constitutional amendments known as the Bill of Rights, which became part of our fundamental charter in 1790. The limitations imposed by the Bill upon the U.S. government were extended to state governments by the Fourteenth Amendment in 1868.

The first clause of the First Amendment to the Constitution reads today as it read in 1790: "Congress shall make no law respecting an establishment of religion, or prohibiting the free exercise thereof . . ."

What Do "Establishment" and "Free Exercise" Mean?

What was (and is) meant by an "establishment" of religion? What constitutes "free exercise" of religion? These terms were readily understood by those born and brought up in colonial America, which includes all the Founding Fathers who wrote both our Constitution and its Bill of Rights. Further, the concepts of religious establishment and free exercise of religion, while essentially at odds with each other, are intertwined and must be explained together.

"Establishment of religion" was a principle of government brought to the New World by those who had either benefited or suffered under the church-state alliances of Europe, some of which exist to this day. A religion (say, Christianity) or a denomination or creed (say, Catholicism, Protestantism, or any of its component elements—the Church of England, the Congregational Church, the Quakers, and others) was "established" when it was designated by law as the official religion of a colony, thus entitling its churches, clergy, and laity to varying degrees of special support and privileges not available to others.

"Free exercise of religion," allowing members of all religious groups to worship as they chose and to enjoy full civil rights without penalties, was as rare in the colonies as establishments were the rule. Where the established creed allowed "toleration" (an enlightened concept for those times), some—seldom if ever all—of the nonestablished denominations could worship freely, although the privileged status of establishment churches and their members remained.

Those who wrote the Constitution and the Bill of Rights lived under church-state dispensations such as these, and it was by no means unanimously agreed that establishments must go and free exercise must be unfettered. Only the determination of giants like James Madison and Thomas Jefferson (opposed on occasion by men of the stature of George Washington, Patrick Henry, and John Marshall) finally cemented these principles into the national Constitution.

Conditions in the Colonies

The Reverend Sanford H. Cobb, a noted Presbyterian minister and scholar, reviewed in his comprehensive work, *The Rise of Religious Liberty in America* (1902), how the establishment of churches declined and freedom of worship expanded during the seventeenth, eighteenth, and nineteenth centuries. The degree of church-state control and of limitations upon worship constantly changed during the period, but religious liberty's cause gained strength until it finally won out, in the form of the First Amendment.

In colonial times, that was far from the case. Whether one was a member of the established faith or not, the combination of governmental authority and church power was not always kind. In Virginia, according to Cobb, the Church of England was established at the outset. Its rules became law; those who failed to attend Anglican services had their allowances stopped (for their first absence), were whipped for the second, and spent six months in the galleys as three-time losers. Those who "broke the Sabbath" suffered the same penalties, except that three-timers were executed.

At one point, Catholics in Virginia were disenfranchised; none could come into the colony, and priests were expelled within five days of discovery. Lord Calvert, the Catholic governor of adjacent Maryland, came to Virginia while organizing his own government. Because he refused to renounce his Catholic faith even temporarily, he was made to leave Virginia.

Only Church of England (Anglican) ministers could perform marriages in Virginia; all others were illegitimate. While some Protestant sects were tolerated, others (including, at various times, Puritans, Quakers, and Baptists) were restrained or persecuted.

The proprietary governments of North and South Carolina controlled the Church of England there, and the state paid for the construction of churches and the salaries of clergymen. No one over seventeen who was not "a member of some church or religious profession" was permitted "any benefit or protection of the law or . . . any place of profit or honor" in these colonies. In what the Carolinians of the time must have considered a surge of toleration, a 1696 act allowed "All Christians . . . (Papists only excepted) . . . to enjoy the full, free, and undisturbed exercise of their consciences . . ."; the law was repealed in 1704.

Plymouth Colony (Massachusetts) levied taxes for the support of the established Congregational Church, which the civil authorities controlled. Suffrage was confined to Congregationalists. No Episcopalian (Anglican), Presbyterian, or Baptist could be a freeman; unauthorized persons were forbidden to preach, while Catholics were not "suffered" to live in the colony; priests found there were banished and (if they returned) put to death. Only Congregationalists could be commissioners to the federal council which organized Massachusetts into one colony.

The Year They Outlawed Christmas

In 1649, Congregationalism was established by law in Massachusetts, and any attempt to institute any other form of worship became a punishable offense; non-Congregationalists were excluded from voting or holding office. In 1656, Quakers were jailed, whipped, and banished; harboring Quakers was punished by fines of 40 shillings per hour. And in 1659, celebrating Christmas was declared illegal in Massachusetts because of "the Puritan horror of all things savoring of popery" (Cobb). It was not until 1691 that the colony allowed liberty of conscience to all Christians except, of course, Papists. As for Jews, they were automatically excluded, as non-Christians, from all pre-Revolutionary acts of "toleration."

In Connecticut, the state controlled the established Congregational Church. Ministers were paid by the state, whose laws made church attendance compulsory; the governor had to be a Congregationalist and the legislature served as an ecclesiastical court. In what is now the enlightened community of Fairfield, ten Episcopalians were jailed in 1727 for declining to pay taxes for the support of the established church. Possessing Quaker books was punishable by a 10 shilling fine per book. Moravians were persecuted. As in Massachusetts, "toleration" eventually came to Connecticut's Protestants, but Catholic Churches were still prohibited.

New Hampshire law specified that only Protestants could be freemen; in 1689, the colony's oath of allegiance demanded a personal declaration against Catholicism and the Pope.

Life Under Changing Establishments

New York's first colonial government was Dutch; it established the Dutch Reformed Church in the colony. Judges were required to be Reformed Church members. Lutherans and Quakers were imprisoned. Jews could come to New York but the anti-Semitic governor, Peter Stuyvesant, would not allow them to worship, found synagogues, buy real estate, or trade.

When the British expelled the Dutch, the Church of England was established in New York, with the governor at its head. Ministers were elected by town citizens, who paid them from tax revenues. Under Catholic James II, Governor Thomas Dongan allowed Catholics to practice their religion; he was deposed when James fell from power in England, whereupon Catholics were banned from voting and holding office. In 1689, Catholics, Unitarians, and Quakers were "excluded from government favors" (Cobb), and as of 1719 no churches other than the Church of England could obtain charters. Moravians were ordered to leave the colony. Liberty of conscience was eventually allowed, except to Papists.

Maryland was originally a Catholic colony, founded by Sir George Calvert, Lord Baltimore. Although there was no Catholic establishment as such and Protestants were allowed freedom of worship, the early legislatures were almost entirely composed of Catholics; however, Cobb tells us that laws were enforced equally, without religious distinction. As Protestants became a majority in Maryland and the Catholic reign in England ended, the colony experienced some unsubtle changes. Only trinitarian Christians were tolerated; there was no room for Unitarians, Jews, "pagans," or "infidels." When the Puritans took over in 1654, a new law held that Catholics no longer were "protected" in the colony. By 1675, only Protestants could hold office; Catholics were not admitted to the assembly of the colony they had founded. The Church of England superseded the Puritan establishment in 1692; 40 pounds of tobacco were taxed from each person to pay its clergy. Catholics, who had earlier been banned from holding public worship, were deprived of all civil rights in 1704; a 20 shilling tax was imposed upon the importation of every Irish indentured servant, "to prevent the entrance of papists"; if a Protestant father died, the children could be taken from their Catholic mother. As late as 1718, Catholics could not vote in Maryland unless they abjured their faith.

New Jersey's establishment was loose. Quakers from Pennsylvania, Presbyterians and Anglicans from New York vied for power. Still, only Protestants could hold public office, and there was no freedom of conscience for Papists. London eventually designated the Church of England as the established church of New Jersey, but churches of all Protestant denominations (except for Quakers, in the later years) were allowed to hold services. Georgia had no established church initially, although Catholics were not extended freedom. When the Church of England was established in 1758, its clergy were paid by the government.

In Pennsylvania and Delaware the Quaker form of Protestant worship was established. Catholics could profess their religion, but had no civil rights; they could not hold office. Jews and Unitarians, as well as Catholics, were disenfranchised. Cobb tells us that even William Penn was denounced as a Papist and a "Jesuit in disguise" for the offense of allowing Catholics the limited freedom they had in Pennsylvania.

Only in Rhode Island was Roger Williams able to maintain freedom of worship and avoid a state-church alliance. As Doyle comments in his *Puritan Colonies,* "To Williams, a State-Church was an abomination, however it might be administered, and whether it abode in Rome, in England or in Massachusetts."

The Slow Development of Religious Liberty

It is important to understand that progress toward the First Amendment was slow and tortuous.

Colonial establishments and their limitations upon freedom of worship were different and changing, not only from one colony to another but from one year to the next. Changes in sovereignty from Holland to England (in New York), changes in the English power structure (in all the colonies, but particularly in Maryland), immigration from Europe and migration between colonies—all these were taking place in the New World. There were steps forward, and steps back, but the movement toward the goal of freedom expressed in the First Amendment was inexorable.

The Revolution and the New States

With the defeat of Cornwallis at Yorktown in 1781 and the expulsion of the British from the former colonies, new rules were written by the now-independent leaders of the United States. Unfortunately, and with some notable exceptions, they did not do away with religious discrimination or preferences.

Virginia was one of the notable exceptions. On the first try (1784), Virginians kept their system of civil taxes to support Christian churches, although allowing the taxpayer to say which church his taxes would help. That provision was later killed. In 1785 the principle of "free exercise" was spelled out in a state statute: ". . . all men shall be free to profess, and by argument to maintain, their opinions in matters of religion, and that the same shall in no wise diminish, enlarge or affect their civil capacities."

The Northwest Territory Ordinance of 1787, covering Virginia's newly acquired lands, specified that "No person, demeaning himself in a peaceable and orderly manner, shall ever be molested in his form of worship or religious sentiments in the said territory."

Others among the new states were less liberal in their concessions to religious freedom. New Hampshire's constitutions of 1781 and 1784 discriminated in favor of Protestantism and required tax contributions for support of churches. Massachusetts' 1780 charter also allowed taxpayers to designate which church should get their tithes; those who indicated no choice paid taxes which were given to the Congregational Church. Connecticut kept its state church (Congregational) until the 1800s; Jews and Catholics were not able to share full religious freedom. New Jersey's 1776 Constitution confined officeholding to Protestants. In its constitution of the same year, Pennsylvania restricted civil rights to believers in God, narrowing it further to a requirement that officeholders be Christians; Delaware (1776) granted equal rights to Christians only. Maryland continued taxing for the support of the taxpayer's church; its 1777 charter allowed religious liberty only to Christians. North Carolina permitted only Protestants to hold public office. Georgia (1777) allowed only Protestants to serve in its legislature.

If there is still any doubt as to what "an establishment of religion" meant in the first years of the American republic, the 1778 constitution of South Carolina spelled it out: "The Christian Protestant religion shall be deemed, and is hereby constituted and declared to be *the established religion* of this State. All denominations of Protestants in this State . . . shall enjoy equal religious and civil privileges." (Italics supplied.)

My own State of New York's Constitution of 1784—which created the Board of Regents of which I was to become the thirtieth Chancellor

191 years later—required all citizens to swear an oath abjuring foreign allegiance in all matters, "ecclesiastical as well as civil"—a reference, as Cobb points out, intended to exclude Roman Catholics from citizenship. It was later repealed.

Why the Framers Wrote What They Wrote

My purpose in recounting at some length the history of church establishments and restraints on religious liberty in the various American colonies which became the states of the new Republic is simply to demonstrate what the framers of the Constitution and the Bill of Rights intended when they wrote the First Amendment's "no-establishment" and "free-exercise" clauses.

Rhode Island, the only colony-state which was Establishment-free, was not represented among the signers of the draft Constitution of 1787, and approved the document only when it was accompanied by the Bill of Rights (on May 29 and June 7, 1790, respectively). All the signatories had thus been born and brought up in a society where state-church alliances and barriers to full freedom of worship were the rule; some had been members of the privileged churches, some of the penalized denominations, but all knew exactly what James Madison and his coauthors intended when they wrote the Bill of Rights. His earlier words, in the Virginia Bill of Rights of 1776, rang clear: "No man, or class of men, ought on account of religion to be invested with peculiar emoluments or privileges, nor subjected to any penalties or disabilities, unless under color of religion the preservation of equal liberty and the existence of the State are manifestly endangered."

How the Court Has Perverted the Bill of Rights

Over almost two centuries since the Bill of Rights was incorporated into our Constitution, a succession of Supreme Court decisions, each building upon earlier errors, has twisted and contorted and misconstrued the meaning and intent of the Bill's authors.

It is clear to those familiar with the history of early America that the Founding Fathers wanted no *one* particular form of religious worship or organization—no *one* creed, sect or denomination—to receive from the federal government any status or privileges or rights which are not equally available to *all* creeds, sects, and denominations. *And that is all that the "establishment clause" means.*

The Supreme Court, however, has misinterpreted this part of the First Amendment to mean that government can extend no status or aid to *religion itself,* that is, to any expression of belief in the existence of a supreme, superhuman power. This absurd posture leaves irreligion—atheism—as the national creed of the United States, by default. This is certainly not what the framers of the Bill of Rights intended, nor is it what any succeeding generation of Americans have believed that their Constitution should or did require.

The Court has compounded this fundamental mistake by holding in effect that when government aid is *offered* on equal terms to every creed, sect, and denomination, a forbidden "establishment of religion" occurs if such aid is not *accepted* and *used* in equal measure by all creeds, sects, and denominations. If Catholics, Lutherans, Jews, and Baptists enroll larger numbers of youngsters in their church schools than other religious groups (including those who choose not to run their own schools), does that enumeration mean that Catholicism, Lutheranism, Judaism, and the Baptist Church are "established religions"? Nobody believes this—except the Supreme Court.

Further, with the exception of *Pierce,* the Court has almost always discriminated against nonpublic *education* in its First Amendment decisions and, as we have mentioned, against nonpublic elementary and secondary education in particular. Can the various levels of government allow tax deductions for contributions to the churches and the synagogues of America? Of course. Can these governments allow tax deductions for contributions to church-operated hospitals? Certainly. Can state and local government exempt church-owned property from taxation? Absolutely. How about property of church-related colleges? No doubt about it. But can government assist church-run *schools* and their students? Usually, *no*.

Consider for a moment government assistance to church-related *hospitals,* as compared to church-related *schools*. Such hospitals (and such schools) are both run under the direction of church authorities, and both receive support from religious sources. Both perform an acknowledged public service (health care; education) which is also available at public facilities. Both usually include places of worship in which religious services are conducted. Those who manage and work in these hospitals and schools are in part members of religious orders and in part lay people; in neither case must those who work in the institution necessarily be members of the religious group which operates it. Both extend their services to individuals whose religious preference is not that of the controlling church, as well as members of that church and members of no church at all.

But when it comes to government assistance, the similarity ends. Your child's medical expenses in a church-related hospital can be deducted like any other medical expenses, but your child's tuition in a church-related school cannot. Government funds can be used for Medicare and Medicaid payments to church-run hospitals, but cannot be used to pay for most services by church-related schools. Somehow, "establishment of religion" is defined differently for different kinds of public service. And that makes no sense.

Get Your Act Together, Justices

Those who have served on the U.S. Supreme Court over the last two centuries have (with some exceptions) managed to turn what the authors of the Bill of Rights built as a clear, straight course toward complete religious liberty into a cross-country steeplechase, over hastily constructed hurdles of sheer invention and through semantic jungles of misinterpretation.

It is time that the course be cleared, and only the Court can clear it. Only the Court can restore the First Amendment to its original, intended meaning. The Court should do it for the millions of kids who are now enrolled or will be enrolled in the many different church-related schools of this country. And if the Justices won't do it for the kids, they should do it for themselves, so that when they meet James Madison in that special corner of Valhalla reserved for those who gave their best efforts in the service of their fellow citizens, they will not have to explain to him what they did to his beloved Bill of Rights.

A School-Prayer Amendment? No.

Since the Court's banning of nondenominational, noncompulsory prayers in public schools (*Engel v. Vitale,* 1962), there has been constant agitation for a constitutional amendment guaranteeing the right to pray in the public schools.

As of now, I oppose it.

Was the Court wrong in *Engel?* Yes. The Court was wrong *twice.* First, the Justices called a nondenominational, voluntary prayer "an establishment of religion," which it was not. Second, they banned it, which is a judicial violation of that which is forbidden to Congress (and since 1868 to the state legislatures) by the "free exercise" clause of the First Amendment. "Free exercise" of religion must mean that citizens cannot be prevented from jointly reciting a prayer to a God, albeit a nondenominational prayer if they are in a public place. If it doesn't mean that, it doesn't mean anything. And if the Supreme Court can order a ban which the Constitution forbids the Congress to order because it violates fundamental human rights, then the Constitution doesn't mean much, either. *Engel v. Vitale* is so ridiculously far off the mark that the editors of zany *Mad* magazine once printed, among a set of wall stickers, one which read: "In the event of atomic attack, regulations prohibiting prayer in this school are rescinded."

I can understand the frustration of many good Americans who have been waiting with increased impatience for the Supreme Court to see the error of its ways and reverse itself on the school prayer issue. But that is not the point. *No document, especially a constitution, should have to be amended to say what it already says.* Nor should constitutions become cluttered with too many matters that do not relate directly to the organization, structure, and conduct of government.

What is needed is far greater vigilance on the part of the United States Senate when nominees for the federal courts are being considered for confirmation. A minimal understanding of the intent of the authors of the Constitution and its amendments should be an absolute requirement for confirmation as a lifetime member of the Supreme Court whose opinions cannot be reversed.

I do not believe a school-prayer amendment to be necessary, *as of this writing.* But I reserve the right to change my mind if the next few appointees to the Court show no more understanding of the Constitution than some of those presently sitting. (Incidentally, if anyone tells you that decisions of the U.S. Supreme Court should *never* be overruled, ask him whether he thinks that the *Dred Scott* ruling favoring slaveholders or the later decision outlawing income taxes should still be standing. Both were overturned by amendments.)

A Vote of "No Confidence"?

What is most troublesome about the arguments against any government assistance for children in nonpublic schools is the oft-repeated refrain by individuals whose names command attention that *any* aid to the independent sector will result in the destruction of public education in America.

To me, this is a trumped-up charge, incapable of proof and inconceivable in view of the substantial size and price advantage of our public schools and colleges as compared with their independent counterparts. Those who echo this scare talk must know that it is nothing more than that; if they are so certain that the public institutions would collapse in the face of, say, $250–$500 tuition tax credits, or vouchers, why do they fight like tigers to prevent a test of their argument? They have killed off even the smallest-scale experiments with these proposals—experiments which, if the scare artists are correct, could prove them correct in time to prevent larger-scale damage to the public sector. The truth of the matter is that they do not want their "destruction" theory tested, because they know it will not hold water.

The real reason for the scare talk is that the specter of the destruction of our public schools provides the adhesive to cement the greatest number of potential allies into a coalition against independent education. After all, who wants to be a party to the demise of the public schools? In that context, the scare propaganda has been very effective.

If I am wrong about this—if those who loudly predict the collapse and disappearance of public education as a result of even the slightest government aid to independent-school kids are actually sincere in their fear—we are in serious trouble. If the public sector is so weak and wobbly that its staunchest defenders register a vote of "no confidence" in their own institutions, those of us who believe in educational pluralism have cause for grave concern.

My Own Commitment to Public Education

But I am not worried.

I have complete confidence in the ability of our public schools to survive their present troubles and to return to their former state of excellence. The public schools of this country have always been good— often great. Those which were fine in the past but are not now can be fine again. Those which once had the confidence of the public but lost it can recapture it, by excellence in terms of performance and results.

My own commitment and that of my family to public education is complete. My wife and I are products of the public schools of New York State; our three eldest children are public-school graduates and our youngest is, at this writing, a public junior-high student in our hometown. Most of our eight grandchildren are in the public schools; the others will be, when they're old enough.

We have laid it on the line for the public schools, with no exceptions and no qualms whatsoever. Public education has been entrusted with our most precious assets—our children and our grandchildren. And that is a lot more than can be said by those "limousine liberals" who loudly extol the superiority of the public schools while their own kids are stowed away in private academies. I have nothing whatsoever against private academies, but I don't like hypocrisy.

What We Can Learn from "Coleman II"

Professor James S. Coleman of the University of Chicago became an instant hero of the liberals in 1966 when his "Coleman Report" seemed to support the proposition that black students learned better when they studied with whites, a finding which was widely used to justify busing for racial integration. He later retreated from that position and was branded a pariah by those who had gleefully embraced his 1966 conclusions.

In 1981 Professor Coleman issued another report, this one claiming that, by and large, private-school kids do better educationally than public-school kids, largely—as *Time* reported in April 1981—"because they maintain better discipline and provide more challenging academic demands." A companion study by the Reverend Andrew Greeley, a Catholic clergyman, found that students from minority low-income families do better in Catholic schools than in public schools. Both Coleman II and the Greeley thesis were roundly attacked by establishment educators of the liberal-modernist persuasion.

And that brings us to the heart of the matter.

Don't Damn 'Em, Learn from 'Em

As a confirmed supporter of public education, I am disturbed (as all friends of the public schools should be disturbed) at the dog-in-the-manger tack taken by too many individuals and groups who claim to have the best interests of public education in mind. They *should* be acknowledging the problems that beset the public schools, problems which are largely self-inflicted and which make it extremely difficult to maintain the quality of public education as it once was. They *should* be mounting a strong effort to scrap or revise those policies, rules, and regulations, federal, state, and local, which make it tough to administer a school or to teach its students. They *should* be devoting all their resources to recapturing the excellence which once made Americans proud of their public schools and ready to support them with their children and their dollars.

But is this what the self-styled propublic-education establishment is doing? No. Rather than address their own shortcomings, they have chosen to mount an all-out attack upon the independent schools. Few of us are so young that we cannot remember when educational pluralism flourished in America; when public and private schools, both of high quality, turned out well-educated young people ready to become productive citizens. *We can have that kind of quality education again,* but only if the public-education establishment stops knifing its nonpublic competition and gets to work setting its own house in order. Once American education gets its act together, once all of its elements join forces to improve the whole, there will be no stopping us.

We're Getting There

There are hopeful signs.

In a recent letter to *Newsday,* Edward A. Thorp, a public school-teacher from Rockville Centre, New York, comes close to the mark when he writes:

"[The Coleman] study that finds that private schools can provide a better education than public schools should come as no surprise to anyone. It certainly will not come as a revelation to the rank and file of public-school teachers. The reasons are simple: Private schools are selective in their students. Private schools are not restricted to the same degree as public schools by federal, state and local laws and regulations. Private schools do not have to contend with the demands of a few, often very insistent and abrasive parents who try to prevent the school from taking actions that are conducive to maintaining a sensible atmosphere.

"How many private schools accept untrustworthy, unmotivated, hostile and rebellious teenagers? How many private schools are without the dress codes that are unconstitutional in public schools? How many private schools cannot keep a disruptive student after school if his parent objects? What private school would keep the child of a parent who viciously attacked the ethics of a teacher because the child failed a series of multiple-choice tests in history? If the last sounds implausible, let me assure you that it happened to me.

"The challenge of the public schools, indeed the miracle, is that we operate with some degree of success under these conditions."

Mr. Thorp, obviously a dedicated and understanding teacher who says "I try to give all [my 143 students] love and discipline, training and affection," is right on target until he states: "Let the private schools of America take [the obnoxious, surly, disruptive student] into their classrooms and deal with him under the same restrictions that the public schools must."

Instead of suggesting that nonpublic schools be made to operate under the same unfortunate, mistaken policies and regulations that have put too many public-school systems in the fix he eloquently describes, Mr. Thorp should be screaming at his union leaders, his Congressmen, his state legislators, and his state and local school board members to get rid of those rules as applied to the public schools. I hope he is.

After all, none of these now-discredited policies and rules has been granted eternal existence. They have all been imposed by ill-considered laws and administrative decrees during the heyday of the permissive liberals. Laws can be amended, and their provisions repealed. For example: The public schools must *admit* students who may prove to be disruptive, but must they *keep* them? If the law insists, change it. Compulsory attendance statutes are not graven in stone. Indeed, *any policy, rule, or regulation can be changed*—and a good many of those with which our public schools are saddled *should* be changed.

As I said, there are hopeful signs.

They come not only from the parents who are unhappy with the quality of the public education their children are receiving, but from the one element of the professional educational community which is suffering most from the intolerable status quo and has the most to gain from a thoroughgoing restoration of standards and authority in the public schools—*the teachers.*

AFT President Albert Shanker, certainly no advocate of nonpublic schools, in a 1981 column headlined "Discipline, Tough Courses, Homework, Tests—Good Schools Put Pressure on Students," comments that there are good and less-than-good public and private schools. He cites historian Diane Ravitch's conclusions from Coleman II: ". . . public schools have lowered their requirements, decreased their expectations, made basic courses optional and learned to tolerate intolerable behavior." Al Shanker adds this conclusion of his own: ". . . it's time to stop making excuses. School boards, administrators, teachers and parents should use these results of the Coleman report as a basis for improving the quality of public education. The American people still support public schools and oppose aid to non-public education. But public school support is slipping. If schools don't offer both a safe and orderly environment and a quality program, the public will surely go elsewhere."

Shanker's frank summation says in general what I have been saying here: In addition to the special advantages offered by nonpublic schools, it is *parents' dissatisfaction with the environment and the academic performance of their public schools* which prompt them to transfer their children to the independent sector. Government aid in various forms merely helps them to make that move. Public-school reform might make it unnecessary.

Only public-school reform can restore the eroded confidence of many Americans in public education. The considerable clout of the educational community should be marshaled to press for that reform—not wasted on fratricidal infighting that can solve nothing.

Summing Up

While we consider higher education and its problems more specifically in the next chapter, my conclusions about educational pluralism generally apply with equal strength to the colleges and to the schools; this chapter has focused largely upon the schools, where formal education begins.

I believe that parents—not government—have the responsibility and the right to decide how their children are to be educated.

I believe that the interests of a free society demand that every child be educated, and that the interests of both the child and society demand that the child's education be of high quality.

I believe that educational pluralism, the healthy and competitive coexistence of public and private schools and colleges, is absolutely essential for the survival of democratic government.

While I believe that no single segment of society should dominate education at any level, I believe that a *government* monopoly in education would constitute the most serious threat to a free nation.

I believe that competition between and within the public and private sectors in a pluralistic system will raise the quality of educational service and thereby produce higher levels of academic performance.

Because I believe that universal education serves the public interest, I further believe that government, as the instrumentality of the public, has the right and the responsibility to provide educational assistance which will benefit every child, no matter where that child is being educated.

To that end, I believe that government has the right and duty to oversee the quality of every child's education, no matter where it is taking place—and that the state is the proper level of government to perform this function.

I believe that society must make free public education at the elementary-secondary level available to anyone who chooses it and who is willing to abide by the principles and rules whereby it can work to the advantage of all who use it.

To that end, I believe that every citizen has a responsibility to support public education through taxes, whether or not he or she has children in the public schools.

I do *not* believe that government assistance to families of independent-school children, or to those children themselves, presents any danger whatsoever to the survival of the public schools, which continue to be the considered, voluntary choice of the parents of nine of every ten American children—including mine.

I believe, on the other hand, that the steady rise in taxes, coupled with independent-school tuition costs, chills the capability of lower- and middle-income families to choose those schools for their children, presenting an increasing danger to educational pluralism.

I believe that government should grant no aid to independent schools which do not meet standards of educational quality, but that such schools should not be penalized on the basis of the values they pass on to their students.

While I believe that most of the constitutional barriers to government assistance to independent schools are grounded in misinterpretations of the Constitution's First Amendment, I do not believe that the Constitution should be further amended at this time to restore prayer in the public schools.

Finally, I believe that if the champions of the public schools and those who are responsible for their governance and successful operation will acknowledge their problems and take the necessary steps, however unpopular, to restore the quality of their educational services, we will return to that era of good will when both public and independent education prospered in a climate of public confidence and support.

5.

Higher Education

The Battle for Bodies, Bucks —
and Quality

DURING the Vietnam War, when I was still the bottom Indian on the New York Regents' totem pole, the Board was invited on a fine spring day to lunch with the retiring president of State University College at Albany. The occasion should have been as warm and pleasant as the day itself, but it wasn't. America's college campuses were in turmoil and Albany State was no exception.

We were instructed not to drive our own cars, which were identifiable by state shields and low-number license plates; we were to ride to Albany State in the unmarked private cars of the State Education Department. Why? It seemed that the students were not in a receptive mood to visiting authority—or authorities.

Albany State is a beautiful college, well conceived and well ordered, the buildings and grounds designed, as Governor Rockefeller intended, to foster contemplation, deliberation, and learning—not much of which was going on during our visit. As we moved through the halls of the new building devoted to the communication arts and equipped with the latest technological gadgetry, two elderly women armed with brushes, pails, and soap scurried to keep ahead of us as they scrubbed at the four-letter words felt-penned on the corridor walls. Outside, on almost every one of the gorgeous white marble slabs which adorn many Albany State buildings, someone had spray-painted black stencils of a clenched fist and the slogan: "Free the Panthers!"

Bypassing a few hundred students playing touch football on the lawns and walks, I stumbled upon an unexpected oasis of tranquillity.

Serenely sitting behind a card table on which lay a pad and pencil was a lovely young woman, blond hair long and straight in the manner of all those students who despised conformity, reading a paperback textbook. Aha! I thought, "Education lives!" Then I read the hand-printed notice tacked to the card table: "Sign Up Here for the Armed Revolution to Counter the Armed Counter-Revolution!"

Such were the conditions and terms of higher education in America during the Vietnam years—not just at Albany State but on most campuses, except for some religious colleges and the military academies.

The Educational Tragedy of Vietnam

Campus disruptions and disturbances were everyday happenings from 1968 to 1974. TV-news programs spread the tidings of campus violence to other colleges and to schools: militants, many not students themselves, freely interrupted the studies of young people whose parents had scrimped for years to pay for a college education, young people who wanted to learn, but who could themselves not maintain intellectual discipline—or even class schedules—without leadership on the part of college authorities.

College students have always been active in support of causes they admire. The great old Socialist Norman Thomas (Princeton class of 1905) was hit by a raw egg during a campaign speech in Jersey City, New Jersey, in the 1930s, prompting me to be one ringleader of a noisy on-campus demonstration against Jersey City's Mayor Frank Hague, boss of the New Jersey Democratic Party.

But the difference between such efforts and the Vietnam disturbances was significant. Back then, we organized, we spoke our minds, and then we returned to the education we were determined to attain. None of us ever thought that closing the college would make our point; there were no cries of "Shut it down!" We held our demonstrations and rallies *after* classes, not in place of them. The notion of boycotting our own education, for which we and our parents paid—more than half of Princeton's pre-World War II students helped to finance their own college costs—made no sense at all.

But in this generation, Vietnam and other highly visible national issues (civil rights, protection of the environment, addressing the grievances of Indians, and others) were catalysts in gaining broad campus backing for actions which had more *local* goals in mind—goals which, unlike peace in Vietnam, could be realized on the spot. Student leaders issued "nonnegotiable demands" for "pass/fail" grading, coed dormitories, more electives in what they considered "relevant" subjects ("black studies"), students on boards of trustees, and scores of other changes, which had to be agreed to, or the college president would remain a prisoner in his office, the ROTC building would be torched, and classes boycotted.

Some faculty members were quick to appreciate that student uprisings were opportunities to increase their share of power in the university communities. If they openly sympathized with student demands, their own demands would be added to the list of final ultimatums handed to the college administration. As a result, the invisible and thin wall between teaching and governance was often breached by faculty members intent upon gaining more decision-making authority.

The Triumph of "El Foldo"

TV star Johnny Carson has a couple of favorite names for those who collapse in the face of opposition: "El Foldo" and "El Choko," the latter referring to "choking" in sports—nervousness that causes one to slow or quit. The college campuses produced their share of El Foldos and El Chokos during the Vietnam-era disturbances.

Were the college presidents and provosts and boards of trustees who yielded to student militancy unworldly? The situation was as new to them as it was to the rest of America; they were simply not prepared for it. Many presidents had accepted their posts as pleasant stopovers on the road to retirement, with no idea that they might be subjected to psychological and even physical harassment. Others had been selected for their fund-raising ability, and soon their greatest concern was that the college's image not be tarnished by excessive violence which might drive away students and contributions. The presidents had no precedents to follow, no game plans for dealing with what amounted to, in many cases, insurrections. Even at that, many reacted with sense and courage.

Yet the final winners seemed to be those who negotiated to buy campus peace at the price of educational excellence. Because the immediate results of settlements—disasters averted, study schedules resumed—were much more visible than were the detrimental effects upon the quality of academic services to be delivered, the El Foldos among college presidents became instant heroes who made bad bargains, somewhat like Prime Minister Neville Chamberlain of England, the El Foldo of Munich in 1938.

The Long Road Back

To their credit, higher education deal-makers of the Vietnam era were wiser than Chamberlain. They bought not only peace but *time,* which was on the side of peace—time to see what their concessions had done to education, time to return gradually to the standards that had been lowered under duress.

We have by no means recaptured the high ground held by our colleges and universities before the "bad period," but we are on the long road back. Speaking at Pace University in 1978, I cited a few chapters and verses:

"Our universities are beginning to lick the demeaning, unfair practice of grade inflation, which dates from the years when college presidents, deans and professors found themselves locked by students in broom closets until their consciousness of some world-shaking problem was properly raised.

"We are getting away from overspecialization in Mickey Mouse courses [weird electives] which have value only when a student takes an advanced Mickey Mouse course in the same subject area.

"Pass/Fail, the cosmetic copout of the late sixties, is fast fading, as word drifts back to the campuses that company personnel offices, studying the college records of competing candidates for a hard-to-get job, will choose the "A" student or the one with an 85% average over the poor fellow whose file shows only that he passed."

Mine was a commencement address. It was hard to resist a smile when, at another college commencement in 1979, the student government president—since Vietnam, a required commencement speaker—attempted to rabble-rouse his fellow graduates' ire about some perceived shortcomings of the college administration and was roundly hooted off the stage in rhetorical mid-flight.

Despite constant goading about "apathy" from the media, the college student of today has his or her mind on education, not agitation. Today's students have revised yesterday's priorities. Consciousness-raising has given way to scholastic achievement as the number-one goal of one's college years. *Excellence is returning to the campus.*

Spillover into the Schools: The Teachers' Role

Elsewhere in this book, I've observed how college-campus violence on television makes its impression upon youngsters of all ages. There *was* a spillover. High-schoolers *did* try to ape their college counterparts and were frequently successful (where unchecked), and the learning process at the secondary level suffered. What's more, schools have not managed to recapture discipline and order, in the aftermath, half as well as the colleges.

One troublesome phenomenon is the role that *teachers* played in school demonstrations. We know that at all levels teachers often are role-models. I can recall some faculty members at Princeton who so commanded their profession that they led classmates of mine into teaching. Teachers have opinions, of course, and they have every American's right to voice their views. *As teachers,* their responsibility remains this: to temper their own views by having their students examine different sides of a question. Whether the issue is an unpopular war, the Equal Rights Amendment, or handgun control, teachers must take care to keep controversial subjects a matter of exposition rather than indoctrination. During the bad period, a minority of teachers—in schools as well as in colleges—refused to accept this distinction, taking sides openly, appearing often in the vanguard of student demonstrations, not only those about matters of national concern, but also those involving disputes between student leaders and administrations over governance and internal operations of their institutions, which in the past faculties left to deans, provosts, presidents, and chancellors.

The new "involvement" by teachers aggravated the problems of college presidents and school superintendents who were faced with student disruption. Teachers could no longer be relied upon to remain neutral or disinterested: too many of them were ready to become part of the problem rather than part of the solution.

Intellectual Incest

In the traditional division of labor which allocates to faculty the primary role in development and organization of college courses of study, new full-time faculty members are usually chosen by the existing faculty in a department. What sometimes results is that new members of the teaching staff are ideological clones of the professors already established. It is, of course, understandable. Many college communities, particularly those in small towns or suburbs of large cities, are entities unto themselves and tend to be insulated from the outside world, even intellectually inbred. Job security, which is in fact "tenure," is crucial; a low-ranking pedagogue on the way up or an eager job hunter is not likely to risk his or her individual future (especially as reputations follow people from one campus to another) by shooting down those principles and positions held by senior faculty members who largely influence who gets employment and tenure and who doesn't. Speaker Sam Rayburn's advice to new Congressmen applies with even greater validity to new and prospective faculty members: "If you want to get along, go along."

It is no surprise that many of our college faculties are not a reflection of the political spectrum in the "real" world. Princeton alumni friends were aghast when a faculty poll gave Hubert Humphrey a tremendous majority, with the remainder of the votes being shared equally by Richard Nixon and Dick Gregory! I wasn't surprised. One needed only to check the list of speakers invited to Princeton's campus to know where political sympathies of the faculty resided in 1968—and perhaps still do.

Biting the Hand That Feeds You

There is nothing wrong with teachers holding and expressing their own opinions so long as those opinions are not clamped upon their students as eternal verities. I would indeed be wary of a teacher who claimed not to hold personal views. It is not a sin for collections of teachers (i.e., faculties) to think pretty much alike on important issues, even if their consensus is 180 degrees from the public's. While an imbalance of opinions may mean that students are not equally exposed to all sides of a question, an even split on every subject is impossible to attain and unnecessary to the purposes of teaching and learning. Only *unanimity* should be suspect. As long as there are some professors who do not share the majority's views and are willing to defend their own, intellectual competition will survive.

The tendency toward conformity of thought in a faculty is not necessarily a liberal phenomenon. My own observation is that neither liberals nor, say, Moral Majoritarians are given to open-minded impartiality. But should colleges and universities disdain the values of those families whose sons and daughters will as alumni be asked to provide the institution's lifeblood—financial support?

One reason why traditionalist colleges are so successful in raising endowment and operating funds is that their political and intellectual posture is acceptable in large part to those who commit their children and their dollars to these institutions. Yet no college is expected to parrot what seems to be a dominant American public opinion at a given moment. Academe is not supposed to be a mirror of society. It is an open forum for examination of ideas and principles and issues and proposals, no matter how unpopular they may be. But some people simply do not believe that the liberal-modernist universities fulfill that definition of academe. They are convinced that liberals are not liberal about those views which challenge their own; they see *conformity* to be a liberal vice— as it may also be a reactionary one.

The question is really one of *options*. A college community can choose to accept and reflect whatever consensus its members form. On the other hand, those whose assistance may be vital to the institution's survival have the choice of withholding that assistance if they disagree with the consensus.

For quite a while, the liberal establishment stifled criticism of their own faculties' hostility toward American business and finance. It raised the specter of "threats to academic freedom" to silence critics. A drumfire on noisy campuses rose against oil companies and firms importing materials from South Africa and Rhodesia, although I recall no newsworthy protests against entrepreneurs who brought in Russian vodka and caviar, Czech Christmas-tree ornaments, or Havana cigars.

The curtain of silence has finally been breached. It has been suggested by the inventive industrialist David Packard, former Deputy Secretary of Defense, that those who make the American system work have no obligation to finance those institutions which become launching pads for attacks upon that very system.

The antibusiness slant of faculties is not the only cause—let alone the major cause—of current unhappiness over higher education. Perhaps a broader restlessness comes from the loss of control by college authorities and the resulting lessening of educational quality during the Vietnam era. This malaise becomes evident in the refusal of older alumni to continue giving to their colleges. Colleges can produce figures showing higher dollar totals each year, but no statistics will tell how much *more* might have been given if the loyalty and confidence of old friends had not been sacrificed.

Nostalgia aside, the hard and ironic fact is that American universities and colleges have lost support at the very time they have the greatest need for financial help from individuals and businesses.

Pluralism: A Different Ball Game

We should be concerned over the continuance of educational pluralism at all levels of formal learning, but pluralism in postsecondary education is not affected primarily by debates on whether public institutions or private ones offer better discipline—there's no real difference between the public and private—or more rigorous academic opportunities, for there are plus and minus examples in both sectors. Nor is the constitutionality of government aid to nonpublic institutions a major issue.

There is, obviously, a lively contest, not only between public and private institutions, but also within both sectors, for enrollment and gain of both public and private dollars. The impact of this struggle is more clearly seen when we keep in mind two conditions: (1) higher education is not compulsory; (2) public colleges and universities can charge tuition as well as receive tax monies.

Government Needs the Colleges

Government has a direct *need* for the extensive research capabilities of American higher-education institutions, a need which cannot be supplied at the elementary and secondary-school level. Government contracts for national defense benefit the universities in many ways, including their ability to hire more and better faculty, who in turn attract top students.

Church versus State? No Big Deal for the Colleges

Perhaps mutual need is the most compelling reason why independent (private) colleges and universities have been less troubled than independent schools by judicial strictures against government dollars because of the "separation of church and state." Private higher-learning institutions are allowed a greater degree of federal and state dollar support than are schools, which convinces me that "separation," far from being a constitutional principle of universal, immutable, and eternal application to education, is nothing more than a handy weapon in the ongoing fight against government aid for independent *schools* and their clients.

Another reason why we seem to have shied away from restraints upon government assistance to higher education is the fact that so many Americans want to attend college and, thanks to tuition requirements, need some form of direct or indirect public help to do so.

The G.I. Bill of Rights: A Voucher System That Worked

Millions of veterans returned from service after World War II anxious to begin or complete their college educations. Instead of the World War I expedient of handing veterans a few dollars as a "bonus," we put into operation a sensible and practical reward for service: the celebrated G.I. Bill of Rights, whereby veterans attended the college of their choice, if admitted, with the U.S. government picking up most of the tab. The G.I. Bill was an even better deal than the tuition tax credits now being proposed for colleges and schools—it was a higher education voucher system. It worked! The modern-day wolf-criers against tax credits and vouchers might note that the G.I. Bill helped institutions as well as individuals, and that not one public college was damaged by it.

Other Federal and State Assistance Programs

The federal government has a variety of aid programs available for college students who need financial help. Federal data for 1979 show (in addition to $2.5 billion in research grants and facilities) roughly $5.9 billion in student assistance, not including $1.1 billion in student loans. Although amounts have been reduced, both grants and loans are available regardless of the kind of college the student attends. As with G.I. Bill funds, the colleges retain their right to reject applicants on appropriate grounds—a practice always cited as a reason why nonpublic elementary and secondary *schools* should receive *no* state help.

The same strident voices that insist that no public funds be given to independent schools (or to those who attend them) also clamor for government money to help needy students in both independent and public universities. What's more, a major argument raised by the anti-private-school lobby against tuition tax credits for private-school students is that credits will divert government funds which should be going to help *college* students in private as well as public institutions. These paradoxical contentions may have a logic which escapes me, but they play holy hell with the "separation-of-church-and-state" argument. If there were any validity to it—there isn't—there could be no state funds for either private schools or colleges or for those who choose them.

In New York, aid from Albany is funneled through two principal conduits: Bundy Aid and the Tuition Assistance Program (TAP). Bundy funds (named for McGeorge Bundy, who chaired the state commission which recommended the program) go directly to independent colleges and universities, based upon the number and kind of degrees awarded. TAP funds go to the colleges (public and private) through their students and are administered according to family income levels and to varying college tuition rates in each case. In addition, the state Dormitory Authority provided low-cost construction support for university buildings and facilities during the "college explosion" in the years after World War II.

Bundy aid would not have been authorized by the New York State Legislature unless it were available to the state's church-related colleges as well as to secular independent colleges, which would otherwise have acquired a competitive advantage over the denominational colleges sufficiently great to endanger the pluralism which has been New York State policy for years. But there were problems involved. Not the federal Constitution (which does not mention education) but the nineteenth-century Blaine Amendment to the New York State Constitution (barring state funds for "any school or institution of learning wholly or in part under the control or direction of any religious denomination") seemed to stand in the way of Bundy assistance to the church-related colleges.

The Blaine wording itself suggested a way out: secularization. "Control or direction" would not be the case if boards of trustees could be restructured and repopulated with majorities of lay people rather than clerics (including laymen of faiths other than the dominant denomination of the college), and if governance were altered to reduce clerical authority over administration. A carefully worked out agenda of secularization requirements was proposed by the legal staff of the State Education Department, and put into practice by most of the state's church-related colleges and universities. Although secularization was not intended or arranged to produce a final divorce of these institutions from their religious heritage, Bundy Aid has not been successfully challenged in the courts. All this reinforces my opinion that "separation of church and state" in education is a phony issue.

Only a very few religiously oriented colleges can claim the status of ultimate independence by being sufficiently well endowed and supported to thumb their institutional noses at Bundy money and the forced secularization it entailed. I have said many a silent hoorah for these few (which included small Molloy College in my home county).We owe them a vote of thanks for making a point which had to be made and which their sister colleges were not in a position to make: Blaine Amendments are anachronisms traceable to the prejudices of past centuries and they deserve to die.

The Battles Ahead

When the college-age population was mushrooming and public confidence in our educational system was at its peak, the states rushed to promote expansion of higher education—and damn the cost. In less than half a century, the State University of New York has grown from almost nothing to the biggest institution of its kind in the country. All sorts of government assistance were granted to every kind of college, in response to the swelling demand for higher education.

Those days are history now. Higher education in the United States is fighting a rugged two-front war, while at the same time trying to stamp out a fratricidal struggle on the home front. One source of trouble has been predictable for years: a smaller college-going population. Births in the 1960s were low. The rate improved very slightly in the late 1970s, but that baby crop hasn't even reached kindergarten yet, and it won't help the colleges until the 1990s. The New York Regents' 1980 predictions for higher-education master-planning saw a 27 percent decline in the number of eighteen-year-olds between 1979 and 1991. This situation is typical across the country, except in those Sun Belt states where immigration more than compensates for lower birth rates. As public school districts (particularly in the Northeast) struggle to decide which elementary schools must be closed for lack of youngsters, the competition among colleges for students becomes fiercer and less friendly. Having built their "plant" for full enrollment, the colleges cannot permit their student bodies to decline in number, for overhead has been cut to the bone in most cases. If a college keeps raising its tuition to cover fixed overhead, quite apart from inflation, it will price itself out of existence.

The Second Front

On the demographic front, as the normal college-going pool of seventeen- and eighteen-year-old Americans dries up, it is a war of attrition. On the second (financial) front, private gifts are harder to come by as economic conditions dampen the generosity of individuals, corporations and foundations, while government reduces grants in response to taxpayer demands for relief.

Since 1965, when somebody convinced President Lyndon Johnson that this country could afford *any* level of public expenditures, the federal government's gift list has skyrocketed. U.S. budgets, including education, which before 1965 had been left to the states, ballooned from $96.5 billion in 1965 to $578.8 billion fifteen years later. In response, taxpayers went for "tax revolts" like Proposition 13 in California and Proposition 2½ in Massachusetts—reforms imposed by personal votes. The sins of federal profligacy were visited upon the smaller members of the federal family: states, cities, counties, towns, villages, and school districts.

I discuss later the story of how federal money has been followed by federal control, how dollars from Washington have become a narcotic habit that many states and school districts have been unable to kick—to the point where some of them regularly sacrifice their responsibility for the governance of education in return for their annual federal "fix." Colleges have fortunately demonstrated more independence.

Resistance to federal encroachment is not easy. President Ronald Reagan emphasized the problem at the University of Notre Dame's 1981 commencement:

"In recent years, as government spawned regulations covering virtually every facet of our lives, our independent and church-supported colleges and universities found themselves included in the network of regulations and the costly blizzard of administrative paperwork government demanded.

"Today, 34 Congressional committees and almost 80 subcommittees have jurisdiction over 439 separate laws affecting education at the college level. Virtually every aspect of campus life is now regulated— hiring, firing, promotions, physical plant, construction, record-keeping, fundraising, and to some extent curriculum and educational programs."

To the extent they have been willing to deny themselves the luxury of federal dollars, colleges have been able to keep relatively free of considerable federal interference, but only relatively so. Even those colleges refusing Washington's money (pardon me: *our* money) are hit by U.S. court decisions authorizing Department of Education bureaucrats to *withhold student aid* at institutions which do not knuckle under to their decrees. This is a cruel and tough system to buck.

The cure is coming from whence it should: Washington. Despite urgent pleas for extension and even expansion of federal spending for higher education, current U.S. policy favors gradual curtailment of federal grants and loans, accompanied by a lessening of federal demands upon the institutions. As part of a whole plan to reduce spending and taxes, this policy would return responsibility and control to the fifty states and the individual colleges, where indeed both belong.

But independence from onerous regulations does not solve the problem of funding or of declining enrollment. Returning funding to the states to handle will be a slow process, especially as it will be difficult to consummate until U.S. tax reductions make enough new revenue available to the states and localities. Meanwhile, the two-front war goes on, as does the internal bickering.

The "One Big Pot" Theory: College Version

Less government funding increases the struggle between the public and private sectors, and between institutions within both, for whatever public funds are available. For colleges, the "one big pot" theory that there is only so much government money available for education has more validity than for elementary and secondary schools. Given the capability of universities to raise their own funds through tuition, contributions and business or government contracts, government assistance is perceived as less seriously needed. Yet college fund raisers are jumping into every ring and scrapping for everything they can take home.

Public universities have a great advantage both in financing and recruiting (which is directly connected to finance). Their *cost to the student* is usually somewhat less than private college tuition, yet the quality of the education they deliver is excellent. There's no magic in this: the difference is made up by the taxpayer, who supports the public universities to a significantly greater degree than he supports the independents.

In a period of declining enrollment, this advantage is quite troublesome to the independents competing for undergraduates, especially when government-run colleges "go public" with comparative figures aimed to put down their nonpublic competition. One such campaign (mounted in newspaper advertising by the State University faculty union in New York in 1980) told potential students that they could "have a quality education and save $3,000 each year" by attending SUNY, "as opposed to private colleges." And there is icing on the cake: "In fact, the savings in many instances can be $5,000 annually." I don't know whether they're comparing Columbia with Squeegee County Community College, but no matter: differences like this are not chick-enfeed, especially in a period of inflation, and particularly since any student, regardless of family income level, can apply for State University.

Unity — Coming Apart at the Seams?

Austerity has produced at least one negative result: the public-private alliance to gain government undergirding for both sectors is slowly coming apart. There is a new dog-in-the-manger attitude: if I can't have it, he can't have it either. Of course, this helps nobody.

State aid for construction (particularly in the public sector), tuition assistance money for use at any type of college, grants to independent colleges based numerically upon degrees granted—these and other declining forms of public assistance to higher education are now pawns in a chess game in which there are only losers. To their credit, the independents have shown restraint in not criticizing their public counterparts in noisy slugfests on TV or in newspapers, probably because they figure to be the losers, given the public institutions' greater size, larger clientele, and (at least until lately) bigger political clout. But attacks and charges are made and the tempo of battle rises.

Adversity can end friendships and destroy cooperative efforts. Divide and conquer is an effective strategy. If the public and private sectors each insist that their own needs be served first, government budget trimmers have a quick solution: *cut both.* And if cuts are made with a sharp ax, they can create imbalance and undermine educational pluralism in the college field.

Solving the Money Crunch

It is plain that current economic difficulties affect the private sector more seriously than the public colleges and universities. In *U.S. News and World Report* (April 1981) it is noted that about 60 percent of college students now receive some form of federal dollar assistance, and it relates how various colleges plan to substitute their own assets for U.S. money which may no longer be available for student aid. Roger J. Fecher, Vice-President of Kalamazoo College in Michigan, comments on present-day stopgap practices of switching scarce funds from other necessary programs and increasing tuition in order to cover dollar aid for students who need it: "Just as the government makes transfer payments from the productive to the nonproductive sector of the economy, colleges have found themselves in the same screwy business. They're soaking the full-pay students more and transferring it to the needy students."

Finally, it reports: "Perhaps the most serious consequence of the inflation squeeze for colleges is the deterioration taking place in campus buildings and grounds." The report mentions a study which concludes that higher education is "mortgaging its future" by failing to repair roofs and sidewalks and postponing work on landscaping, painting, and other maintenance. The Association of Physical Plant Administrators of Universities and Colleges estimates that $55 billion would be needed "to make all the necessary repairs and replacements at the nation's colleges."

A thought occurs: Why not marry the two needs—the students' need for funds and the colleges' need for maintenance, repairs, and replacements? Why leave necessary work undone? Why pay more in insurance premiums because the physical plant has been allowed to deteriorate, thus increasing the risk of accidents? Every college has some form of student employment program—or should have one. Students should be offered the opportunity to earn discounts from their tuition, and room and board bills, by working on maintenance and repair jobs.

Of course unions will scream, but what would they lose? If the students don't do these jobs on a barter basis, the colleges can't afford to hire anyone to do them. If student labor does the basic work, the colleges' maintenance budget can be devoted to those union jobs which students are not qualified to do.

The value of working for what one receives cannot be overstressed; it is vastly better preparation for life than being handed a free education. And there's a bonus: grounds and buildings kept in shape by the students themselves should sharply reduce vandalism.

A New Philosophy — and Its Byproducts

Earning your college education is not a novel concept. In the thirties "Working Our Way Through College" was not only a popular song but the one avenue (other than scholarship funds) where young people of limited means could pay for their tuition, room, and board. Lots of us did odd jobs during the short-of-cash 1938 recession and the years before World War II. I made a few bucks-for-books writing college news and sports for metropolitan newspapers, managing the Princeton debating team, editing a literary magazine, and typing papers and theses for classmates who couldn't even hunt-and-peck.

Students still work hard to pay for education. But somehow the approach is different, for reasons devolving from society's present situation. Skyrocketing college costs eventually led to state and U.S. assistance grants and loans for needy students. However helpful these are, a new and different philosophy seems to have been born, the idea that: (1) society *owes* students the aid which it now provides through government; (2) students therefore have a personal *right* to that aid, so (3) any means necessary to acquire all that is theirs by right is justified. Not all college-age young people have accepted this line of thinking by any means—but many have.

Defaults on low-interest guaranteed student loans are so numerous that the federal government is starting to use private collection services. In view of the millions of dollars already lost to deadbeats, I'm surprised that Uncle Sam hasn't made the effort before. Toleration of delinquency is the surest way to encourage more of it. Postgraduate personal bankruptcy has become a new phenomenon in disposing of student-aid loan responsibilities. There have been cases where students from well-to-do (therefore ineligible) families entered an out-of-town relative's address as their own on their aid applications in order to claim the "emancipated" status of having no family support and requiring maximum dollar assistance. Falsification of income data is not unknown.

It is no accident that the rise of governmental power and publicly dispensed largesse to hitherto-unknown heights has had a negative effect upon public morality. Whenever government has goodies—permits or licenses or contracts or grants or loans—to dispense or withhold, whenever government can tax or impose or waive fees or penalties, the result is to encourage bribery, favoritism, and cheating. This erosion of commonly held values has reached the ranks of young adults, tomorrow's citizens.

Ideology and Investments: A Bad Mix

The ability of colleges to help their needy students is impaired by revenue shortfalls. That's the fact. So it is time to take off the ideological blinders and the hobbles fastened onto the managers of college investment portfolios during the Vietnam War, when left-liberal notions about good guys and bad guys were allowed to determine where a university put (or didn't put) its money-earning reserves. Maximizing investment income was a casualty of campus unrest during the bad period, but it must be resurrected now—quickly. Colleges cannot now afford to tie their financial future to someone else's selective moral judgments, especially since many of us seem to have difficulty distinguishing between friends and foes abroad. It is questionable wisdom to cut off a source of institutional vitality in order to make a dubious ideological point which has in fact little influence upon outcomes. The students who forced those decisions are long gone, but the colleges' problem of survival remains.

Educational institutions can and should be free to promote discussion and debate about all issues, and to broadcast what their faculties and students believe pro and con. But the translation of moral judgments into practical terms, when public policies are involved, should be a function of the people through their government's decisions, external and domestic. For their own survival, our colleges and universities must be free to put their money in legitimate enterprises where it will help them most without ideological hindrance.

Should Remediation Costs Be Charged to the Colleges?

Deterioration of academic standards in many of the country's secondary schools has caused a new problem for colleges, especially those like City University of New York which, under a policy of "open admissions," will accept any city high-school graduate as a freshman. Simply stated, the problem is that many incoming students cannot handle college-level work. The schools' failures must then be remedied by the colleges at a substantial cost in the salaries of faculty, who are diverted from teaching college subjects to remedial instruction. There is another cost: Students have lost college time by having to learn there what they should have learned back at Lenient High.

The problem does not arise solely in low-income area urban schools, nor does it turn up only at the big public universities. It affects the whole spectrum of secondary and higher education. Even with the screening of standard aptitude testing in the college admissions process, graduates of "good" high schools find themselves attending remedial classes in English or math at "good" colleges, public and private. The recent tendency to admit on the basis of membership certain subgroups of the nation's population, using demographic quotas rather than depending upon academic excellence, has aggravated the problem.

Should colleges be asked to pay for what the schools failed to do? Are colleges responsible for raising to basic levels the skills of those they admit to their classes? I do not have a pat answer. I doubt very much that there is one. Faced with unprepared first-year students, a college is presented with this dilemma: either spend valuable time and resources on "crash" remediation, hoping to equip the subpar freshman for college-level work, or forget remediation and steer the unprepared student through a curriculum which, although substandard and plainly not designed to raise expectations of students, will lead to a degree. In either case overall quality declines.

Top-heavy Tenure

For educators, tenure is the ultimate guarantee of employment security. Those who have tenure are protected from all sorts of unhappy eventualities, including being relatively protected from firing when the college falls upon hard times. Those colleges and universities which now find themselves overloaded with high proportions of tenured faculty have lost one means to tighten their financial belts. Discussing the "crisis in engineering education" (*Newsday*, June 1981), Daniel S. Greenberg points out that "the shortage of [engineering] teachers is matched by a shortage of up-to-date equipment for training students." He quotes Dean James J. Duderstadt of the School of Engineering at the University of Michigan, who outlines the principal reason: "Our equipment situation is dismal. In the past, we've responded to financial problems by foregoing the purchase of new equipment *so that we could keep our tenured staff intact.* And we've fallen very far behind." [Italics supplied.] Duderstadt also said, "We're so out of tune with industry that on-the-job training is usually essential for new graduates."

Tenured professors certainly add luster to faculties, and they improve the image of a university, but this is at the cost of scrimping and corner-cutting in other ways—equipment, grounds, buildings, and maintenance. As the danger to the quality of education is evident, an expert hand is needed to maintain balance.

Educational Oliver Twists

At this point, we might remind ourselves of a cardinal principle of human nature: that which is freely given again and again comes to be viewed by the recipient as his right, not a gift. Try reducing the amount of a periodic gift, or eliminating it entirely; try charging for something that was free, or charging more for something that was dirt cheap—and watch for the outraged reaction.

Those involved in education, like all who rely heavily upon government for funding, eventually become institutionalized Oliver Twists, always pleading hunger, always asking for more. Faculty and students differ only in their approach. Once, I saw an angry mob of public university students at the New York State Capitol at Albany break the glass doors and savage priceless historical objects on display in the lobby. They screamed imprecations at anyone in authority—all because their tuition rates had been increased. I have recounted a similar instance in New York City, also because of increased tuition. Professors are, of course, more dignified, but they are no less determined and persistent. What's more, they have capable union specialists to bargain for them.

My point is that colleges are well advised to avoid prodigality, even at the price of unpopularity, because when hard times require budget cuts that threaten vested interests and encrusted habits, the cutting is hard to carry out.

The Loyal Alumni to the Rescue?

Earlier I noted the disinclination of some alumni to support their colleges' annual fund-raising campaigns or capital-gifts drives, because they disapprove of what occurred on campus during the Vietnam War, or indeed what is happening there now. It seems to me that some of these recalcitrant alumni have not thought the matter through. If their concern for alma mater is real, none will be happy to see its doors close or its independent status vanish. Yet such a result is inevitable if the colleges' private revenue sources dry up. To remain in operation, colleges would then require vast infusions of government money, which would invariably be followed by government controls and, finally, government ownership. It is my observation that very few of the grumpier alumni are socialists, in education or anything else.

Alumni support is more important today than at any time since the college explosion of the 1950s and 1960s, especially in the independent sector. Smart college presidents and boards of trustees defuse their detractors by bringing some of their number into the governance of the institution, instead of stonewalling them; the rules can be easily amended to end the kind of attitudinal inbreeding that so angers alumni who have their own ideas about how their college should be run. Responsibility is the best cure for chronic dissent. Who knows? Broadening the base of governance may produce some good suggestions, and good friends, for the college. Similarly, a healthy development of recent years is the organization of alumni support for some *public* colleges which earlier made no attempt to supplement government funding with private contributions.

A fact of my own college years is still a fact: a student never pays, in tuition, room, or board fees, the *full* cost of his college education. Endowment income, alumni giving, corporate and foundation contributions, government contracts, and other revenue go to cover the student's college costs. It makes a great deal of sense to appeal to the former student (now presumably enjoying the fruits of a college education) to repay in part the institution which provided that education. That is the eminently logical rationale behind all alumni-giving drives. The success of this approach, however, varies with the closeness of the individual's ties to the institution and the recollections (positive or negative) of his or her days there. It is my experience that college fund-raising drives are not wholly predictable on the basis of college careers. The biggest BMOC (big man on campus) may be a dismal flop as a giving prospect, while the Wistful Willie whom nobody knew may come in with the big bucks. You never know.

An Early-Warning System for Money Problems

No institution in difficulty advertises its troubles. That would dry up contributions and scare away potential students. Financial setbacks are kept top secret until they are forced into the public spotlight. Students, faculty, and alumni, many for the first time, learn of serious trouble when the administration announces at commencement that the college will not reopen in the fall.

To protect the interest of both colleges and students, New York (under a system set up by Joe Nyquist when he was Commissioner) now receives regular financial statements from nonpublic institutions. When things look bad, the Commissioner suggests private meetings with the college president to discuss plans so that the college may be restored to health. A sick college is sometimes urged to merge into a healthier university. At the worst, it is phased out of existence with the least damaging effect on students and faculty. The entire process is completely confidential.

New York is able to do this because its Regents have jurisdiction over all levels of education, but a similar "red alert" could be created under other governance systems.

Expanding the College Clientele

Small independent colleges, especially church-related women's colleges, are already dropping by the wayside; some are merging into the nearest university that will have them. While the women's college woes have been particularly severe because of the spread of coeducation into the major established universities of the East, the culprit for all higher education is the down-curve of America's birth rate in recent years, which bodes ill for those institutions which fail to attract more and different student publics as well as their proportionate share of the shrinking college-going age groups. The declines have already swept over elementary and secondary systems; the colleges are feeling the pinch. A new baby boom (there is a boomlet now) will not help the colleges for a number of years.

Thus the name of the game is expanding the college clientele. There are a number of ways that higher-education institutions are doing exactly that.

Articulation: Helping the Transition

The sharp line of demarcation between secondary and higher education is in many ways artificial. College freshmen are three months older than the graduating high-school student. It is the academic environment, and the learning modes, which are quite different, but even these do not justify a sudden interruption of instruction. Many young people in high school at seventeen and eighteen are quite capable of mastering freshman or sophomore level college work in their best subjects. Why let the clock, the calendar, and outmoded habit hold them back? Instead of going unprofitably through the torpor of "senioritis" during their final high-school semester (or semesters)—after college admissions applications have long since been filed—schools and neighboring colleges can arrange for able seniors to take college courses for which they are best qualified, imposing a fee for so doing. Successful completion of those courses can produce credits toward college degrees. Even though they may not attend the college where their "articulation" (as the practice is called) has helped them win credits, their part-time presence (and their fee payments) help the local colleges. And the college may influence students eventually to enroll there. Where it has been tried (as in New York State), articulation works.

Reaching Past the Traditional Students

With the traditional college public—residential students between seventeen and twenty-two years of age—dwindling, it makes sense to recruit other people who seek a college education, a process familiar to American higher education for some time. It works. *Part-time students,* commuting from their homes before or after work, make up an increasing proportion of our college and university student bodies. *Older people* can combine newfound leisure time with a desire for higher education—and a degree to help start a second career. *Foreign students* still clamor for a chance at an American college education, the chance to spend four years in a democratic land. Of the Iranians who once comprised the largest single segment of foreigners in our universities, George Kane wrote in *The New Republic* in 1981: "Even the militant Iranian students, who believe that America is Satan and that Khomeini is God's vice-regent on earth, disclose a curious reluctance to leave the American hell and return to the Iranian heaven."

You Don't Have to Be Present to Win

Have you ever wondered how many people have the capacity to earn college degrees but never had the opportunity to attend college? There are tens of thousands of Americans young and old whose family and job responsibilities prevented them from attending a university even on a part-time basis. Recognizing this, Commissioner Nyquist, when he was inaugurated in 1970 as President of the "University of the State of New York"—not a college with a campus, faculty, and students but, rather, a constitutional concept covering all education in the state—proposed that this underserved public be given a practical chance to earn college degrees by enrolling in the Regents' External Degree Program. This is a fully accredited system of extension courses which permits individuals to study outside of classrooms and to earn degrees by passing exams devised by college faculties. By 1980, my final year as Chancellor, more than 10,000 New Yorkers had won USNY degrees through the Nyquist program.

One of my most rewarding duties as Chancellor was to shake hands with and pass diplomas to those degree-winners who were able to gather at Albany every September, several hundred men and women as diverse as seemed possible. I greeted heroes of the uniformed services, men convicted of murder who studied in prison, housewives who pored over assignments in the wee hours after their day's work was done, and others—truly a cross-section of the American people. Not all the 10,000 came to the ceremonies, but, in the spirit of the curriculum itself, could stay home and receive their degrees.

I cannot forget the exhilaration I felt in sharing their moment of triumph with all these hard-working Americans where desire for education, oftentimes at great personal sacrifice, was an inspiration to all who saw and heard.

And I will confess something to you. The pride and gratification demonstrated by the people who had earned their external degrees delighted me more than I was able to express because they offered such a sharp and welcome contrast to the unappreciative, discourteous, surly, sometimes disruptive students who marred the college commencements of those days by refusing to stand through the national anthem, or by shouting down or walking out on speakers with whom they disagreed, proving they had not learned the meaning and the purpose of a university.

The Regents' External Degree Program (and State University's comparable Empire State College, which is in the same mode but requires some direct contact during study) benefits New York institutions through nominal tuition fees which reimburse faculties for preparing courses and examinations. Every little bit helps, and the external degree programs have been vigorously supported by the higher education community in New York. Other states have emulated them. The idea is spreading.

Let Them Be What They Want to Be

As competition for the available pool of students becomes keener, college administrators play a life-and-death game of anticipating demand for certain types of specialized courses. During the late 1970s, for example, the Regents received a barrage of applications for the right to grant new degrees in business administration and business law—and these applications produced counterbattery fire from nearby colleges which already had such programs and feared dilution of their market. Whenever new programs of any kind were proposed, the question of *need* was always raised: Do we need more doctors in this or that part of the state? Is the market for new lawyers growing or declining in the region served by a college applying for a law school? Will a building boom enable new architects to find enough jobs in the coming decade? Don't we already have too many degree programs in business? *Need* always seemed to be defined on the basis of somebody's estimate of future job placement prospects, or perceived social requirements in years to come.

That's not my idea of what need should mean, or of the proper criteria for authorizing degree programs. Need for college programs should be defined as *demand.* Are there sufficient applications or indications of interest to warrant offering degree courses in the subject area? Can the college mount a good curriculum—if so, at what cost? Is the faculty able to provide high-quality instruction? Can the library support the study requirements of the courses? If the student decides what he or she wants to do in life, and if the college can offer a good degree program which will help the student enter his or her chosen field, the only concern of government should be to assure the student that the program will be of excellent quality, within the proven capabilities of the institution, and that there is enough demand so that neighboring colleges will not suffer unduly from competition.

Educators should not be social engineers, tailoring human aspirations and talents to fit *anticipated* future societal needs or requirements. Young people should not be told that they cannot be trained as veterinarians because society is going to need accountants. Should that be done, we could end up with a generation of disgruntled third-rate accountants whose chief merit is that they love animals.

Young people are not stupid. They understand the economic risks of choosing a career, of risking future job prospects. And they know that

what they *like* to do, what they are *good* at doing, is what they are likely
to do best at as a career. Let them decide for themselves what they want
to become—then help them to be outstanding in their chosen field.

One of Our Greatest Mistakes

Should everyone go to college? Hell, no. One of our greatest mistakes,
one made at times by all of us, egged on for obvious reasons by those of
us in education, has been to promote the notion that every young person
is capable of mastering college-level work, needs the kinds of learning
that colleges impart, and therefore should work toward a college degree.
The argument ends with saying that today it is as necessary to have a
college diploma as it was to have a high-school diploma twenty-five
years ago. This trilogy of fallacies has spawned a fourth: that everyone
has a right to a college education.

Our exaltation of higher education and a college degree has succeeded at the expense of dignity and pride in that kind of work which
does not require college training, work that calls for the mind and the
hand to collaborate in craftsmanship and creativity. During an Albany
dinner at which the Regents were hosts to labor and minority-group
leaders, a black masterprinter spoke eloquently of the satisfaction and
rewards of his trade. When he sat down, a black woman across the table
rose and denounced him as a Jim Crow, a Judas-goat for the white majority. "We don't want those pick-and-shovel, broom-and-mop jobs for
our children," she shouted. "We want them to be bankers and lawyers
and doctors!"

On later reflection, I accept that her attitude was of *our* making.
Society has glorified the professional and executive status which supposedly is attendant to college degrees, and in so doing we have silently but
effectively downgraded the value of those jobs which require talent and
expertise but are assigned a lower standing in the pecking order of
American society. It is no wonder that the woman accused the established order of trying to perpetuate the second-class citizenship of minorities by directing them into work not requiring a university degree,
ergo, into inferior careers.

What Has It Cost Us?

By failing to treat manual, physical, and sometimes routine desk work
with the dignity it deserves, we have contributed to a decline of pride in
one's own work. Those of my generation remember how we laughed at
cheap foreign-made gadgets that broke down or blew out quickly, so

quickly that an ingenious American importer advertised them as "guaranteed to last indefinitely." Today we rush past U.S.-made cars and TV sets and cameras and other expensive items to buy imported versions. Why? First, because so much of what is made in America today is of shoddy workmanship that we fear it will conk out without warning, perhaps dangerously. Second, it is difficult to find people nowadays who are able and willing to fix our costly machines, a situation which *Time* capsuled as "Buttonhook Service in a Pushbutton Age."

All of us have heard the plaintive query, "If we Americans can build space vehicles to carry men to the moon and back flawlessly, why can't we build flawless automobiles and television sets? Why is it that, as our technology improves, our craftsmanship seems to worsen?" Unless and until we attach as much dignity and worth to craftsmanship as we do to technology, the situation will not be corrected.

Don't Blame the Unions

Are labor unions guilty of the decline in the quality of manufactured goods and of services? No. It is true that labor union contracts can protect workers against dismissal because of inferior performance—and human nature tells us that such protection may contribute to carelessness—but I consider that only part of the story. We had labor unions long before there was a discernible deterioration of quality in American-manufactured goods. Grandpa told my dad in 1915 that he would be wise to become a labor lawyer (he became a newspaper reporter). Repair and maintenance people are as likely to be nonunion as union members, and their ability to cope with breakdowns and stoppages seems to have suffered equally.

Union leaders are acutely aware that their membership totals have been declining. They know that the unions' continued strength depends upon a steady and uninterrupted flow of capable, talented people into the trades. They know, too, that such flow depends upon the value that potential workers place upon their jobs, not only in dollar terms but also in dignity and expressed worth to society. They have heard that angry woman at Albany, and it hurts.

For these reasons, unions have been very helpful in organizing career-oriented programs in secondary schools, hoping to encourage young people to train for entry into the job market as, for example, carpenters, auto mechanics, cooks, and appliance-repair experts. In Nassau, New York, labor unions share the credit for the success of our Board of Co-operative Educational Services (BOCES) in offering a variety of training programs which few, if any, school districts could afford to operate on their own.

Open Admissions: A Costly Experiment

One inevitable result of a misplaced stress upon making college degrees available for practically everyone is the proliferation of "open admissions," that is, allowing every holder of a high-school diploma to matriculate at certain colleges without further qualification. Open admissions appear to confirm the impression that *all* high-school graduates are "college material"; the policy invites them to choose higher education rather than undertake specialized training for entry into the job market. Once lubricated by generous state and federal grants for tuition and expenses, open admissions loosed the floodgates: thousands upon thousands of unprepared and unqualified young people swarmed into colleges and universities which were not ready to receive them.

When the New York Board of Regents okayed in late 1969 an open admissions policy for City University (CUNY), they advanced its effective date from 1975, the original date, to the 1970–71 college year. Although it was obviously impossible to prepare for the rush of students, this precipitate action was justified, sub rosa, by fears that to insist upon the 1975 date would certainly invoke physical violence. The Regents gave their permission reluctantly with a warning that open admissions was not to become a revolving door moving students out as quickly as they came in. That was a warning easier given than heeded.

What happened? An educational disaster. The facilities of CUNY could not be expanded fast enough to meet the swollen student body's requirements; every available square foot of space was pressed into use as makeshift classrooms. It was discovered almost immediately that the city's public schools had done such a poor educational job that many of their graduates who were now open-admissions college freshmen were unable to meet the basic English and mathematics standards of competency expected at grade-school levels. High-salaried, tenured professors were shanghaied to teach remedial classes in reading and arithmetic. CUNY estimated its costs for remediation during the first year of open admissions at more than $50 million.

Writing in the *National Review* (May 1981) about an unnamed open-admissions university, William F. Buckley reported the following conversation with a professor, who said of his students:

". . . I would guess that half the blacks and half the lower quintile whites can't (a) add fractions, or (b) read a newspaper."

"You're kidding," [Buckley replied].

"I am not kidding."

"How do they pass their exams?"

"They don't. But the administration doesn't expel them, because to do so means one less body against which to claim the annual subsidy from the state capitol."

"So what happens to them?"

"They are put on probation. It isn't easy for a student here to know what the difference is between being on probation and not being on probation. Life goes on exactly as before. After about two and a half years they have to weed out. The student leaves, and he's mad at the college, mad at his teachers, mad at the state, and probably mad at the truck-driving firm that gives him a job."

Why shouldn't he be mad at the world? For several years of his life he was conned into believing that he would receive a degree; now he finds that he will not—worse, he suspects that everybody else knew it all along.

In another institution with which I am personally familiar, some students became accustomed to college as a semipermanent way of life. They and their wives and their children lived in the dormitories; some of their kids were born into the college community. While a generous government provided all the necessities, these students leisurely carried a couple of courses each semester, until the authorities finally had to break the logjam by requiring passage of a specified number of courses per year for a maximum number of years. Their awakening was rude.

The revolving door may revolve slowly, but it is still a revolving door—and it wastes those years young people could have been spending on learning productive trades and crafts. It is a cruel hoax, as well, upon the taxpayers. Years will pass before anyone can total the enormous waste of federal and state funds spent in subsidizing and thus encouraging college experiences which were doomed from the start—doomed, that is, unless the colleges lowered their standards to the level of secondary schools, which to their credit they refused to do.

The trouble is that we are still pouring millions into the support of unqualified degree candidates. We do it because some of us have not yet understood that college cannot and should not be for everyone.

Government grants and loans for college tuition and allied expenses are "entitlement" funds; the total amount which must be spent depends upon the number of those who claim the assistance for which their matriculation qualified them. When we finally summon the sense and the guts to limit college entrance to those who can master college-level work and have a reasonable chance of earning a degree, we will at least have the satisfaction of knowing that our tax money for higher education is being well spent. Then, young people who otherwise can become productive members of society without college degrees will not be tricked.

Light at the End of the Tunnel:
Guess Who They're Recruiting Now!

Before World War II, when the major qualification for admission to college was academic achievement, top students vied with each other for acceptance at the most prestigious universities; every college-bound secondary-schooler worked his or her hardest to get into a "good" college. As far as scholars were concerned, it was a sellers' market. Promising young athletes, on the other hand, were part of a buyers' market, with colleges competing for the best high-school graduates.

During the 1960s and 1970s, a new dimension was added to college recruiting. Academics and even athletics took a back seat to demographics, for now universities struggled to shed their "elitist" reputations—assets which suddenly became liabilities in the liberal ledger—by recruiting women, blacks, Hispanics, and American Indians (newly labeled Native Americans, since John Wayne seems to have made Indians a bad word). The recruiting of "minorities" was the sine qua non of college policy in those years; although women have been a majority of our population for some time, they are included, because "minority" in this context is not quantitative but a synonym for "cheated." Under the new dispensation (which was more sternly enforced as each new Vietnam-era graduating class produced new members of the admissions staff), a college was not considered properly balanced (and surely not "liberal") unless its student body was more or less proportionate in racial and male-to-female ratios to the U.S. population. Indeed, minorities were sought *beyond* this number as redress for grievances of the past.

The kind of person you are and what you can do gave way to emphasis upon your sex, your skin color, your ethnic heritage. Questions on application forms now sought to find "qualified" persons quite apart from scholastic standards and basic competency.

But times are changing. The *U.S. News and World Report* (April 1981) says, "With lures from big scholarships to private labs, universities are competing for the brightest high school graduates—and stirring heated controversy." Scholarships are again being offered on the basis of academic standing rather than need; Texas A & M University, for example, gives $2,000 per year President's endowed scholarships "based strictly upon academic achievement." Acting A & M President Charles H. Samson explains: "We are going after the brightest of the bright students more diligently than ever—in a manner not unlike that in which we pursue blue-chip football players and star faculty."

Michigan State University offers up to $22,000 cash each year to ten high-school seniors, awarded on the basis of a very demanding examination. The prime contenders in recruiting competition for high scorers are the large state universities, because high-caliber scholars help to convince tight-fisted legislators that the college is performing well and thus qualifies for increased state assistance.

Whatever the motivation, whatever the tactics, the one most salutary and refreshing aspect of this post-Vietnam shift in emphasis is that *excellence*—in academic achievement and potential—has resurfaced in so many places as a (no, as *the*) primary qualification for admission to higher education.

I do not contend that *only* the very bright should go to college. We have come a long way from that outmoded concept. Those who look forward to lifelong careers in those types of work which require college degrees, and who are capable of doing college-level work in those subjects, should have an opportunity to prove themselves and acquire those credentials. When they need more than self-help to finance their college or university tuition, room, and board, the public should be as generous as their pocketbooks permit.

What I *do* say is that the renewal of our time-tested system wherein a premium is placed upon academic excellence—in terms of preferential admission and financing—is healthy for America. Not only will it sustain the standards of teaching and learning in our colleges, it will also impress upon high-school students that good grades are well worth working for and can reap substantial rewards, that college is not a right which belongs to everyone but rather an earned privilege, and that society has once again placed a high value upon superior intellectual accomplishment.

If you can think of a better way to breathe new life into the whole educational system, tell me about it.

Summing Up

I believe that the campus disturbances of the Vietnam era lowered the quality of American education in several ways:

First, the authority of college administrations to run their institutions in an atmosphere of disciplined learning, coupled with a free exchange of ideas, was severely impaired.

Second, the inception of such negative practices as pass/fail grading, grade inflation, lowered diploma requirements, more useless electives, and so on, depressed academic achievement and inhibited a true assessment of it.

Third, the spirit of disruption spread from the colleges to the high-school campuses.

I believe that the majority of earnest students were cheated of part of their education by campus disrupters who were allowed to interrupt class schedules and even close down the operations of entire universities during the bad period of Vietnam.

I believe that too many teachers, by taking the side of the disruptive student (and nonstudent) leaders, became part of the problem instead of helping to maintain learning discipline and order on campus.

I believe, however, that today's college students (like most of their predecessors) are determined to acquire an education and a degree to equip them for their future careers, and that they will not tolerate the disruptions which interrupted the schooling of earlier student bodies.

I believe that allowing existing faculties to have the final say as to who will be hired to teach at a university can produce a kind of intellectual incest, creating a philosophical-political imbalance that may be passed along to the students.

I believe that some colleges have lost the allegiance and support of some alumni and other benefactors because they project an air of ill-concealed hostility, not only to the business-commercial-industrial community upon which they depend for contributions and contracts but also to the generally accepted values of the society in which the college exists and from which it must draw its students.

I believe that nobody is obliged to support any institution, college or otherwise, which is openly critical of or inimical toward his own values, position, or career. But I also believe that withdrawing one's support from an institution will not necessarily help it to become or to be again what one might want it to be.

I believe that the problems of educational pluralism in higher education are different from those of the schools, in that, generally speaking, there is no real difference in the quality of discipline between public and private universities; there is no real difference between them in the quality of educational opportunities offered, and there is no serious question about the constitutionality of government assistance to nonpublic colleges.

I believe that the danger to educational pluralism in the college field is largely demographic and financial in origin, in that: (1) the normal college-going age group in America is shrinking, and the decline will not bottom out until the 1990s; (2) no law requires young people to go to college; (3) although both private and public colleges charge some tuition, a far greater degree of taxpayer support enables the public institutions to offer an excellent education at much lower cost to all who qualify, regardless of their income status, and (4) the costs of operating universities are skyrocketing.

I also believe that there are important offsetting factors that can help colleges survive, many of which have been enumerated in this chapter.

I believe that the increased availability of government funding for college students has led to unanticipated fraud and cheating by students at a substantial cost in tax dollars, a situation which should not be blamed upon the colleges but upon the state of public morality.

I believe that not every young person should go to college, and that our continuing overstress upon the value of a college education and degree has led to a decline in dignity and pride in craftsmanship and creativity among those whose careers do not require college training.

I believe that admission to college should be limited to those who demonstrate the potential to master college-level work and who therefore have a good chance to graduate, regardless of their sex, race, creed, color, national origin, or income status, and that any "open admissions" or other programs which may result in the matriculation of unqualified students are unfair to those students and demeaning to the institutions.

Finally, I believe that the recent turn to recruiting bright students, encouraging college admissions on the basis of scholastic ability rather than financial need or "deprived" status, will have a beneficial effect both in maintaining high academic standards within the colleges and in reestablishing the idea that society does place a high premium upon academic achievement and intellectual prowess, which, in turn, will improve the quality of the entire educational system.

6.

From Topeka to Cleveland, from Desegregation to Quotas

After More than 25 Years, Has Busing Been Worth the Price?

DONALD WALDRIP's name may never become a household word, but he should be remembered for a unique contribution to life in these United States.

Waldrip, the U.S. court-appointed administrator of desegregation for the Cleveland, Ohio, public schools, observed late in 1980 that while the city's school enrollment is about 35 percent white, there was only one white basketball player on Cleveland's fourteen high-school teams. Accordingly, Waldrip ordered that at least 20 percent of every twelve-man squad must be white; inasmuch as 2.4 basketball players of any skin hue are hard to find, he directed coaches to recruit a minimum of two white players per team.

Waldrip's decree ignited an uproar in Cleveland and across the country. An Indianapolis newspaper snorted: "The players don't have to be good, they just have to be white." Columnist James J. Kilpatrick dubbed the order "lunacy." President Albert Shanker of the American Federation of Teachers observed that "suddenly, picking people on the basis of race—black or white—rather than skill or accomplishment appears ludicrous"; commenting on the defense that quotas may have a place in education aside from sports, Shanker replied tartly that, if so, we should pick basketball players on the basis of their skills and surgeons on the basis of their color. He called the Waldrip order "just plain dumb." Black columnist William Raspberry added that if Cleveland's best high-school basketballers happen to be black, "there is no problem [for Waldrip] to fix." *Reason's* Thomas W. Hazlett predicted that "the federal micro-heads" would soon seek further refinements—a fixed quota of white players on court at all times, and 65–35 percent sharing of scoring between blacks and whites.

The Lessons of the Waldrip Affair

But let's not blame everything on Waldrip. I agree that his silly decree was everything that his critics said it was—yet Donald Waldrip was simply carrying out the decisions of his bosses, the U.S. courts, as he understood them: It is an unconstitutional deprivation of equal protection of the law for a public body (such as the Cleveland public-school system) to condone a situation whereby opportunity (e.g., the chance to play varsity basketball) is not simultaneously and jointly exercised in proportion to the racial mix of the population served (in Cleveland, 65–35 percent black and white).

If Waldrip's order was absurd (and it was), its absurdity must be debited to the judicial directives on which it rests. I said earlier that Donald Waldrip has made a unique contribution to American life—and he has.

First (and I discuss this aspect elsewhere), Waldrip focused our attention upon a new phenomenon in American society: the petty proconsul, endowed with the virtually limitless powers of the federal courts and charged with governance over some vital element of our daily lives—in this instance, the public-school system of a great city (Waldrip made headlines again in 1981, when he had two Cleveland school officials hauled off to the slammer in a dispute over pay increases for his small army of desegregators).

Second, Waldrip's ridiculous basketball order dramatized in terms understandable to every citizen the present bankruptcy of our federal judiciary's desegregation posture, brought to the point of absurdity by a quarter-century of expansion and distortion of the Supreme Court's majestic affirmation of human rights in its unanimous 1954 decision, *Brown v. Board of Education of Topeka.*

Finally, Waldrip has forced us to face up to a fundamental choice in education: *quality* or *equality?*

As Waldrip discovered, quality and equality are not always compatible. Sometimes (as in the case of Cleveland's basketball teams) equality of opportunity can be achieved only at the expense of quality in performance. Waldrip chose equality, as that seemed to be his mandate. Must we all do the same?

What Should Be Our National Goal?

After eleven years of experience on the directing board of the oldest, largest (and in my view, best) unified educational enterprise in the United States, I am more firmly convinced than ever that *our national goal must be the attainment of educational excellence* as a first priority, superseding all competing considerations. Over the years, our search for that goal has made our educational system great; we cannot abandon it now.

Educational opportunities must be made available to all on an equitable basis; that has been the New York Regents' policy for years. But opportunities must be *real*. They must have not only merit but *value*. An opportunity to attend an inferior school is meaningless, worthless. Our resources (and they are limited) must be committed to the maintenance and improvement of the *quality* of our educational offerings. We cannot let those resources be diverted to other things, however high-purposed they may be.

Is this how we're handling educational priorities in these United States today? Unhappily, no. That's the cause of much of our present problem. Let's see what we're doing wrong.

What Brown Said — and Didn't Say

This chapter has to do with desegregation, integration, affirmative action, and racial quotas, as applied to America's educational system. I do not for a moment contend that the effort to end segregation in education is wrong. It is both morally and constitutionally correct, and it was long overdue when *Brown v. Board of Education of Topeka* triggered our national policy. What I *do* contend is that the judicial mutations which have distorted *Brown* since 1954 have led to substantial diversions of our resources from the betterment of educational quality to a massive reshuffling of students in order to achieve what the shufflers consider a better racial mix.

And that is not what the *Brown* decision intended.

Brown, with Chief Justice Earl Warren speaking for the Court, overturned an 1896 ruling in *Plessy v. Ferguson* that states could segregate blacks from whites in public facilities if both enjoyed facilities of equal quality. Wrong, said the Chief Justice: *separate is not equal.* State-mandated segregation (in this case, of public schools) violates the Fourteenth Amendment's "equal-protection-of-the-laws" requirement and must be ended "with all deliberate speed."

The logic of *Brown* was clear and compelling. Where society (through government) deliberately separates black children from the white children with whom they would normally attend their local schools, the black youngsters realize that this official ostracism reflects their inferior status as blacks, which realization lessens their impetus to succeed in school and in life, knowing that they will always be black.

The *Brown* Court relied heavily upon sociopsychological evidence to which my friend and colleague, Regent Kenneth B. Clark, contributed and which indicated that segregated black kids have a low level of self-esteem because of their color. Some critics have contended that the Court should not have considered this evidence, that the case should have decided purely on law and precedent. I disagree. To be realistic and enforceable, judicial decisions should take into account the facts of life as they are, as well as the likely effects of rulings upon society.

That is one of our problems. While the *Brown* Court did take into account the practical effects of school segregation, successor courts at all levels have generally refused to consider the results of earlier court-ordered desegregation and the probable effects of each new decision being pondered. *Brown* said only that segregated school systems which exist as a matter of governmental policy and practice must be dismantled.

Did *Brown* mandate that every school—indeed, every classroom, every team—must have a proportion of blacks to whites substantially equal to the black-white percentages of the district's enrollment?

No, but that is the discipline that Waldrip and others like him have been directed to impose upon schools across the country.

Did *Brown* mandate that school attendance boundaries or school district lines, not arbitrarily drawn to separate blacks from whites, be redrawn, and districts combined, to produce a greater racial mix?

No, but attendance zones have been arbitrarily altered for this purpose, and heavy pressure is building to impose a "metropolitan" combination of city and suburban districts which would provide a fresh supply of white students to "desegregate" city schools whose former white pupils have left.

Did *Brown* mandate that classroom assignments be made in proportion to white/minority enrollment in the school building, rather than based upon the individual child's ability to master instruction at a given level and pace?

No, but the last vestiges of "ability tracking" are disappearing before the onslaught of desegregation orders, as teachers struggle to educate classrooms of youngsters who vary greatly in their capacity to absorb what is being taught. The result: brighter children are bored, slower ones (who need more individual attention than such a situation can provide) cannot keep up, and those in the middle cannot move ahead as fast as they should.

Did *Brown* mandate abandonment of standardized tests as a measure of academic achievement or ability, or as a diploma requirement, if such tests regularly produce minority failures out of proportion to minority enrollment?

No, but legal challenges have been mounted in many states, alleging that tests deny "equal educational opportunity" in that high rates of minority failure prove bias. Florida's competency testing program is struggling through litigation as this is being written, with the outcome in doubt.

Did *Brown* mandate the imposition of discipline (punishment, suspension, expulsion) upon minority students only up to the proportion of minority enrollment in a school?

No, but the federal bureaucracy, in 1980, monitored the disciplinary records of schools in racial-ethnic terms, presumably on the theory that disproportionate punishment of minority kids proved racial bias on the part of administrators.

And There's More

Did *Brown* mandate that "Black English," a jargon spoken by young blacks at home and at play, be given standing when teachers determine school curricula?

No, but that's what a federal judge ruled in an Ann Arbor, Michigan, case in 1980.

Did *Brown* mandate that special classes designed to help foreign-language-speaking students learn English also include an appropriate number of English-speakers in order to meet desegregation standards?

No, but that's the case in many classrooms under desegregation orders. One case (I've changed the numbers to protect the identity of the district) involved teaching English to eighty Hispanic students whose proficiency in our language was limited or nonexistent. The district was required to assign *forty English-speakers* to sit in the classroom, learning nothing, wasting time they could have spent studying other subjects. Thus the class was "desegregated." The excess cost to the district was $50,000, for which better uses could surely have been found. The cost in wasted study time for the forty English-speakers cannot be computed— or recovered.

Did *Brown* mandate that faculty members be distributed through a school system on the basis of race, rather than assigned where they want to teach, where they are most needed, or where they are likely to produce the best results?

No, but despite the importance of role-models with whom youngsters can quickly identify, and despite findings like those of Bailey's 1970 study of school disruption that a predominantly black faculty can best maintain discipline in a predominantly black school, New York City (for example) has been under federal orders to assign teachers on the basis of a racial-mix formula.

Did *Brown* mandate that policies and standards governing admission to colleges and universities be disregarded if they do not produce a federally fixed minimum of minority students?

No, but the federal bureaucracy mounted strenuous efforts to force institutions of higher learning (under pain of losing U.S. grants and aid) to integrate their student bodies on the basis of U.S.-determined formulas.

Brown mandated none of these enumerated policies and requirements, yet some of them have become harsh realities and others may follow—all claiming the moral, constitutional, and educational fatherhood of *Brown v. Board of Education of Topeka.*

A wise jurist once observed that the Constitution is what the judges say it is; now a new breed of federal judges (who would rather be caught in public without their trousers than without their liberal credentials) vies for honorable mention in the Establishment history of our times by adding fancy new variations on the desegregation theme and imposing them on people who have been proved "guilty" of segregation only by the wildest convolutions of circumstantial evidence—all, of course, in the revered name of *Brown.*

Brown and Scholastic Achievement

Before we leave *Brown,* we must note one pertinent fact about the landmark decision:

The Supreme Court did NOT base its *Brown* ruling upon a finding that black youngsters achieved better scholastically if they were enrolled in racially mixed rather than all-black schools. The Court simply held that deliberate, official segregation damaged black children's self-esteem and thus diminished their incentive to achieve.

Certainly the Justices hoped and believed that desegregation would enhance blacks' educational performance. So did I. That hope and belief was the very practical (as distinct from constitutional) rationale for eliminating segregated schools: providing equal educational opportunity would break the vicious circle of discrimination preventing black Americans from gaining equality in jobs and housing. But it remained a hope and a belief, not a finding of fact.

After more than a quarter-century of school desegregation in the wake of *Brown,* there is still no such finding of fact. There is still no substantive evidence that desegregation or integration per se significantly improves the scholarship of black youngsters.

Black achievement improves after desegregation, *sometimes.* But sometimes it does not. The academic performance of white students does not suffer after desegregation, *usually*. But sometimes it does. Throughout the extensive research on the question of changes in educational outcomes subsequent to desegregation, one adjective pops up again and again: the findings are *inconclusive*.

The 1974 Nyquist Report

In June 1974, as the New York Regents prepared to update their position on school integration, Commissioner E. B. (Joe) Nyquist (himself devoted to desegregation) provided the Board with a "report on the research results on the effects of desegregation-integration projects." There were positive results and negative results. The report cited a 1973 paper by the U.S. Commission on Civil Rights covering the results of integration of ten formerly minority schools. Better black achievement was noted in three of the ten; nothing was said about the other seven. A 1972 University of Chicago study of 32,000 students in eight hundred integrated Southern schools found that "no effects on educational achievement were noted as a result of either busing or racial and school attitudes."

A Buffalo, New York, study showed black gains after integration, as did one national study, but an analysis in 1974 of integration results in Boston, Massachusetts, White Plains, New York, Ann Arbor, Michigan, Riverside, California, and Hartford and New Haven, Connecticut, indicated that "in terms of academic achievement . . . the black children showed no significant improvement as measured by standardized tests. In the Boston study, in fact, a 'control group' of elementary school pupils kept in the predominantly black neighborhood schools performed slightly better than those bused to middle-class suburban schools, although not significantly so." An early Washington, D.C., survey surprisingly indicated that "the desegregation experience could negatively affect scholastic performance . . ."

A 1965 California report "concluded that the achievement of bused pupils did not increase. The achievement of pupils desegregated in grade 2 or earlier neither increased nor decreased. And, the achievement of pupils desegregated after grade 2 decreased in comparison to that of other pupils." A Washington State study suggested that "neither pupil race nor racial composition of a school per se . . . seemed to have a substantial effect on academic performance . . ."

Two Cracks in the Wall of Certainty

It was in the Nyquist report that two cracks appeared in the previously solid wall of certainty that desegregation inevitably improved the academic performance of black youngsters.

A California study suggested that the *quality of schools* was a major factor in minority achievement: "When minority children in school 'A' read significantly better than minority children in school 'B,' and all the minority children are substantially from the same socioeconomic background, it is because of the difference in the *schools,* not the difference in the children." Profound? No. Obvious? Yes. But what was worth noting was the admission that the *comparative excellence* of one school vis-à-vis another (not merely the fact of desegregation in those schools) could affect the scholastic achievement of minority kids.

And . . . the first discernible retreat from an immutable belief that school integration is essential to the improvement of black achievement was noted in this statement quoted from a 1968 professional report: "It is felt [a favorite expression of educators, which fuzzes the distinction between the writer's opinion and the profession's] that school integration should be viewed as a means of producing human beings who can cooperatively confront and mutually resolve crucial social issues, and that the purely academic justification for integration is less relevant and less important." Translated from educationese, this copout says: "Research doesn't prove that blacks do better in integrated schools. So let's dismiss that fact as irrelevant and say that integration is worthwhile because it encourages black-white cooperation."

The 1975 St. John Study

A year later, in 1975, Dr. Nancy H. St. John of the University of Massachusetts published *School Desegregation Outcomes for Children,* a comprehensive review of the results of more than a hundred programs across the country.

Dr. St. John's initial ventures into desegregation research reflected her hope of proving that racial mixing in schools produces higher academic achievement among black pupils. She started in 1962, in New Haven, where "unfortunately, that hypothesis was not confirmed." In Pittsburgh, in 1969, Dr. St. John found that "again, the results were disappointing. No difference was found in the reading scores and self-attitudes of desegregated and segregated youth, aspirations were significantly higher in segregated schools, and only arithmetic showed the expected boost from early desegregation." Her third disappointment was in Boston, where in 1974 "again the findings did not strongly support the basic hypothesis that desegregation confers clear benefits."

Turning to research by others, Dr. St. John noted that the longest-running survey of desegregation results in a given community (Riverside, California, from 1965 to 1973) had proven inconclusive; she commented: ". . . as it stands, neither the Riverside evidence nor that of any of the other longitudinal studies provides strong support for the hypothesis that desegregated schooling benefits minority group children." Of a 1967 study of 4,000 junior and senior high-school youngsters in the San Francisco Bay area, conducted by Alan Wilson, she concluded that ". . . the study is impressive in design and quite convincing that in this community, at least, racial integration per se was not significantly related to the academic performance of blacks."

In Boston, Dr. St. John reported, "bused pupils did not show significantly greater gains than their brothers or sisters." In Hartford, bused pupils made "significantly greater gains" than their nonbused peers in grades K-3, but "in grades 4 to 6 the difference in achievement favored the segregated." In Goldsboro, North Carolina, desegregated kids did better on arithmetic, but not in verbal achievement. Dr. St. John summed up these studies: "Taken together . . . they suggest that the achievement of black children is rarely harmed by desegregation, but they provide no strong or clear evidence that such desegregation boosts their achievement."

Effects on White Students

As for the claim that desegregation does not lower the scholastic achievement of whites, she observed that "desegregation has rarely lowered academic achievement for either black or white children," but that while "the evidence appears convincing that the achievement of white students is not adversely affected by the addition of a few black students to their classrooms, classrooms over 50% black are quite possibly detrimental to white achievement." In sum, says Dr. St. John, "white achievement has been unaffected in schools that remained majority white, but significantly lower in majority black schools."

Blacks and Busing

Brown postulated that black self-esteem was lowered by racial segregation, a logical conclusion from scientifically reached evidence. But does desegregation as it has been imposed in the United States raise the self-esteem of black students? Dr. St. John's review found that "the evidence . . . is that the effect of school desegregation on the general or academic self-concept of minority-group members tends to be negative or mixed more often than positive. Moreover . . . the most careful study . . . found that self-esteem was significantly lower in desegregated schools."

Black parents, according to Dr. St. John, do not necessarily believe that their youngsters can be educated only in classrooms with white kids; blacks supported integrated schools largely because "they believe that a majority-white school is inevitably better equipped and better staffed than a majority-black school." To paraphrase a blunt black school official: "Whitey will put his money where his kids are."

"It does not follow," Dr. St. John continued, "that most black parents want their own children bused out of their neighborhood to a mostly white school." Blacks were never greatly enthusiastic about busing, and recent polls indicate that black support is waning. Said Dr. St. John, "As the black population of a city grows in numbers, political power and militancy, its interest tends to shift from desegregation to adequate funding, accountability and community control of its schools. The closing of ghetto schools and mandatory outbusing of their pupils is viewed by many blacks as a way of perpetuating white supremacy."

St. John: End Forced Busing

Assessing her overall findings after reviewing more than a hundred existing desegregation studies, St. John opted against forced busing: "Should families be allowed to refuse assignment to a school that is very distant or in a totally different neighborhood? Should a child be allowed to transfer out of a school in which classmates are predominantly of the other race? I am not sure what the answers to these questions should be, but [I] tend to feel that such refusals and transfers should be allowed."

She believes that *voluntary* methods of school integration will produce better results than we've seen so far. "During the past twenty years considerable racial mixing has taken place in the schools, but research has produced little evidence of dramatic gains for children and some evidence of genuine stress for them," she says, adding, "What is needed now is a period of vigorous experimentation in ways of achieving equality of educational opportunity. School boards, principals and teachers must have the freedom to examine alternatives in all aspects of schooling, not merely ethnic ratios."

My Rochester Proposal: Dudsville

In October 1975, I was invited (as the new Chancellor of the Board of Regents) to address the New York State School Boards Association at their convention in Rochester. The gist of my remarks can be simply stated:

1. I spoke for myself, not for the Regents or the state.

2. Like many others, I had become increasingly troubled about the ill effects of busing for racial integration, which in my view was "dividing our society, pitting some groups of our citizens against others, generating intense emotional heat which too often has flared into vio-

lence, disrupting human lives and educational careers, and substantially weakening the faith of many Americans in the responsiveness of their government and in the fairness of their system of justice."

3. The rationale for forced integration of the public schools, and therefore also for the imposition of involuntary, massive transportation requirements to achieve racial "balance," is the idea that black children do not have "equal educational opportunity" unless they attend school with whites, which contention is in turn based upon the theory that black children cannot do their best scholastically unless they are taught in concert with white children.

4. Although I and many others in government had accepted the theory as logical, coinciding as it did with moral and constitutional principles we had already embraced, studies of desegregation outcomes in the twenty years since *Brown* were at best inconclusive. *The theory had not been proved.*

5. Because it was so important that we know the truth about the educational outcomes of desegregation, I announced my intention to ask President Gerald Ford to convene a task force of unbiased, scientifically trained individuals to measure and report on the educational impact of school integration upon both black and white youngsters.

My proposal was greeted with the reaction one might have expected had I moved for repeal of the Emancipation Proclamation. Odoacer, as he began the sacking of Rome in A.D. 476, probably got more applause than I did in Rochester in 1975. I had done the inexcusable: *I had questioned an established belief.*

Yes, I had—and I wanted answers.

A Proposal to President Ford . . .

Some months later, I wrote as a private citizen to President Ford, who promptly bucked my letter to a good friend, Vice President Nelson Rockefeller, with whom I had worked when he was Governor of New York. Through a counselor, Rocky sent my suggestion to HEW Secretary David Mathews. The net result: I was given some hope (not subsequently realized; 1976 was late in the Ford Presidency) that HEW would create a commission, and I was put on the Department's mailing list for copies of all their school-desegregation publications. For small favors, I was thankful—but not satisfied.

. . . and to President Carter

Being a persistent cuss and thoroughly convinced of the importance of a study, I wrote in 1977 (again as a private citizen) to newly elected President Jimmy Carter, repeating my proposal. A prompt response came from a member of his domestic policy staff, a Ph.D. who managed in one paragraph to misspell "privileged" and misuse commas twice: the National Institute of Education (NIE), research arm of HEW, was conducting "several major studies that hopefully address your concern." I would get copies of the studies. Period.

A Question of Bias

But NIE and HEW were not part of the solution I was seeking. They were part of the problem.

Desegregation research is virtually worthless unless it is conducted by a qualified, *unbiased* panel—and the in-house "experts" of NIE/HEW are not unbiased. Indeed, they wear their hearts on their sleeves; most of them are absolutely convinced that school desegregation *does* improve educational performance by black children without hurting that of whites, and they regularly downplay and discount any evidence to the contrary.

Even reports which they themselves have commissioned—reports by prointegration scholars—are snubbed by the forced integrationists in the federal bureaucracy when they seem to substantiate the conclusion that desegregation does not necessarily improve black scholarship.

NIE Publications

There are such reports. In 1976, the NIE published a booklet entitled *The Desegregation Literature: A Critical Appraisal,* in which the following statements appeared under the bylines of "distinguished researchers" (so described in Ray C. Rist's preface):

"Racial balance did not seem very effective in eliminating discrimination or in producing better educational opportunities.

"Research on educational outcomes . . . [does] not readily support the notion that simple desegregation will improve educational outcomes for black children.

"Local officials were told to implement specific plans narrowly focused upon achieving a certain degree of mixture by social race. *Not able to argue the plan on educational merits* . . . the officials could only present the plans as directives from higher and not always valued government sources . . ." [Italics supplied.]

"Superintendents also have no educational basis for advocating desegregation since the research findings on academic outcomes are inconclusive.

". . . findings from the desegregation research to date suggest that social race mixing alone has little consistent effect on black-white outcomes.

"Overall, findings are mixed on the question of whether or not desegregation significantly improves the scores of black students. No adverse effects on whites' achievement scores have been reported *except in cases where they attend predominantly black schools.*" [Italics supplied.]

On questions of educational attainment (the number of years students remain in school), results are again inconclusive. "Whatever gains some black students are making in educational attainment are more than offset by the increased number of black students who drop out, are pushed out or are expelled from desegregated schools."

And as for individual aspirations, "Findings have shown that black students in segregated schools tend to have higher aspirations than those in desegregated schools." Composite findings "show no significant differences in self-concept as a result of desegregation," although a sense of environmental control was posited as a positive outcome of desegregation. Of attitudes on race, the HEW study declares that "the findings are that racial attitudes are affected by desegregation *but the direction of the change is unclear.*" (Italics supplied.)

As for the requirement to mix faculty on a racial basis, "What evidence there is suggests that black students feel closer to and are more accepting of black teachers and that the presences of black teachers and other staff members in the school may reduce black drop-out rates and alienation."

Did Nyquist's report, or St. John's, or their own round-up of survey results discourage the government from pressing even harder for more racial integration in the schools? Not on your life.

Why the NAE Report Was Quashed

In May 1979, a quarter-century after *Brown,* HEW planned to issue a commemorative report entitled *Prejudice and Pride,* commissioned through the National Academy for Education, of which my distinguished colleague, Regent Emeritus Stephen K. Bailey, was president. Because Bailey insisted that the report include submissions by James S. Coleman and Nathan Glazer critical of desegregation tactics, Richard Beattie, executive secretary to HEW Secretary Joseph A. Califano, refused to release the report in time for the *Brown* observance, commenting: "I didn't think it was written well. It was just a hodgepodge." Bailey defended the report. "It's a report that indicates there is more than one position beside the HEW position on the issue of desegregation." Coleman added: "Some people would like to maintain the fiction that there is a high degree of consensus about the benefits of school desegregation policies."

In the end, the forced-integration zealots of HEW had their way.

Because the Bailey-NAE report included views incompatible with their own, they refused to give it general distribution. I am on their mailing list; I never saw the report, which (according to Gene Maeroff of the *New York Times*) went only to those who specifically requested it.

To suggest that such people could be entrusted to conduct a scientific, unbiased research study of the educational outcomes of desegregation is ridiculous. Whatever money might be spent on such a project would be completely wasted.

Is *any* research study needed today? I am no longer convinced that it is. Evidence already accumulated over more than a quarter-century of experience tells us that the academic performance of black youngsters is not significantly raised by integration. I very much doubt that more research would tell a different story.

Busing Isn't Worth the Price

To put it bluntly, forced integration, of which massive busing is an integral characteristic, is not worth the price we pay for it.

Important people who should know better, including one nationally respected college president whom I know personally and therefore will not name here, often justify their support for busing with sheer sophistry, to wit: Millions of youngsters take buses to and from schools every day, with the blessing of their parents—but when buses are used for racial integration, the same parents howl in protest, which doesn't make sense except as an expression of racism.

Wrong. It isn't the bus riding that is at issue. Most buses provide convenience and safety by carrying pupils to and from the *nearest* school for their grade—their neighborhood or district school. Busing for integration carries kids *away* from their nearest school, usually on a much longer run, to a school other than the one to which they would normally go. It's the effect upon their children that upsets parents, not the big yellow bus.

Like Prohibition, massive involuntary busing for school integration was a noble experiment. Like Prohibition, it has failed. Prohibition did nothing to stop Americans from drinking; it kindled a national disrespect for law and law enforcement that persists as a source of our social problems today. Forced busing has not produced significant scholastic improvement among black youngsters, which was its purpose; it has proven tremendously costly in terms of children's time which could otherwise be devoted to study or recreation, in terms of precious dollars which could be spent on improving the quality of education for all kids, and in terms of community disruption and resentment which have set back the cause of interracial amity by years.

Having been created as a U.S. constitutional amendment, the Eighteenth, Prohibition was killed by a repealer amendment, the Twenty-first. Forced busing is the creation of federal court decisions and administrative orders; it can be wiped out by intelligent judicial reconsideration in light of its failure and by the immediate firing of those bureaucrats who have, by their extremist interpretations, made a travesty of desegregation. After fourteen years, we had the good sense to put an end to Prohibition. After more than twenty-five years, will we have the good sense to end massive forced busing?

The Heart of the Matter Is Quality, not Race

It was once said that "white flight," the wholesale movement of white families out of urban centers, was racist; the implication was that whites leave because they do not want their children educated with blacks. That allegation seems to have faded; even David S. Tatel, a prominent backer of involuntary busing, concedes that "what parents—both black and white—flee are poor schools."

In this, Tatel is correct. People who can afford to do so have left the cities because of *the deterioration of the quality of life* there—not only declining performance levels in city public schools, but broken-down city services, decrepit transit systems, filth in the streets, unclean and unsafe parks, high (and rising) crime rates, astronomic municipal taxes, discourtesy and indifference at every turn, plus a myriad of other indications of urban decay.

If more whites than blacks have left a city and its public schools, that is in large part because more whites than blacks have the economic option of leaving. But when they can afford it, blacks leave, too: witness the growing migration of upper- and middle-class blacks to the suburbs.

City public schools are not being abandoned because their enrollment is largely black. Both blacks and whites leave them when they can because *they cannot find in those schools the quality of education which is their children's birthright.* A child passes through schooling just once, and every parent wants that one experience to be the best. The heart of the matter is QUALITY. It is not race.

A perfect illustration of the point was reported by the *New York Times* of September 20, 1981, describing a boycott of new integration lines in Chicago by both black and white parents whose youngsters were slated to be shuffled between two nearby schools:

"On the other side of the track the black parents were just as adamant. 'Our kids are not going to get any better education over there [in the mostly white school] than they are over here,' said Mosemae Ellison, as she shivered in the rain outside the Hendricks School. 'I don't mind my kids going to school with whites but they've hooked up two poor schools here. That's not going to do anybody any good.' "

Fred Reed, writing in *Harper's* magazine in February 1981, makes the point vigorously:

"An obvious observation ... is that blacks suffer less from racism than from poor education. Harvard does not reject black applicants because it dislikes blacks but because they are badly prepared. Blacks do not fail the federal entrance examination because it is rigged against them but because they don't know the answers. Equality of opportunity without equality of education is a cruel joke: giving an illiterate the right to apply to Yale isn't giving him much."

And the quality of education is not a function of some statistical racial balance. In a seventies' study, the New York Regents found that two New York City schools populated by almost exactly the same racial-ethnic-social-economic mix differed sharply in the educational performance of their pupils as determined by standardized tests. One school was (and may still be) a better school than the other. Its principal was a better administrator and a more forceful leader; he supported his teachers, who were more dedicated, better prepared, and happier in their work. Discipline was more strictly enforced and obeyed. Parental cooperation was more aggressively solicited and freely given. As a result, the achievement of that school's pupils was measurably better than that of their contemporaries in the other school a few blocks away. The difference was *quality*.

One of the more successful devices for promoting voluntary integration of a mixed public school population is the "magnet" school, a designated building into which special resources, including first-rate teachers, are committed in order to attract biracial or multiracial transfers from other schools. Admission controls assure racial mixing in the magnet school, and its ability to turn out well-educated youngsters guarantees a continuing supply of applicants. Quality is the magnet.

The old *Plessy* doctrine of "separate but equal" facilities was a farce. Separate black schools were not equal; to those who considered blacks inferior, it made no sense to put as much money into their education as was put into the education of whites. Black Americans are justified in their belief that predominantly black schools have not commanded the educational resources given to mostly white schools. It is no wonder that black parents want white kids bused into their schools; they are convinced that the presence of whites will bring all sorts of improvements.

We therefore have an obligation to commit the best resources at our command to the predominantly minority schools. Most of them have been shortchanged for too many years. It will not be enough to spend the same number of dollars-per-student on mostly black schools that we spend on mostly white schools; we must give them *extra* assistance until they are the *qualitative* equals of any "white" school in our state, city, or district.

Compensatory Efforts Do Seem to Work

Those who insist that minority children cannot reach their academic potential without school integration and that integration cannot be achieved without wholesale busing are reluctant to admit that *compensatory* education—the provision of extra, special resources: teachers, materials, learning aids, and facilities—can effectively improve the scholastic achievement of these youngsters, *whether they are in integrated or segregated schools or classes.* If it can be proved that such added efforts do help underprivileged children to learn, the rationale for racial integration of schools as an absolute necessity is weakened.

It has been proved. Compensatory education does help. A recent study cited elsewhere in this book shows that newly integrated kids moved ahead faster *with* special help than without it. A 1981 study by the National Assessment of Education Progress in Denver shows that youngsters in schools eligible for Title I aid (compensatory, by definition) were doing better in their studies and moving ahead faster than their contemporaries who received no extra help. Roy Forbes of the NAEP, discussing this definitive evaluation of Title I with a group of which I am a member, said that "compensatory education has a positive impact." Their studies show it, and we should be happy that they do.

I do not oppose school integration, but I do not believe that it is the *only* solution to the problems of the disadvantaged.

Color Does Not Determine Ability

If you believe—as I believe—that the color of a child's skin or the language his parents speak at home has *no* bearing upon his own innate ability to learn, then you must believe—as I believe—that the child's eventual mastery of learning will be determined not by the racial background of those around him but by the *quality* of the schooling he is offered.

A school's enrollment may be in perfect proportion to the racial and ethnic makeup of the community it serves—and it may be a third-rate learning institution. Racially mixing students in bad schools may provide equal educational opportunity, but it is equally worthless.

As reported, various desegregation studies tell us that some black pupils have done better scholastically after moving to majority-white schools. Others report that some white students' academic performance declined when they transferred to majority-black schools.

It is my belief that both these outcomes—one plus, one minus—reflect the *quality of schooling* in the new environment as compared to the old. I am not ready to say that blacks do better because they study with whites; neither am I ready to say that whites do worse because they study with blacks. When the move is from a weak school to a good one, the child does better; when it is from a strong school to a poor one, the child's performance suffers. One study of a control group of black youngsters newly placed in a desegregated school showed that half (who simply took their places in their new classrooms) did little better than they had done before desegregation, while the other half (who received special compensatory help) did quite a bit better.

Whatever the case, our course of action is clear.

Placement Should Be Optional

The placement of children should be *optional* with parents. If black parents become convinced that their child will get a better education at a white school, and are willing to have the child bused to and from that school for that reason, they should be entitled to do so. Conversely, no white pupil should be sent to a black school unless his or her parents are convinced that there is a better educational opportunity at that school.

How to Fill Those Empty Seats

The new phenomenon of declining enrollment in our elementary and secondary schools offers us an unexpected chance to help black youngsters achieve equal educational opportunity and (more important by far) *better* educational opportunity, by making places available for them at majority-white schools, which they may attend if their parents choose.

Some years ago, when the late Bernie Donovan was the boss of New York City's schools, he attempted to persuade a suburban district adjacent to the city to accept black children from nearby city schools, with the NYC system paying the tab for their education. The deal fell through, but the idea was brilliant. Today, as irate mothers and fathers picket to save this school or that from being closed because the district has too many desks for too few kids, threatened schools may be kept open by accepting bused-in minority youngsters, paid for by the city. Schools will be majority-white; some survey results indicate that such a relationship has proven best for all the pupils involved.

Certainly the idea is worth trying.

Business and Industry Can Help

Every businessman knows the importance of having a well-educated workforce. In New York City, this realization has prompted a leading business-and-industry group to lend its best talents to the practical improvement of city public schools. Executives are paid by their firms and released for work with school officials. They are quick to recognize problems and adept at contriving solutions. Business people in every community should be called upon to help; the schools—and the kids—will be better served.

The New York Regents' Voluntary Program

We do not lack specific suggestions for the voluntary integration of local public-school systems. In their 1968, 1972, 1974, and 1975 statements on the subject, the New York Regents proposed no less than seventeen affirmative steps to that end:

Revise intradistrict attendance zones to provide a broad cross-section of the district's population; involve local citizen groups in preparing district integration plans; include nonpublic schools in the area's total integration effort; gain the support of other agencies, public and private, whose actions can affect school attendance patterns; work out voluntary transfer arrangements with neighboring districts (Bernie Donovan's idea); cooperatively modify district boundaries which impede desegregation; increase financial assistance for integration efforts; acquire textbooks and teaching materials that reflect our ethnic and cultural diversity; increase the awareness of teachers, administrators and school board members about their desegregation responsibilities; train teachers-to-be in college to master the special requirements of integration; plot the opening of new schools and the closing of unneeded old schools to advance integration; devise optional transfer programs between schools; arrange for open enrollment (that is, enrollment in a given school made available to any child in the district); expand magnet and specialized schools; establish compensatory education programs to equalize the quality of schooling within the district; recruit qualified faculty from various racial and ethnic backgrounds, and, when it is "the only instrument available to enable local communities to meet constitutional requirements and educational goals," to arrange for ". . . the judicious and reasonable transportation of pupils with due consideration that the health, safety and access to high quality education of pupils are not imperiled, and with particular consideration that children of elementary school age are not transported for more than moderate distances. The child's rights to health, safety and quality education are paramount."

The Lone Regent

Because I had fought a lonely battle since 1969 for the priority rights of students expressed in that latter sentence of our 1974 proposal (and became known as "The Lone Regent" for so doing), I gladly introduced the statement, which was approved overwhelmingly. Commissioner Nyquist moved quickly to instruct school boards that grievance procedures designed to protect these rights were to be set up whenever desegregation plans went into effect.

It is evident from the Regents' wording that the transportation envisioned here as a last resort is to be undertaken only within "local communities." That does *not* mean big cities which are viewed as one district for busing purposes. It means minor rerouting of buses to accommodate attendance zones revised for integration; it means that no child may be forced to attend any school where his health and safety may be endangered (broken-down buildings, poor facilities, a record of disruption and violence), and—most important—it means that children shall not be trucked from their present school to one which (on the record) does not provide educational opportunities as good as those in the school they attend. The burden of proof is, as it should be, upon the objecting parents, but the policy itself, spelling out the grounds for objection, paves the way for voluntary integration by removing those major concerns about their children's well-being which often prompt parents to fight *any* integration effort.

Compulsion versus Voluntary Action

Those who favor forced integration of the schools, the kind that is backed by court orders, threats to withhold funds, and (years ago) federal bayonets, believe that voluntary integration will not work in America today because racial animosities are still too strong to allow it to work. They don't believe that we have made much progress since the resistance of the fifties. Voluntarists (I am one) counter with two basic principles of human nature. One holds that forcing relationships upon children, especially if dangers to health and safety or the prospect of inferior education seem involved, will heighten rather than reduce animosities against those on whose apparent behalf those relationships are forced. The second maintains that if you believe that you will be ordered to perform a given action and told exactly how you must perform it, you will be wise not to perform it at all until ordered to do so.

The Curious Case of the Grimes School

Consider the unhappy lot of the Mount Vernon, New York, school district. Enrollment in city schools was majority-black when the board reconstituted its Grimes School as an extra-endowed magnet school, with a fifty-fifty black-white enrollment ratio designed to foster optimum voluntary integration. They thought they were successful until 1978, when the forced-integration mixmasters of HEW suddenly hit the district with a court action, claiming that some qualified black students had been unconstitutionally discriminated against by being denied admission to the enriched curriculum of Grimes (the penalty for this "discrimination" being a cutoff of all U.S. school aid for Mount Vernon unless the district shaped up). I later learned that those rejected for enrollment at Grimes at the time, obviously because capacity was limited, included six blacks and eight whites. HEW did not suggest that the eight unadmitted *whites* had been the victims of discrimination, a distinction which excapes me. What finally happened? Mount Vernon buckled and did what it was told to do: Grimes will admit all qualified blacks who apply.

So much for one American city's honest effort at voluntary integration. But things need not be that way.

Desegregation and Integration Are Not the Same

Commenting on the Waldripian nonsense in Cleveland, columnist William Raspberry suggested: "Send Donald Waldrip to the blackboard and make him write 100 times: 'Desegregation and integration are not the same.' " That's true, and one cannot have a firm grasp of the problem without knowing the difference.

There are two kinds of racial segregation, *de jure* and *de facto*. When acts or omissions of government deliberately separate black pupils from their white contemporaries—by busing them away from their home neighborhoods to all-black schools, by purposely locating new schools to draw a heavily black enrollment, by establishing attendance zones to concentrate blacks in certain school buildings, or by refusing to eliminate such deliberate barriers to joint black-white participation in the schooling process—that is *de jure* segregation. When separation of the races occurs through private and individual decisions—as when members of an ethnic group settle in one neighborhood—that is *de facto* segregation.

While *desegregation* is theoretically the process by which either type of segregation is eliminated, it usually refers to those actions which end official, *de jure* segregation. The courts continue to rule that it is only *de jure* segregation which is an unconstitutional violation of the Fourteenth Amendment by government.

Integration, on the other hand, is not a remedy for the acts or inaction of government. It is the name given to those positive efforts voluntarily undertaken to erase the effects of *de facto* segregation by providing minorities with equal (i.e., joint) access to opportunities in education, in jobs, and in housing. Integration does not carry the force of law as desegregation does; integration is essentially a function of fairness and good will, not a remedy for deprivation of rights.

Although we have come to use the words almost interchangeably, the distinction is important to us because the more zealous advocates of racial equality in all its forms bend every effort to give *integration* the authority of law—imparting the element of compulsion to what is and should be an essentially voluntary action.

When Compulsion Fails, Use More Compulsion: Try the "Metropolitan Solution"

Twenty-six years after *Brown,* the sorry story of massive busing for desegregation was eloquently capsuled by U.S. Supreme Court Justice Lewis F. Powell, Jr., in his 1980 *Estes v. Dallas NAACP* dissent, which was joined by Justices Stewart and Rehnquist:

"It is increasingly evident that use of the busing remedy to achieve racial balance can conflict with the goals of equal educational opportunity and quality schools. In all too many cities, well-intentioned court decrees have had the primary effect of stimulating resegregation. . . . The promise of *Brown v. Board of Education* cannot be fulfilled by continued imposition of self-defeating remedies."

Wise words, but liberalism's answer to the failure of one compulsory program was predictable: more compulsion.

The failure of busing for racial integration has produced not an end to the practice but the "metropolitan solution," which is an *expansion* of busing to bring suburban white pupils into the city schools to replace those whites who have left the system or the city. As of this writing, the application of the Metropolitan Solution to most cities is hampered by two elements: (1) the united opposition of suburban voters, and (2) the absence of deliberate segregation in suburban schools. In *Milliken v. Bradley,* the Detroit case of 1974, the U.S. Supreme Court held that an urban-suburban busing program could not be mandated unless it could be shown that the suburb involved, or the state, had engaged in segregative practices.

Nevertheless, the hot-to-trot integrationists continue to press for metropolitan busing by constructing professional "findings" which tend to support the idea as educationally sound, in the hope that some federal judges will buy it.

A Catholic University think-tank in Washington, D.C., has come up with the novel proposition that expansion of racial-integration busing to a city's surrounding suburbs will eventually eliminate all racial busing, because families who would otherwise flee the city to avoid integrated schools will then stay put, knowing that they cannot escape the system by moving to the suburbs. Nifty, eh? This is a typical push-'em-around product of the to-hell-with-what-the-people-want school of public affairs—whose proponents will still insist that they are liberals who believe in democracy.

But is it racial integration that draws people away from the cities? We have already suggested that the deterioration in the quality of urban life is a prime mover. To that, a planner with the National Committee Against Discrimination in Housing adds the fact that whites—and blacks—leave cities to obtain better jobs and better homes, rather than to escape integrated schools. He points out that between 1970 and 1975 twice as many childless households moved out of Chicago as households with children, and that thousands of black families also decamped to the suburbs.

Yet the forced-integration fanatics continue to press for the metropolitan solution. Before any judge decides that it makes great sense, however, I suggest that he or she consider carefully the Fourteenth Amendment question of equal protection of the laws.

Metropolitan Solution: Equal Protection?

As the integration-at-any-price zealots push ever harder for a Supreme Court decision overturning *Milliken v. Bradley* by okaying forced city-suburban busing with or without a finding of *de jure* segregation in the suburbs, we can foresee a remarkable scenario.

The U.S. judiciary's desegregation rulings have been based upon the Fourteenth Amendment to the Constitution, which forbids states to deny their citizens "equal protection of the laws." Presumably this protection extends as well to acts of the federal government, of which the U.S. courts are an agency. Very well. Can those courts *deny* equal protection of the laws *in the name of equal protection of the laws?* Catch-22.

I pose the question because the involuntary busing of school kids away from their own school district and into another district raises some very pertinent questions about equal protection.

Suppose you and your neighbor in the next house or apartment each have a fourth-grader enrolled in your neighborhood public elementary school. Your surname begins with D, E, N, W, or Z, his name does not; on that basis, your child (not his) is tabbed to be transported to another school district for purposes of racial integration (don't laugh; that's how they do it with black fourth-graders in Louisville, Kentucky). Are your child and your neighbor's going to enjoy equal protection of the laws?

Your neighbor's child gets up after a full night's rest, takes a short bus ride to his neighborhood school, participates in after-school activities if he likes, hops on the bus for a quick ride home, and has plenty of opportunity for healthful outdoor play, homework, or whatever free-time action he chooses.

Your child must rise earlier to catch a special bus for a longer, tiring ride to a distant school. He must grab the bus for home as soon as the final bell sounds (precluding extracurricular events); he arrives home too late for recreation.

Your neighbor's child associates in school with his pals from your neighborhood; he makes friends, puts down roots, and builds a social life.

Your child's fellow-students are most likely kids he neither knows nor cares about. As the Louisville experience showed, he becomes alienated and estranged in his new school; he is likely to act more belligerently, perhaps to vandalize. At home, he has little common experience to exchange with his neighborhood peers.

If your neighbor's child should fall ill or be hurt while at school, your neighbor can reach him quickly.

If *your* child takes sick or is in an accident, you may not be able to be with him when he needs you most; his school is too far away. This is particularly troublesome for families in which both parents work and those without their own means of transportation.

Your neighbor finds it a simple matter to participate in parent-teacher meetings, to visit school on open-house days, to attend plays and concerts in which his child participates, and to talk with his child's teachers on conference days.

You find that distance impedes your ability to support your child's education in these ways. When you do manage to get to your child's distant school, you may realize (as he may have realized) that you and he are outsiders, not really accepted as part of that school's community.

Your neighbor's child enjoys all the benefits that you and your neighbor have paid for by local school taxes: administrators, staff, equipment, facilities, building, and services.

Your child cannot enjoy the benefits you've paid for. The school he must attend is in another district, whose taxpayers may not have been so concerned about the quality of education in their system.

Your neighbor can vote every year on the operating budget for the school his child attends, and for the members of the Board of Education which sets policies for his child's school.

You can't. You can vote in your home district, but your child doesn't attend school there. You have no voice whatsoever about the school he does attend.

If you and your neighbor received "equal protection of the laws" in this government-mandated arrangement, I'll be a monkey's uncle.

But don't be too surprised if my familial relationship to an anthropoid becomes firmly established by some ingenious U.S. jurist unhappy with *Milliken v. Bradley.* After all, in those cases where a finding of suburban or state segregation has prompted court-ordered metropolitan solutions, interdistrict busing arrangements have produced situations similar to those I have described—and have done so in the name of "equal protection of the laws."

As for educational impact, I will let Dr. Nancy St. John provide the rebuttal to metropolitan busing:

"In comparison with integrated neighborhood schools, mandatory, metropolitan-wide busing has many drawbacks. Not only does it incur the determined opposition of parents and expose children to potential social threat, but it also consumes scarce school funds and scarce gas and contributes to highway pollution and congestion. Involvement of working-class parents in school life is inevitably curtailed. Local sense of community may be destroyed and the power of the central bureaucracy increased. Though not inevitable, it is likely that metropolitan schools will be larger, more uniform, more impersonal than local schools, contributing further to the [alienation] of mass society."

And David J. Armor, a senior social scientist with the Rand Corporation in California, who shares my analogy with Prohibition, holds (in *Public Opinion,* Fall 1981) that the social science evidence so widely used to justify school integration during the last quarter-century does *not* support the use of mandatory busing for that purpose:

"At this point . . . there is overwhelming social science evidence that mandatory busing has failed as a feasible remedy for school segregation. It has done so, first, because public opposition and white flight have been so extensive as to increase, rather than to decrease, racial isolation in many cities. Second, desegregation has not produced the educational and social benefits that were promised. Not only does it fail to truly desegregate, it also fails to remedy the presumed effects of segregation.

"Mandatory busing fails, third, simply because it is not an equitable remedy. By rejecting a neighborhood school policy on the grounds of housing segregation, the courts deprive parents of their traditional right to choose schools close to home. Since it is unreasonable to hold schools responsible for housing patterns, the extent of the remedy far exceeds the scope of the violation.

"The basic problem is that the courts have not yet accepted this evidence. Known facts are frequently obscured by social scientists and civil rights leaders who equate any criticism of mandatory busing with racism. Has not the time come to acknowledge these facts, to admit the failure of mandatory busing, and to find ways to end this harmful policy?"

An Antibusing Amendment?

The Civil Rights Act of 1964, passed by the Congress and signed by President Lyndon Johnson, specified what it meant by desegregation:

"Desegregation means assignment to public schools and within such schools without regard to their race, color, religion or national origin, but desegregation shall not mean the assignment of students to public schools in order to overcome racial imbalance."

Plain enough. But since 1964, the federal courts and the federal bureaucracy (which takes its cues from the courts, not Congress) have acted as if that part of the law did not exist.

Should we bypass this judicial-administrative refusal to pay attention to the coequal legislative arm of government? Should we pass an amendment to the U.S. Constitution which would bind the courts and the executive branch to the stated policy of 1964?

As of now, I think not. I am no fan of the constitutional-amendment approach to overturning judicial decisions, even those with which I strongly disagree, which include those on school prayers, abortion, and busing, as they stand at the time of writing.

The American system of justice is precious to me. Despite its many faults, it is still one hell of a lot better than any other system around. Judges are human; that's why they make mistakes. And judges are mortal; that's why they don't stay on the bench forever. It is their mortality which eventually saves us from their human errors. We've managed to live with the system (and to some extent *because* of the system) since my predecessor as Chancellor of the New York State Regents, John Jay, became the first Chief Justice of the U.S. Supreme Court in 1789. I think we, and the Constitution, can make it without too many amendments.

Having taken that stance, however, I would strongly suggest that the U.S. Senate, which has the responsibility of examining and consenting to or rejecting presidential nominees for major U.S. offices, take that responsibility very seriously—not giving their okay *pro forma* or on party lines. Too many lifetime appointees to the federal bench seem to think they have been handed commissions to rewrite our laws. Senators should interrogate each nominee carefully to establish whether he or she understands the proper relationship between the branches of government—and should reject those who don't understand.

What's more, there's nothing wrong about asking a court nominee what he or she thinks about constitutional issues which may be ahead for the federal judiciary. Certainly no promises that a successful candidate will vote this way or that should be extracted—proper decisions must rest upon the facts of each case—but at least the Senate (and the country) should be aware of the thinking of those who will make judgments binding upon us all. We are already too far along the road to an imperial judiciary; the Senators, whom the Founding Fathers made the guardians of the integrity of our courts, should do their job. If the Senators do not do their jobs, if federal judges persist in their blindered commitment to the discredited practice of busing, I reserve my right to change my mind about a constitutional amendment. After all, it took not only a civil war but the Fourteenth Amendment to reverse the *Dred Scott* decision upholding the rights of slaveowners in 1857, and the Twenty-fourth Amendment was required to end antiminority poll taxes in 1964.

But I cannot forget that *Brown* overturned *Plessy*. If that could happen (and it did), I'm willing to wait (for a while) until an enlightened Supreme Court finally junks those elements of former decisions which upheld busing. My patience, however, is not infinite—nor is the American people's.

Higher Education Is Another Ball Game

Why were the public schools the first target of desegregation? Why not colleges and universities? Why not employment? Or housing?

First, elementary and secondary education is compulsory, and public education is the shared experience most common to all Americans; while not all children attend public schools, most do. If the pattern of separatism can be broken at this point as children develop into adults, integration will be accepted as a matter of course later in life. If minority kids enjoy equal (defined as joint) educational opportunity with whites, they will be able to compete for jobs on equal terms with whites and (being paid on a par with whites) will be able to move into the neighborhoods where their white coworkers live and where their children will attend neighborhood public schools with whites, thereby successfully completing the circle of desegregation. So goes the theory—and to me, it has a logical ring.

Second, public schools are instrumentalities of government. They are subject to government control by public agencies at all levels, from the local school board to the U.S. Department of Education. It is much easier to force a school district to do what those with power over it want it to do than to force actions upon colleges, private employers, or residential communities.

Higher education is another ball game. Nobody is required to go to college, nor is any college required to admit everyone who wants to enter (although some come close, like the City University of New York, which will admit any New York high-school diploma holder). Those who do decide to go to college cannot be forced to attend a specific institution; they can shop around among the colleges which will accept them. Their choice is reasonably free, and desegregation of higher education is not as easy a task as the controlling of public-school racial adjustments. Nor are the colleges always willing to take actions which might undermine the overall quality of education offered in a very competitive market.

But the feds did not have to look far to find the Achilles' heel of our colleges and universities: *U.S. government money.*

The extent to which the funding of our higher education depends upon federal grants is greater than most people realize. I was shocked to learn, a few years ago, that Princeton University, one of the great independents, had received *39 percent* of its year's income from Uncle Sam— a percentage which may have changed with reductions in defense research and related grants, but which is still impressive, particularly when we recall that money has a muscular companion called control.

Our American colleges and universities have willingly participated in federally sponsored research projects, collaborating with government to meet the needs of society and being paid to do so—to the point at which the withdrawal of federal funds can mean trouble. That is right where the forced-integration zealots strike: comply with our orders, or your federal grants will be turned off, period.

Not every college takes federal money. One small private institution which accepts no U.S. funds was told by Washington to sign certain papers or face the loss of all federal support. Quite naturally, the college authorities told the government what they could do with their papers, but the bureaucrats were ready for that response: they announced that U.S. educational-opportunity grants which enabled low-income students to attend the college would be cut off if the papers were not signed. The college may still be fighting in the courts when this book appears, but the point is that when their domination is threatened, the Washington power-wielders will abandon compassion for compulsion every time.

As for the courts, they have generally supported the growing use of federal funding to control the internal affairs of colleges and universities. A cloud hangs over the future of our many black colleges, most of them established after the Civil War, which have not only preserved and enriched the black heritage in America but have also turned out scholars of the caliber of my Regent colleague, Dr. Kenneth B. Clark, a graduate of Howard University in Washington, D.C., and probably the most distinguished psychologist in the country today. Some of these colleges (Howard, for one) admit white students now, but we have yet to see the full extent of federally imposed recruiting requirements which could sooner or later destroy the distinctive nature of these institutions.

Meanwhile, federal forced-integration experts have worked over the public universities, demanding that each constituent college meet specific quotas which mirror the racial mix of the college-going population of the state. Maryland has succumbed, although at this writing their best efforts have still not satisfied the federal "goals." North Carolina has its orders, which (says Nathan Glazer in a letter in 1981 to the *New York Times*) "we can predict will be both destructive of educational programs and ineffective in changing the racial composition of the various campuses." Eight other states (South Carolina, Delaware, West Virginia, Alabama, Pennsylvania, Florida, Missouri, and Kentucky) had, as I write, been directed to desegregate their campuses or face the loss of their U.S. funds. Why? The feds found that they had "vestiges of segregation because some parts of their public higher education systems still have mostly white or mostly black students," i.e., purely circumstantial evidence amounting to no more than *de facto* segregation.

But they have forgotten something. College-going students are not public-school pupils who can be pushed around from one school to another as long as they stay in the system. Glazer puts it well:

"The fact is that black and white students are individuals and have much better reasons for deciding which college to attend than satisfying N.A.A.C.P. and O.C.R. statistical goals. . . . There is no reason . . . to countenance this uninformed and destructive effort to force states to attain some fixed proportion of white and black students on each campus."

Those who disagree with Glazer should be prepared to answer the basic question he poses:

"Where is the barrier to education when public institutions are open to all qualified students regardless of race?"

Ujamaa: A Question of Free Choice?

Shortly after I took over as Chancellor of the New York Board of Regents, a situation arose which drew a very sharp line between the individual's right to freedom of association and the state's responsibility to desegregate educational institutions.

During the campus agitation of the 1960s, Cornell University at Ithaca, New York, an outstanding Ivy League college, had been pressured into setting up a living-learning center in which (so the information sheet for incoming freshmen said) those whose primary interest is in the development of the emerging nations could sleep, eat, study, and work together. The special appeal of the facility was tipped off by its title: "Ujamaa," a Swahili term which Cornell translated as "family-hood" but which in Africa refers to a communal style of living.

Why did Ujamaa come to be? In the hearings over which I presided, it became evident that some (not all) of the black students entering Cornell did not want to be scattered through the predominantly white dormitories. They wanted to be together. Their solution: Ujamaa. Cornell was on the spot. If the college administration had in any way encouraged the racial separatism which was the choice of these black students, Cornell was guilty of violating New York State policies and rules against campus segregation. But if Cornell (or the Regents) forced the dissolution of Ujamaa, all hell would break loose at Ithaca, or so we were quietly informed.

Our decision was less than Solomonic, but it resolved the controversy. Cornell had been lax in allowing the residents of Ujamaa (acting as agents for the college) to decide who would live in the facility; Cornell would have to reassert its central responsibility to designate Ujamaa's tenants, and to see to it that white applicants (if any) were not excluded. Cornell had also been lax in allowing Ujamaa's leaders to word flyers distributed by the college to new students, describing the facility— wording which left little doubt that Ujamaa was primarily intended for blacks. Cornell would have to get its act together, and did.

I felt (and still feel) that the name, Ujamaa, is itself a code-word which promotes racial separatism. But Cornell authorities balked at my suggestion that the name be changed; they contended, with some justification, that there is nothing wrong with a living-learning center (there were several such "theme" centers on campus), that concentration upon problems of emerging nations is a legitimate educational function, and that the name Ujamaa is appropriate to that function. I yielded, on the promise that Cornell would see to it that Ujamaa was open to all who might want to live there.

The Ujamaa case points up a fundamental question which is woven through all of our considerations of desegregation and integration: If members of a given racial or ethnic group are not excluded from a facility (Ujamaa had two white residents and no white applicants at the time of our hearing), can it be called segregated, and if so, what must be done about it? Must we shanghai whites into Ujamaas against their will?

Must we disband Ujamaas if no whites choose to live in them? These are real questions, going to the heart of the matter.

My own view is this: In our free society, the individual's right to choose his or her associates remains paramount. Equal justice requires that nobody be kept out of a public or public-supported institution because of his or her race—but equal justice does not insist that someone be dragged unwillingly into an institution or facility just to provide a multiracial flavor.

Affirmative Action versus Racial Quotas

Just as there is an important distinction between desegregation and integration, so there is an equally important distinction between affirmative action and racial quotas.

Affirmative action is a bona fide, organized, *voluntary* effort to increase minority participation in education, business and industry, government—in any facet of American society. It goes beyond antidiscrimination laws and policies, which say only that people cannot be excluded from participation because of their race. It is, as its name implies, an affirmative reaching out to encourage and promote minority sharing of opportunities for advancement. Affirmative action makes sense. It is a *positive* program. Enlightened firms and institutions have undertaken carefully planned affirmative-action drives to expand minority participation. Many have enlisted the help of professional experts in affirmative-action recruiting.

As in any businesslike operation, affirmative-action programs set goals. Those goals may be expressed in terms of comparative percentages, of numbers, of improving upon an existing situation, even of simply trying to do one's best in specific ways—but there must be goals. The point, of course, is that the goals are *voluntarily* established, and no one is penalized if their goal is not reached or surpassed by the day after tomorrow. We do not shoot place and show horses because they didn't win. In a true affirmative-action program, those who make an honest effort and perform reasonably well are not punished.

Because our ultimate criterion is always excellence, those of us who understand and applaud the principle of affirmative action must take care to set those outer limits beyond which further action becomes undesirable because it results in a lessening of quality.

Take the recruitment and training of police officers, for example. Law enforcement is a public service which requires very special mental, physical, and moral qualities and a very strenuous preparatory regimen; the safety of people's lives and property depends upon the quality of police service. Where there is a significant black or Hispanic segment of a population but few black or Hispanic police officers, the benefits of an affirmative-action recruiting drive to increase their numbers seem obvious. If blacks or Hispanics do not apply because they feel that they cannot pass the stiff entrance exams, affirmative-action principles would urge them (and pay them) to enroll in courses which begin by testing their innate abilities and suitability for police work (as all candidates are tested) and then provide intensive training for likely recruits until they can pass the regular entrance tests.

If there are more applicants of all backgrounds than there are openings, a simplistic solution might be to select the top-scoring qualifiers until all vacancies are filled—a method that might exclude qualified but lower-scoring blacks and Hispanics. But is test scoring the only criterion? I suggest that it may not be. Having served in law enforcement, I know that there are advantages to having police officers work in areas and on cases wherein those with whom they deal have the same ethnic background as they do. To me, this factor can be more important than relative standing on a test, insofar as the end result—the quality of law enforcement—is concerned.

In education, we have observed that there are benefits to be gained by employing black teachers and administrators in schools with high proportions of black students, and the same would apply to Hispanics. The positive impact of available kindred role-models who generate greater mutual understanding and confidence cannot be shrugged aside. In addition to its moral impetus, there is a practical underpinning to affirmative action.

The linchpin of all this is *qualification.* If an individual is qualified for the job or promotion he or she seeks, or can become qualified with proper training, affirmative action can provide this assurance of an opportunity to serve. But judgments must be made on an individual basis in each case. If we say "take all qualified black applicants first," we run perilously close to the borderline of quality selection, and we risk losing first-rate people because they aren't black.

What I am saying here is that the practical application of affirmative action, in order to assure greater minority participation in a given function at all its levels, must be carefully orchestrated to provide not only social justice but quality safeguards for the public served, and to do so with sufficient popular support to render it an essentially *voluntary* program.

Quotas, on the other hand, are *requirements.* Whether they are called goals or something else, they set specific, fixed results which must be achieved to escape a penalty. Make every school in your district racially balanced in proportion to the racial makeup of the entire system, or you will lose your U.S. aid funds. There is nothing voluntary about quotas. They are imposed.

Does the Constitution's Fourteenth Amendment require racial quotas in the public schools?

The U.S. Supreme Court says *no*. Commenting upon a lower court's support for quotas, the Justices spoke clearly in their *Swann v. Charlotte-Mecklenburg Board of Education* decision in 1971:

"If we were to read the holding of the District Court to require, as a matter of substantive right, any particular degree of racial balance or mixing, that approach would be disapproved and we would be obliged to reverse. The constitutional command to desegregate schools does not mean that every school in every community must always reflect the racial composition of the school system as a whole."

Unfortunately, that message has been lost upon the zealots of the federal bureaucracy, who continue to impose penalties upon districts whose schools are not statistically "balanced."

I favor affirmative action, and I am dead set against quotas. Affirmative action is designed to produce equal *opportunity* for minorities; quotas are intended to produce equal *results*—or else. Society is not obligated to guarantee equal results, to assure that every runner finishes first. Society's responsibility is to give everyone an equal chance to finish first. No more than that—and no less than that.

The Supreme Court said much the same thing in its *Bakke* decisions, which struck down a university's racial quotas for admission to a graduate program but made it clear that the institution had every right to pursue the recruitment of minority students.

Familiarity Can Breed Contempt

As more evidence piles up to show that school integration is no guarantee of better scholastic achievement by the black youngsters it is intended to help, promoters of forced integration are shifting to other, more socially oriented grounds for imposing racial mixing upon the schools.

The diversionary rationale is this: If students of different backgrounds work together on a daily basis, they will come to understand each other better, thus to like each other more and to cooperate in joint efforts more effectively. Undoubtedly that is true in some cases but, like most well-intended theories, it doesn't necessarily work every time. There is a history of interracial friendships formed in the primary grades which have dissolved by junior or senior high as blacks form their own associations. At the college level, there is the Ujamaa syndrome. Merely knowing people better can emphasize differences which were not obvious earlier.

My point is not that familiarity breeds contempt, but that it can. We should not expect too much from the better understanding that results after integration. And we certainly should not accept the "better understanding" theory as justification for compulsory integration. It is a valid purpose of *voluntary* integration, but not for pushing people around against their will, which could be self-defeating in the context of better racial relations.

Are We to Be Governed by Reason — or Fear?

No consideration of the problems of racial integration in America can avoid mention of the ugly undercurrent of threatened violence which permeates the subsurface of debate on the subject. One seldom sees direct threats in print. They are passed by subtle suggestions in conversation. They are made clear in confidential discussions. They are there. And we take them into account when we make decisions—like it or not.

Cornell was concerned about the possibility of violence if the Regents insisted upon dismantling Ujamaa. Nobody said it, straight out. But the word got around. Don't impose a solution that could trigger another racial confrontation like the one in April 1969, when black students armed with rifles seized a student center, alleging harassment of black coeds and a cross-burning on campus. They left after concessions were made by the administration.

When the Regents were asked to advance the start of "open admissions" at the City University of New York from the 1975 target date to 1970 (which we did, although CUNY was far from ready for the massive influx of open-admissions students) it was quietly made clear that further delay, even to enable the university to prepare for the new undergraduates, could ignite the torch of violence.

The specter of Watts and Detroit is sneaked out of history's closet almost every time a decision must be made which affects race relations and integration.

Sometimes threats are less than subtle. In 1979, California's voters approved a proposition which forbids state courts from exceeding federal school-desegregation guidelines and from ordering busing where there has been no intentional segregation. In 1980, the California Supreme Court upheld the constitutionality of this new law, eliciting an intemperate reaction from the American Civil Liberties Union's attorney, as reported in the press: "Calling the Supreme Court's actions 'White Wednesday,' ACLU attorney Joseph Duff said . . . that the ruling could prompt protestors to take their frustrations out 'in the streets.' Asked if that meant violence, Duff said: 'This is a violence-prone society. The people in the streets are very frustrated. They are going to take direct action in every form possible.' "

The ACLU is supposedly dedicated to equal justice under law; it is therefore quite surprising to hear its representative making remarks which are as much an invitation to violence as a prediction of violence: the negation of lawful resolution of differences.

The cause of racial integration is immeasurably damaged by threats of violence "in the streets" if this or that is not done. Like every other element of public policy, racial integration and the means of achieving it must stand the test of reasonableness. And it can stand that test, if properly conceived. Threats serve no other purpose than to kindle racial animosity and make it more difficult to bring about acceptable integration.

Summing Up

After eleven years of grappling almost daily with the knotty problems of desegregation and integration in education, I have reached certain conclusions based upon that experience.

Fundamental to all of my beliefs is my conviction that black and minority students, given the same opportunities as white students, can achieve just as well as white students. In other words, minority youngsters are not intellectually and scholastically inferior by virtue of their racial or ethnic background.

I believe that we, as Americans, have a moral responsibility to provide equal educational opportunities for minority students.

I do *not* believe that minority students are unable to do their best scholastically unless they attend school or college with whites. The preponderance of evidence indicates that desegregation of educational institutions does very little, per se, to improve the academic performance of minority youngsters, and can damage that of white pupils.

I believe that our best bet for helping minority children *and* white children is to devote all the resources we have at our command to the improvement of the *quality* of the schools they attend.

For these reasons, I believe that we should stop wasting our resources and the limited time available for children's learning and recreation on the wasteful and unproductive busing of pupils, black and white, to schools away from their home neighborhoods and districts, in order to attain a better racial "mix" in those distant schools.

I believe that schools whose students are underachieving in comparison with other schools (whether predominantly minority or predominantly white) should be helped to improve their quality by infusions of extra resources and the imposition of better discipline upon all involved in the educational process.

I believe that the right and duty of government to eliminate school segregation is limited to erasing deliberate, intentional acts, policies, and procedures of government which promote separation of the races.

That being so, I believe that government oversteps its proper bounds when it attempts to force integration where no deliberate segregation exists.

I believe that every effort should be made to encourage the *voluntary* revision of any plan, regulation, or action which abets or does nothing to eliminate *de facto,* unintentional segregation of schools and colleges.

I believe in affirmative action to increase the participation of minorities in all aspects of American life—as a voluntary, bona fide effort to reach specified goals which are realistic and sensible.

I believe that the imposition of racial quotas, accompanied by threats of penalties for failure to meet or exceed those quotas, runs counter to American principles of equal opportunity without regard for race, creed, color, national origin, or sex, and should be abandoned as a tool of desegregation.

I believe that our national responsibility is to assure all our citizens of access to equal opportunity—not to guarantee that they will achieve equal results.

I believe that a citizen's right to associate freely with those of his or her own choosing is fundamental, as long as that association does not involve the exclusion of others from public or public-supported facilities because of their race, creed, color, national origin, or sex.

I believe that there is no place for violence or threats of violence in the attainment of racial and social justice and equal opportunity.

I believe, finally, that there are better ways of achieving racial integration in America than those which have been forced upon us in recent years — that those better ways have been pointed out to us by people of good will, and that if our country is truly a democratic Republic, the voice of its people cannot forever be ignored.

7.

Sex Education

Whatever Happened to Mom
and Pop?

NOT too many years ago, there was no such thing as sex education in America's public schools.

Today, every state includes teaching about sexuality somewhere in its recommended curriculum. Several states require students to take the course; others are being urged to do so. Sex education isn't always *called* sex education. Just as we boys used to sneak girlie magazines into high school back in the thirties and forties and fifties, school authorities now sneak sex education into their course offerings, disguised under some bland title so not to arouse the ire of those who feel that young people should learn about sex from traditional sources: the walls of the boys' rest room, the conversation outside Mr. Dunkel's candy store on Saturday night, and the rather innocent (by today's standards) girlie magazines.

Does anyone call sex education what it is? The District of Columbia and six states did, at last reading. Elsewhere, a bit of digging will unearth it under such soothing labels as Health Education, Home Economics, Family Life, Survival Education, Personal Living, Personal Growth, Career Education, Parenthood Education (that one comes close to spilling the beans), Biology, Human Development, Personal Development, and (here's a nifty one) Family Consumer Education.

Why the deception? For two main reasons: (1) to avoid bitter public controversy; (2) well, I'll get to that one if you'll first indulge me in a personal reflection.

When I was growing up in the 1920s and 1930s in a Long Island

146

suburb of New York City, human sexuality was not mentioned, much less discussed, either at home or at school. For me, Princeton was not any different. There were no coeds at Tigertown then; the young ladies we imported for our infrequent dances and parties (at least, those whom *I* imported) had been well trained in self-defense. As for me, good marks never did come easily, and it was study, study, study if I was to excel. And my field was public and international affairs, not biology.

The Army Way

My own introduction to sex education occurred after I enlisted as a private in the Army in October 1941. Once I had taken the oath, a grizzled sergeant handed me my orders and a small pamphlet, which turned out to be about sex, written in simple and unmistakable terms (the Army was good at plain English—indeed, one hell of a lot better than many educators I have known). It began with the statement that one's male organ is not a muscle, and therefore does not have to be exercised regularly to prevent atrophying. In those pre-WWII days, pamphlets were written for men: Title IX, ERA, and even the WACs were in the future.

Watch out, the pamphlet warned: If you do have haphazard sexual contact, you can catch a venereal disease, which could take various forms, all dangerous to your health and that of your family. Your own physical suffering and the painfulness of the extended cure were stressed.

There was, however, no moral or religious angle to the pamphlet. Sex was your business, not the Army's. But venereal disease was the Army's business, because it meant *"downtime."* A soldier being treated for VD could not give the Army a day's work for a day's pay (even at the stingy $21-a-month recruits were paid in 1941). The Army was unhappy about this, and to show its unhappiness, it docked the VD victim's pay—as if the disease itself was not enough.

If all of these deterrents didn't work, there was the required visit to the prophylactic station before "going into town," to obtain government-issue rubber contraceptives, and after coming back, to be treated with VD-preventive medication. Those who failed to observe these rules could find themselves condemned to use the "love seats" (labeled FOR VENEREALS ONLY) in the company latrine . . . which indeed they did, for hours on end (a pardonable pun).

Then there was the VD movie, which all were required to attend. The VD movie was to sex what "Frankenstein" was to brain surgery; it tended to dampen enthusiasm for the subject. We gulped at the swollen genitals of VD sufferers and blanched at the monstrous syringe used to propel antidotes into the punctured buttocks of soldiers who had been careless; we erupted from the theater vowing a lifetime of celibacy. But did all this psychological warfare work? No. Particularly overseas, VD continued to be a problem.

"Miracle Drugs" = No More VD?

Then came sulfa and penicillin, the "miracle drugs." VD was disposed of quickly and easily, with no painful, long-drawn-out treatment needed. The VD victim was back on duty in short order—and the Army was happy. But was VD eradicated? Hardly. With the easy cure, the Army's VD rate escalated; some units filed monthly VD-rate reports of more than 100 percent, which meant that some soldiers managed to contract the disease more than once during a month, thanks in part to the "miracle drugs."

Removal of the deterrents of physical pain and loss of pay did nothing to wipe out VD then, and the same effect prevails today, both in the service and in civilian society. Gonorrhea has become virtually epidemic in those age groups which are the source of most recruits for our volunteer services, a dangerous development. It is quite evident that we should be doing something that we aren't doing now.

Have We Learned Anything?

The military's experience can help, if we interpret it right.

We learned that most young men seemed to know the *mechanics* of sex—how to do it—but that very few understood the ramifications of sex: moral, physical, psychological and social, anything beyond the momentary pleasure of the act. Further, there was a surprising "knowledge gap" about sexuality—a vacuum quickly filled with popular misconceptions and silly folklore which soldiers too often paid a high price for accepting as fact.

These personal observations convinced me long ago that wide availability of sex courses, if properly presented, would help young people. Both public and independent schools can offer to those mature enough to understand not only information about sex, but also a comprehensive overview of all aspects of this personal and sensitive subject.

And I learned something else: *moral factors count.* Soldiers who entered military service forearmed by a serious, responsible family upbringing and religious training—with their own codes of personal conduct, based upon their own moral convictions—had little difficulty coping with the vagaries of military life. Others were less lucky.

The Army's record is of only nominal value now, as the WWII program was not really sex education. Its objective was limited: the elimination of downtime as a result of VD. The Army (aside from its hardworking, determined chaplains) was not concerned with the effect of unfaithfulness upon a wife or best girl at home, the psychological damage to one's love partner, the probability of fathering a child to be left in some faraway place when the war ended. Two words describe the Army's program: incomplete and inadequate.

Yet, we will be ahead of the game if we have learned one lesson from WWII—that concentration upon the physical and mechanical side of sex, excluding other considerations, is the *wrong* way to educate young people on this subject. It can do more damage than good. That, precisely, is what happens too often in American society.

To Mandate, or Not to Mandate

I mentioned earlier that sex education is frequently smuggled into other curricula, in part to avoid the public controversy which always seems to ignite when the subject of sex is mentioned—and for another reason. What is that reason?

Quite often, a legislature or a state education authority, exquisitely sensitive to the political explosivity of the issue, will refuse to *mandate* sex education (that is, to order that all children take it in school), preferring that it be offered as an elective, if offered at all. In such states, educators who want to see sex education made compulsory for everyone take shrewd evasive action: they weave sex education into some other course which *is* mandated for every student. For example, New York parents often ask, if they are so inclined, why their child must be formally excused from sex education when in fact sex education is not compulsory in the Empire State. The answer is that in their school district sex education has been folded quietly into, say, health education, which is mandated for all. That's the trick. Many a mom or dad has suffered through an early-September "Parents' Orientation" at which not one word is spoken about sex education, only to find later in the year that innocent little Filbert knows a heck of a lot more about procreation than they thought he did.

Well, *should* the states require that every child take a course about sex? It is a legitimate question. If there are sound reasons for conducting sex education, as I believe there are, isn't it logical to insist that every youngster study the subject?

The liberals, of course, will respond with a resounding "Yes!" If you have trouble reconciling liberalism with government compulsion, all will come clear when you realize that the modern American liberal is not by classical definition a person who fears government's interference in life and commerce. Despite their assumed and loudly touted role as guardians of your personal and civil rights, most liberals do not give a damn for your right to choose the kind of education your child will receive. As far as they are concerned, your child (and everyone else's child) should have the kind of schooling *they* consider "democratic" or "universal" or "open." And they want compulsory sex education—for every kid.

Those who say "yes" to mandated sex education argue well. They hold that a proper understanding of the place of sex in our lives is necessary to our happiness and well-being and is, accordingly, good for society. They believe that knowledge of the physiology of sex is needed to eradicate VD and reduce the incidence of unwanted teenage pregnancies. To the counterargument that sexuality is an extremely complicated and personal subject best left to discussion between parents and children, the promandate people reply that it doesn't work that way in practice. After all, parents seldom tell their youngsters about sex.

On this point, they may be right. How long is it since you gave (or heard) the Birds and Bees lecture?

Oh, yes, parents freely acknowledge their duty to tell their children about sex. A recent *Newsday* survey asked parents of Long Island children aged thirteen to nineteen the question: "Do you think it is the responsibility of parents to educate their children about sex?" Ninety-two percent said "yes," seven percent said "no," and one percent didn't know. The survey team did not press on to ask the 92 percent what they actually *do* to help their children learn about sex. (Of course, such surveys cannot handle lengthy, multifaceted replies—it is a fault with many such "educational polls.")

It is my observation that most parents don't discuss sex with their youngsters of any age. Sex never was a subject that came easily to dinner-table conversation; the generation gap of the 1960s and 1970s made parent-child communication that much tougher. Some parents still try to compile and impose one-shot lists of "don'ts," which may work but which hardly qualify as sex education. A few encourage their youngsters to read suitable literature about sex in the context of moral, natural family living, but I am afraid that these are in a minority. The rest figure that their kids will learn . . . well, somewhere.

Letting Mom and Pop do it didn't work in my time, and it doesn't work now. Not that it shouldn't, or couldn't—it just doesn't.

That, of course, is a very general statement, and it runs the risks that all generalizations run. I am certain that some conscientious parents do an effective job of acquainting their offspring with a healthy knowledge of sex, and I applaud them. What I do say is that *most* parents are not willing to take on the assignment.

The Age of Porn

The need for sex education is made more urgent by the glorification of sex everywhere we look—in print, at the movies, on TV. There are wishy-washy laws about selling pornography to minors (adapted from wishy-washy U.S. Supreme Court decisions defining pornography on the basis of "community standards"—New York City's could make Forty-second Street's "Porn Capital" a candidate for enshrinement as a national monument). Young people find the stuff of sex at prices they can pay. Slick-paper magazines with millions of readers titillate their prurient interest not only with pictures and drawings, but with letters to the editor which make Balzac and Boccaccio read like Saint Paul's Epistles.

Edmund Fuller, writing in the *Wall Street Journal* (August 1980), says: "There are those, nowadays, including authors of best-selling 'how-to' sex books, not to mention the outright porn merchants, who measure the quality of life and the success of one's femininity or masculinity by orgasm count. We are exhorted to be in continual tumescence from youth to old age. Sex is treated as an end in itself, unless in a distortion by which so-called 'love' is understood only on the sexual plane."

To correct this unreal, amoral, scientifically incomplete, and antisocial view of the role of sex in our lives, a comprehensive sex-education program is needed for our young people.

But should it be *mandated* upon them, as a *required* course? Despite what I've said above, I think not.

Remember that parents, not schools, or governments, are fundamentally responsible for the education of their children. This principle is accepted in every democratic nation on earth—and enunciated by the United Nations.

Those parents who *do* want to teach their own children about sex, on their own terms, should have the right to do so. They might feel that the sex-education courses offered in their schools approach the subject in the wrong way. It may be that school sex-education classes discuss aspects of sex that are repugnant to a family's religious beliefs.

No child of such a family should be required to participate in mandated courses. The school should make its sex-education curriculum and supporting materials available to parents who ask, and those parents should then have the right to *elect:* (1) to have their kids take the school courses; (2) to have their children excused from those classes if matters objectionable to the parents are discussed, or (3) to have their children excused from sex education entirely. The parents are responsible for their children's education. It allows that they should therefore be responsible for the choice here—and for the consequences.

VD and Unwanted Pregnancy: Does Sex Education Help?

Those favoring mandated sex education will complain that elective sex courses cannot protect society properly. Will young people whose parents object to such courses become more liable to contract and spread VD and to become unexpectedly pregnant?

Before World War II, there was neither sex education—nor widespread venereal disease—nor a plague of unwanted pregnancies among school-age children. The point is well taken, and should tell us something, but by itself it doesn't help much in this age of the sexual revolution and "doing your own thing." We must contend with the facts of a permissive society as we find them for as long as we choose not to change that society. Those facts tell us that despite the broad push for universal sex education in every state as a preventive or antidote to the rising tide of VD and unwanted pregnancies, *sex education has not been effective in reducing their incidence.*

New York State has encouraged sex education in its schools for years. There is no "prescribed" state curriculum, but state guidelines urge local districts to include such instruction in health-education courses. The controversial "Strand III" state guidelines relating to sex education, for kindergarten through sixth grade, appeared in 1970. Yet the New York Departments of Health and Social Services reported in 1979 that there were more gonorrhea cases and more teenage pregnancies than ever before.

This widespread adversity is a national phenomenon. In a 1980 broadside, Planned Parenthood, itself a leading advocate of sex education, cites a "rampant 'epidemic' " of one million teen pregnancies a year. *Newsweek* in 1980 corroborates that, adding that venereal disease is "rampant among adolescents, accounting for 25 percent of the 1 million reported gonorrhea cases every year."

Sex-education courses have not reduced unwanted pregnancies or VD or (the worst tragedy of all) both at once, for a very simple reason: *they have not reduced the incidence of sexual promiscuity which is the cause of these effects.*

Do not buy a sex-education program for your schools in the belief that, by itself, it will end VD and teenage pregnancies. *It won't.* It hasn't done so anywhere. Nothing will do so until promiscuity itself declines.

Let Sex Education Sell Itself

It seems to me that any program should be required to prove itself on a voluntary basis, that is, to sell itself on its own performance record before we think about imposing it by fiat upon our children's instruction.

Sex-education curricula which have sprouted so profusely across the land should be considered *experimental*. They should be dissected and analyzed and evaluated and refined and polished and made more practical and more logical and more acceptable. Who knows? We may find that *elective* sex education is so popular that almost everyone will take it. Does that seem eccentric? Maybe my forty years of involvement with all kinds of government has ingrained into my psyche a massive distrust of faceless, unelected bureaucrats who are allowed to impose their personal predilections upon the citizenry simply becuase they are credentialed as "experts."

It is impossible to deny that while government *policy* may change as the will of the people moves elected officials either into or out of office, those appointed public servants who are protected by Civil Service or life tenure continue to rule you and me as they choose. That's not democracy. But that's how it is.

I don't want sex education courses laid upon our children by people whose decisions cannot be countermanded or reversed—people who are ultimately responsible to nobody.

Public Involvement Is a "Must"

It is quite true to say that in a representative democracy like ours, elected school boards allow people access to how all school programs are conducted. But when a Board of Education is dealing with a controversial subject like sex education, something more is needed. The smart district superintendents will suggest, and the smart boards will create, citizens' advisory committees which include parents, clergy, and interested community civic representatives; they should be involved in program planning and in curriculum or materials review, and should be kept informed of all developments as the program moves along. These are the New York Regents' proposals and they make a lot of sense.

Sex Is Not Mechanical Drawing

One of my crucial worries on the mandating of sex-education programs is that so personal and so sensitive a subject, bristling with moral and ethical issues which public schools are not equipped or are not even allowed to take into account, is readily entrusted to technically minded, fact-oriented pedagogues. Such persons are inclined to regard mechanics as "safe" or "neutral," as one might teach the assembling of a folding chair: "Step 3. Place Male Organ M into Female Organ F (see diagram)."

New York State issues a guideline specifying that a teacher who is not "comfortable" discussing sexual attitudes with students should not be required to do so. This plainly is not adequate to meet the objection stated here. One *can* be coldly comfortable in a flat-out, mechanical presentation, but that is precisely what we do *not* need.

How Old Is "Old Enough"?

I am troubled by currently popular notions of the ability of young children to absorb sex education in its usual, current modes.

The conventional wisdom today is that sex education should begin in the formative years. Dr. Mary Calderone, President of the Sex Information and Education Council of the U.S. (SIECUS), told a Racine, Wisconsin, audience that "sex training begins with pre-adolescence" and that "a child's sex education is essentially complete by the time he is 5 years old."

Whether Dr. Calderone is right or wrong, the trick is to form-fit the curriculum to the absorptive capacity of the child at various stages of maturity. A good program will keep the youngster's age in mind; if not, it isn't good.

I've seen a picture textbook on sexuality which is apparently a big hit with the kiddie trade in Europe, whose experts have assured *our* experts that it is just great for "early-on" use. The book embarrassed me! Not only does the text tend to promote masturbation and fornication, but its pictures are overly explicit: the centerfold is a bed-level photo of a couple copulating. Is this for eight-year-olds? The text is but a few notches above the level of "Look, Jane. See Spot run!" If the young reader, later searching for a dumptruck or a Barbie doll, stumbles upon big sister and her boyfriend engaging in something other than conversation, he or she will know from the book what they're doing: having fun. Grammar school is not the place to teach Hedonism 101.

Why Should Sex Ed Be Coed?

Apparently standard academic theory is that sex education should be coeducational. New York State's pedagogic gobbledygook is in support of this view. (I confess this slipped past me during the early months of my Chancellorship of the State Board of Regents.) It goes this way:

"Education for development of responsible social values requires a mutual understanding of relationships and interactions between people of both sexes. Separate classes for boys and girls create an artificial social situation that (1) does not provide for this interaction in the controlled classroom setting and (2) is not relevant to the real social conditions of life."

Translated, this says simply that if they're going to be doing it together, they should study it together. Baloney.

Is a bull-session of, say, twenty-five boys and girls led by an adult whose approach to the subject of sex may be that of a mechanic or a comic or an amateur psychologist "relevant to the real social conditions of life"?

One angry father of a junior-high girl—we'll call her Janet—told me of an incident in a darkened coed classroom during a sex-education slide show. The instructor was projecting a picture of a young male with an erect penis, when a boy's voice boomed from the rear of the room: "How'd you like a piece of *that,* Janet?" Talk about traumatic experiences! Coed sex-education classes can be every bit as rugged as the Army's VD movie. As a matter of fact, some school courses do include VD movies, although with apparently little success in reducing VD rates.

It is neither necessary nor particularly sensible for sex-education classes to be coeducational. Aside from demonstrations and practical exercises (a point at which I hope we have not arrived), there is nothing to sex education which cannot reasonably be taught in single-sex classes.

The (Wo)manly Art of Self-Defense

There *are* elements best conveyed to a single-sex audience. For example, every young person should know there are effective ways of rejecting the unwanted amorous advances of another person. When I was young, this seemed to be the essential element of every young woman's home indoctrination. Now, with the move of sex education from home to school, it should be a part of every young *man's* armor as well. To have any value, it must be taught in a single-sex classroom.

I am surprised that those concerned about a rising birthrate, with teenage pregnancies, and with VD do not seem to understand that "how *not* to" is just as important as "how to." The best method of birth control and prevention of disease may be to know how to say "No" and make it reasoned and firm. That advice is best taught to one sex at a time.

Is it imperative for a youngster to know all the inner workings of the other's sex's reproductive system? It is helpful to a point, but only if we are bent, after all, upon creating generations of urologists and gynecologists, junior-grade. I'm not.

Here I'll let you in on a little gimmick we in education often use to get our way. It's "educationese," a language barely understandable, like the wordy New York guideline I've cited above.

You see, the American people rightly place their educational system apart from the political pushing and shoving which could ruin it.

We believe (correctly) that the best educational system is one run by professional educators under the direction of a board of lay people, thus combining specialized expertise and training with responsiveness to the public interest and the public will.

So, when what we want to do does not have very strong arguments in its favor, we lapse into "educationese," telling the world that the subject is strictly pedagogical and axiological, off limits to anyone but educators. If someone objects, we make a few rumbling noises about "academic freedom," and the objector will, being brought up to respect freedom, usually back off.

The real reasons for New York State's foggy guidelines which push coed sex-education classes are *practical,* not educational, which is why they are couched in educationese to avoid challenge:

(1) If you want to slip a politically unmandatable subject like sex education into an existing curriculum—in New York, it is health education—that other curriculum is always coeducational; trying to teach one element of it (in this case, sex education) in segregated classes would be awkward.

(2) Teaching the same subject to two classes, one of girls and one of boys, doubles the cost of teaching.

(3) No school district wants the government threatening to cut off U.S. aid money because one class alone is not sexually integrated—no matter how much sense it makes to keep it segregated.

My primary concern is the proper education of the children, not the convenience of the educational bureaucracy. I'll stay with my point: no coed sex-education classes.

The Big Question: How Do We Handle Abortion?

Those who believe that sex education should be mandated for all schoolchildren have the burden of explaining how they would teach information about abortion to youngsters whose religious beliefs and moral criteria reject abortion. Such youngsters would be prisoners in a compulsory class.

Liberals have no problem with this. After all, abortion is legal during certain stages of pregnancy: the U.S. Supreme Court has said so. Abortion is widely discussed in public print, possibly so widely that any intelligent child must hear of it and wonder about it. Students, therefore, should be taught about its purposes and its legal use. They should know the process of abortive surgery, the psychological and physical ramifications of abortion, and the availability of abortion advice and services.

But what of those students whose family standards or religious beliefs hold abortion to be reprehensible and repugnant? Must they be forced to listen? Yes, say the liberals.

No, say I. My critics will be quick to snicker: "What else could we expect? After all, he's a Catholic. We know how Catholics are obliged to feel about abortion." Yes, I am a lifelong Catholic. But there are other Catholics as well as Protestants and Jews to be found on *both* sides of the abortion issue. I am not always happy with all of my church's views—for example, what I understand to be its position on contraception in married life—but I do agree with the Catholic Church's firm opposition to abortion. Abortion is not only a "Catholic issue." Can you name *one* major denomination with an appreciable following in America which officially condones abortion? I can't. The most eloquent plea I have ever heard for the restoration of antiabortion laws in this country was delivered by a Jewish spokesman. Some of the most vocal battlers against abortion are Protestants. Abortion is a *human* issue and a *moral* issue, not narrowly a "Catholic" issue.

Important Questions About Abortion

Will our sex-education instructors teach that there is a fundamental difference between a "fetus" and a human baby? There can be no new life without conception. Life begins at conception. An unborn baby is no less human because some people call it something else. Does a mother-to-be say "the fetus is moving"? Never; she says "I feel *life.*" It makes as much sense to try to fix a moment during pregnancy when the "fetus" becomes human (and entitled to constitutional protection) as it does to argue the number of angels who can dance on the head of a pin.

Will we tell young women that their right to "control their own bodies" entitles them to elective abortion at will? Of course a woman has a right to control her own body. If she exercises that right properly, she won't get pregnant until she wants to. But it isn't the woman's body that's sentenced to be aborted; it's her child's body, which has been entrusted to her temporary custody by God or nature or whatever force of life worked out the continuing miracle of human reproduction.

Will we inform children approvingly that the government will pay for abortions if the mother can't afford them? As an Army counterintelligence officer who entered Nazi Germany in September 1944, before everything could be swept under the rug, I *saw* the Holocaust. I've *seen* what can happen when government is given a role in deciding who lives and who dies.

That is the issue: the deadly precedent set by the deliberate involvement of the state in making such final choices. Government always decides how its money will be spent, and on whom. Today it may be spent to abort the children of the poor. Tomorrow, it may be spent to end the life of . . . whom?

Audrey Antoine of the Black Family League and the Right-to-Life movement put it this way on CBS Radio in New York:

". . . the poor ask for housing, education, job training—cries for help to a society that gives them abortion instead . . . that gives them elimination, which always discriminates against the developing child, rich or poor. The poor don't ask for abortion. The elite abortion forces say they do. . . .

"We don't want them telling us that pregnancy can hurt us, but abortion can't . . . telling teenagers that their age makes pregnancy dangerous, not the lack of prenatal care . . . telling us that the answer to high infant mortality is killing our infants *before* birth. . . ."

How, indeed, shall we explain to a fifteen-year-old pregnant girl why the same government which would throw her into prison if she were to abuse her infant child will cheerfully pay the cost of snuffing out the life of that child before it can come into the world?

How do we answer when a youngster asks if an unwanted pregnancy is a disease? If we answer "No," how do we explain why it can be medically terminated, like excising an infected cyst?

How can we be sure that teaching *about* birth and babies by instructors who place birth control high on their list of human imperatives will not permanently prejudice young women against childbearing? It can happen, if the discomfort of pregnancy, the pain of childbirth, and the nuisance of infant care are overstressed.

There are too many unresolved questions—too many elements on which American opinion is deeply, almost hopelessly, divided. As long as such divisions exist, and as long as the personal predilections of the instructor can and often do creep into his or her instruction, sex education should be an *elective* subject, not mandated.

Muscle from Outside

One of my major concerns is the possibility that outside pressure groups will exercise undue influence in planning and presenting sex-education courses, causing a one-sided program.

Writing in *The Public Interest* of July 1979, Jacqueline Kasun noted that partisan intervention occurred in Humboldt County, California. In considerable detail, she described how Planned Parenthood, SIECUS, and the U.S. Department of Health, Education and Welfare combined to create a distinct bias in the sex-education program in Humboldt's schools. This is bad news. Many states (New York is one) allow their public-school districts wide latitude in drawing up their own sex-ed curricula. Most states suggest the involvement of community groups in the process. Yet, anyone who has ever attended a Board of Education meeting knows the potential for pressure tactics. When Planned Parenthood says (as it has done), "Pack the board room with your own supporters," the results are unduly influenced.

No single group should dominate the process of organizing a sex-education program—not Planned Parenthood, not SIECUS, not the Catholic Church, not the Evangelicals. Their voices should be heard, but the program most likely to gain the support (or at least the acquiescence) of most of the community will be a meld of sensible and logical points proposed from many sides.

PP — or PAP?

Planned Parenthood, Inc., began years ago as a well-meaning, civilized effort to help married couples to space the births of their children and limit their families. It believed that many parents needed help in planning the future of their children. "Planned Parenthood" was probably a legitimate descriptive title back then.

But it isn't so now. The name should be "Planned *Avoidance of* Parenthood," as the organization's considerable energies are devoted to promoting every conceivable method of preventing births. Given our American penchant for acronyms, that title, I suggest, would be shortened to PAP—and "pap" is baby food, hardly an apt sobriquet for an outfit that is almost hysterically antibaby. A 1980 PP fund-raiser mailing illustrates the point. In astonishingly intemperate terms studded with more exclamation points than one of those anti-Semitic "Wake Up, America!!!" hate-sheets that surfaced in the 1930s and 1940s, this broadside teems with denunciations of the "dogmatic bigots" (a common anti-Catholic code term for Catholics) and "right-wing fanatics" who oppose abortion. The central goal of PP is now fighting people who oppose abortion. This is a time-tested technique. Call your enemies "right-wing fanatics," and you conjure up mental images of bully-boys in brown shirts or white hoods, bearing truncheons and torches to terrorize decent citizens.

But who are the fanatics? On my desk before me as I write is a copy of a Planned Parenthood document distributed to editors of college newspapers—a document containing scurrilously anti-Catholic cartoons which would warm the heart of the KKK's Grand Kleagle (or whatever they call the Head Bedsheet these days). And if you've missed the point of the cartoons, the text nails it down, damning the "tiny, vocal minority of religious fanatics, led and financed by the Roman Catholic Church . . ."

Is that a fact? Is abortion opposed only by a "tiny minority" of Catholic "religious fanatics"? You can't prove it by the 1978 elections in New York State, when the new Right-to-Life Party, on the single plank of opposition to abortion, gained a six-digit vote for its little-known gubernatorial candidate and thus displaced the hoary Liberal Party (how ironic!) as the Empire State's fourth largest, behind the Democrats, Republicans, and Conservatives.

It's not relevant to debate here the value of single-issue political parties. I don't like them, whether they're Prohibitionists, Greenbackers, Right-to-Lifers, Free Silverites, or Know-Nothings. The point is that there are lots of us who don't like abortion, but who prefer to vote for multi-issue party candidates.

George F. Will, writing in *Newsweek* in 1980, speaks of the growth of the evangelical Christian movement which opposes abortion. "Don't blame evangelicals for inflating abortion as a political issue. The Supreme Court did that by striking down 50 states' laws that expressed community judgments about the issue. Those who opposed those judgments got them overturned by fiat, not democratic persuasion. There were 1.4 million abortions last year, and the forces that made that possible want subsidies for abortion, knowing that when you subsidize something you get more of it. Yet we are told that it is the evangelicals who are aggressive about abortion."

A fundamental question is this: Can the Planned Parenthood mentality (as it is presently revealed by its own words) be trusted to guide and direct calmly, impartially, sympathetically, and rationally, the presentation of sex-education courses in our schools?

The evidence says no.

That doesn't mean that an opposing group should dominate the field. No group should do so. What it means is that Planned Parenthood has disqualified itself as professionally expert, or at least it has done so until such time as it recaptures its early promise as a genuine family-planning organization.

The Advantage of Independence

Don't fall into the error of presuming that because a religious denomination opposes abortion, it also opposes sex education. Far from it. The National Council of Churches, the Synagogue Council of America, and the U.S. Catholic Conference all defend the essential role of the school in this aspect of child development. Indeed, in the independent schools run by various faiths sex education is oftentimes an important part of family-life instruction.

Here are the words of the Second Vatican Council:

"Children and young people should be assisted in the harmonious development of their physical, moral and intellectual endowments. . . . They should be helped to acquire gradually a more mature sense of responsibility through ennobling their own lives by constant effort, and toward pursuing authentic freedom. As they advance in years, they should be given positive and prudent sexual education."

A bit wordy, but the point is made. It is sharpened by the Catholic bishops of Connecticut when they remind us that

". . . the Catholic Church has long supported prudent, timely and moral sex education of young people. By moral sexual education we mean not merely the teaching of sexual information but also the presentation of moral values, so that the young people know that even in this pluralistic society some people hold that certain things are right and that other things are wrong."

Think about it. *Moral* sex education. The introduction of value judgments. Independent schools, church-oriented or not, can freely incorporate moral values into their sex-ed curricula. Can the *public* schools?

I wonder. One Supreme Court session after another continues to misinterpret the First Amendment of the U.S. Constitution to require that public schools be free of "religion." If religion is the foundation of personal morality, is it possible to talk about *values* when sex is discussed? Or when any other social subject is discussed, for that matter? George F. Will put it this way: "The modern 'night-watchman' theory of government is that it exists only to protect persons and property. It can be ubiquitous and omniprovident regarding material things, but must be neutral regarding values. It can concern itself with nurturing soybeans, but not virtue."

Until that obstacle is removed—until there is a reacceptance and an affirmative assertion of those moral values we have allowed to slip away—whatever else we do will not be enough.

Summing Up

I favor sex education. I believe a program that involves not only information but an overview of all the values in our society which are commonly expressed on the subject would be of great help to young people.

I believe that sex education in most cases cannot be left to parents alone, although those parents who can and will make the effort to educate their own children about sex and sexuality should do so.

I believe that instruction about human sexuality should not be mainly or solely factual and mechanical, that it should be tailored to the age and maturity of the student, and that it should not be taught to coed classes.

I believe that no student should be subjected to instruction which offends the religious beliefs of the student or his or her family. There should always be an excusal option. In short, I believe that sex education should be *elective,* not mandated.

I do not believe that sex education can (or should be) expected to wipe out unwanted teenage pregnancies or venereal diseases, although it should include instruction in avoiding both.

I believe that whatever is taught about controlling birth should deal with contraception (prevention of conception) and should not deal with abortion (prevention of birth after conception and the beginning of prenatal development).

I believe that no group or groups, religious or otherwise, should be permitted to dominate or control a public school sex-education program. In this respect, I believe that no sex-education course can be adequate unless it includes some examination of several and serious value judgments, including questions of morality.

Finally, I think we are skirting the edges of a huge national problem when we try to address sex education. Ours is an age of flaunted, amoral public sexuality. Sex is displayed everywhere, for everyone to see. It is pushed and peddled and promoted *ad nauseam* in every printed or pictorial medium callous and greedy enough to profit from it. The form in which sex makes contact with the individual mind, at almost every age level, is a hedonistic, pleasure-centered, almost animalistic, erotic reaction which in no way portrays the values of human sexuality as found in great literature, philosophy, and art.

Until we Americans somehow reverse the present nationwide glorification of physical sex—its presentation to young and old as a repetitive, sometimes clever dirty joke—the ills of promiscuity will not be cured. We should not expect the schools to do that job.

What *can* work is a citizens' counterrevolution.

Shall we entrust the job to government? Good Lord, no! Even if the courts would approve (which they wouldn't), censorship is not the answer. I'm thinking about those faceless bureaucrats again. Give them the power to tell a publisher what he cannot publish, or a TV station what it cannot show, and we have given them the power to tell *us* what we cannot read or watch. Why, they might even tell you that you shouldn't be reading this book, because of the unkind things I say about them. Forget censorship! There must be a better way.

There is. If each of us says, like the character in a recent popular movie, "I'm fed up—and I'm not going to take it anymore!," that's Step

One of the Better Way. Join others or act as an individual. Hit the smut-merchants and porn-peddlers where it hurts: in their wallets. Refuse to buy books or magazines which flaunt prurient sex; don't watch sex-oriented movies or TV shows. Learn who pays to sponsor such things, and if you stop buying their products or services, let them know *why* you've stopped.

"Sexploitation" has succeeded because it is profitable. *Make it unprofitable.* Nothing dies faster in the world of commerce than something which no longer brings in the bucks for its promoter.

Describing "a wholesome reaction to excess," Edmund Fuller believes that the tide has already turned for some people:

"Sex may be a magnificent component of love, but in itself it is not love. It can become an obstacle to love. By itself it cannot bring fulfillment. Men and women, singly and in couples, married or unmarried, are beginning to rediscover some of these truths long known to the wise but lately overwhelmed in the sexual blitz. Some are searching for the real nature of loving relationships, a search that can be restorative of sexual morality and sanity."

If a counterrevolution in the marketplace can help to restore proper balance to our national views about sex, without leading us into another Victorian age of prudish hypocrisy, so much the better. And sex education *can* help to recapture for the coming generations of adults these old-new, ever-valid perceptions of the proper role of sexuality in human affairs.

8.

Financing Education

Where Excellence and Equality Meet — Head On

WINSTON CHURCHILL in 1939 referred to Russia as "a riddle wrapped in a mystery inside an enigma." He could have been describing the way we finance American education in the 1980s. I say "way" because what we are doing can hardly be called a system, which Webster defines as being "united by some form of regular interaction or interdependence; an organic or organized whole."

For more than two hundred years, we have been trying to find the best way to pay for elementary and secondary education in the United States.

We are still trying.

In 1778, Washington's troops weathered a winter at Valley Forge, and a treaty guaranteed French help against the forces of George III. Little colonial kids in Massachusetts were being taught in church-governed schools subsidized by local public funding.

Two hundred years later, in 1978, Congress created an Advisory Panel on Financing Elementary and Secondary Education, a fifteen-member body commissioned to explore all facets of the matter for both public and private schools and report back by the end of 1982.

That sounds like plenty of time for such a study. But President Carter didn't bother to appoint the panel's members until late in 1979, at which time I became a panelist and a "consultant" to the U.S. government. We spent more months paring our budget to $11 million from the $21 million proposed by the staff; an ungrateful Congress said we could do it for less and fudged on our appropriations. Then control shifted from HEW to the newly created Department of Education, with a new Secretary, Shirley Hufstedler; we paused politely until the myriad bureaucratic details of the transition could be arranged. There was a turnover of our staff and a relocation of our office. Then the 1980 elections upended the wheelbarrow, and Secretary Terrel Bell took over; our shaky budget was more up in the air than Icarus. We struggled along, meeting and talking and listening. Where the Advisory Panel and its project will be when this book is in print is impossible to predict.

In any event, I am not going to prejudice the work of the panel or my own freedom to adjust my views on the basis of new data which may be produced. My ideas as expressed here and elsewhere in this book will be limited to those which I believe represent a substantive position required by my commitment to excellence and quality in education.

"United" Doesn't Mean "Identical"

Among the many advantages of our federal system, under which the United States has grown strong and prosperous, two are of special importance for education:

First, while the central government performs those functions which the Constitution says it can do best (and which do not include education), the individual states and their numerous local governments of all kinds are able to reach independent decisions as to what nonfederal services are necessary, given local circumstances, and how they may best be made available to the citizenry.

Second, the fifty states and their subdivisions (all local governments are the constitutional subordinate agencies of states) form a galaxy of civic laboratories wherein the science of government is constantly being explored and developed, with the results of each made available to all others and to the federal union in which they are all partners.

Nowhere are the differences among those partners more evident and more pronounced than in the area of financing public education. A brief examination of some elements of the question proves the point.

Who Raises the Money?

There is an ongoing argument about the *source* of educational funds: who should provide more, who less, and how much or how little authority and control should accompany federal, state, or local contributions. The dust raised by such flaps often obscures the fact that every individual is a citizen taxpayer, directly or indirectly, in *all three* categories—that local, state, and U.S. tax dollars all come out of his or her pocket. We also tend to forget that there are constitutional inhibitions involved in the money game, that spending money carries authority only to the extent that such authority is constitutionally permissible.

The latest (1979–80) figures (as of this writing) prepared by the Education Commission of the States tell us that the federal government, with all its muscle stretching, gives only 9.2 percent of the funds for elementary and secondary schools; the states provide 48.9 percent and local school districts 42.0 percent.

But those are *totals*. The mix of contributions varies widely from state to state, with U.S. shares generally (but not always) highest in the South and Southwest and the state-local division inconsistent. It is my general observation that local contributions seem greater in the more industrialized states. The variety of approaches is illustrated by citing the extremes:

Federal funds provide 24.1 percent of Mississippi's education money, 16.6 percent of New Mexico's, 15.2 percent of North Carolina's and 14.9 percent of South Carolina's—but only 4.1 percent of New Jersey's, 5.0 percent of New York's, 5.1 percent of New Hampshire's, and 5.5 percent of Wisconsin's.

Exclusive of Hawaii, which has no local districts, *state* contributions range from California's 71.2 percent, Washington's 70.8 percent, Alaska's 70.2 percent, and Kentucky's 69.7 percent on the high side to New Hampshire's 6.8 percent, Nebraska's 18.2 percent, South Dakota's 20.8 percent, and Vermont's 28.0 percent on the low side.

Again excluding Hawaii, *local* shares are highest in New Hampshire (88.1 percent), Nebraska (73.9 percent), South Dakota (65.3 percent) and Vermont (64.2 percent)—an exact match with the lowest state contributions—and lowest in Alaska (16.9 percent), Kentucky (17.8 percent), Alabama (18.4 percent), and California (19.1 percent), an evident but less exact correlation with state shares.

The state-local differences result largely from state-level decisions by popularly elected legislatures and governors as to what the state contribution will be, and for what purposes. Support for the schools originated as a state-imposed local responsibility, but the states have continued to play a greater part, usually at the urgent pleading of the beleaguered localities, many of whose taxpayers have simply refused to commit more dollars to local schools. It goes without saying that the local districts, citing state responsibility for education, demand more money but insist that it have no control strings attached. In 1970–71, the state share of educational revenues (schools only, not colleges) was 39.4 percent, with the districts carrying 52.1 percent of the burden; by 1979–80, ten years later, the onus had switched to the state capitals, as the states bore 48.9 percent and the districts only 42.0 percent of the whole load. Federal money, on the other hand, is mostly Elementary and Secondary Educa-

tion Act funds, intended for special compensatory and remedial purposes; the extent of the gap between high federal shares and lower state
shares of school money usually reflects the inability (or unwillingness, or
both) of the states to deal with the problems addressed by U.S. programs.

How Deep Do We Actually Dig for Our Schools?

Do we make enough of an effort to supply our public schools with necessary funds? As one might expect, the answer is "Yes," and "No." Some
of us do, some of us don't. Some of us are heavily taxed, but competing
demands only allow a small share for schools.

In April 1981, the Education Commission of the States published
some pertinent figures about state and local tax revenues. Per $1,000
personal income, the top taxers were Alaska ($175), New York ($172),
Wyoming ($159), California ($158), and Massachusetts ($151), while
the five lowest-taxing states were Ohio ($99 per $1,000 of personal income), Missouri ($99), Arkansas ($102), Alabama ($102), and Indiana
($103).

For education, the top *per-capita* spenders were Alaska, at $1,406,
Wyoming at $762, Utah at $684, Washington at $670, and Oregon at
$663; bringing up the rear were Missouri ($424), Arkansas ($426), Ten-
nessee ($428), New Hampshire ($441), and Florida ($449). But the top
spenders *per pupil* were Alaska ($3,943), New York ($2,800), New Jersey
($2,570), Massachusetts ($2,519), and Connecticut ($2,407). At the low
end were Arkansas ($1,301), Georgia ($1,339), Idaho ($1,424), Missis-
sippi ($1,430), and Alabama ($1,436).

For the United States as a whole, the states and localities collected
an average $127.53 per $1,000 of personal income and spent $543 per
capita and $1,961 per pupil on schools, paying out an average $16,001
per annum per teacher.

The ECS statistics also tell us that the percentage of total state-local
expenditures devoted to education has slipped slightly, from a national
average of 27 percent in 1972–73 to 26 percent in 1978–79, a six-year period. Most states hover within a few percentage points of the U.S. average, the highest being Utah, at 31 percent, and the lowest Hawaii, at 18
percent. Between surveys, education's biggest losses in share of total dollars spent occurred in Minnesota (−6 percent) and Delaware, Iowa,
South Dakota, and Wyoming (all −5 percent). Gains were minor; Vermont, Alabama, and Oklahoma led with +3 percent each.

These figures suggest the possibility that other demands upon state
and local treasuries cut into education's share. Certainly education
funds have not declined in dollar terms; they simply have not risen as

fast as other expenditures. A clue to *which* other expenditures might be fingered as pushing education aside can be found in the whopping quantum jumps in health and welfare spending at almost all levels of government in recent years.

How the States Collect Their Taxes

There is no uniformity among the fifty states in the types of tax whereby their revenue is obtained. ECS figures show that, overall, they derive 49.4 percent from sales taxes, 27.1 percent from individual and 9.7 percent from corporate income taxes, and 13.8 percent from "other" revenue sources, such as real and personal property taxes and, in some states, severance taxes levied upon the extraction of mineral wealth from the earth.

The states relying most heavily upon *sales* taxes include Nevada at 82.1 percent, Tennessee at 75 percent, Washington at 74.6 percent, Florida at 73.8 percent, and Connecticut at 72.1 percent of revenues. Those depending least upon sales taxes cover a wide range, from Alaska (3.8 percent) to Oregon (11.8 percent) to Delaware (14.4 percent) to Montana (21.8 percent) to Massachusetts (34.4 percent).

Highest *individual income tax* contributions to state revenue are made in Oregon, where 59.6 percent of state money comes from this source, Massachusetts (47.4 percent), Delaware (45.7 percent), New York (45.4 percent), and Wisconsin (42.5 percent). South Dakota, Florida, Texas, Wyoming, Nevada, and Washington collected no funds from individual income taxes in 1980. As for *corporate* taxes, they provide 39.3 percent of Alaska's revenue, 23.5 percent of New Hampshire's, 15.3 percent of Michigan's, and 13.4 percent of Connecticut's and Massachusetts'. Again, Texas, Wyoming, Nevada, and Washington levied no corporate income taxes.

In the "other" category, which is mainly composed of *real and personal property* and *mineral severance* taxes, the states relying upon these sources most were Alaska at 49.9 percent, Wyoming at 44.6 percent, Montana at 36.7 percent, Oklahoma at 36.4 percent, and Texas at 35.4 percent. To me, that spells o-i-l and g-a-s as major revenue producers. States counting least upon these kinds of taxes include Hawaii (2.3 percent), Georgia (4.0 percent), Massachusetts (4.8 percent), South Carolina (5.4 percent), and Utah (5.9 percent).

The message conveyed by all these statistics is that states will tax whatever seems most easily and painlessly taxable, and will lean heavily upon their own particular resources with little or no regard for what the experts consider "fair." What's more, they keep a sharp eye peeled upon their fellow states to see if their own tax system is driving business, industry, and other tax generators next door. Those who do not pay attention to interstate competitiveness do so at their peril.

Within the states, there are substantial differences among local school districts in terms of taxable wealth behind each pupil and expenditures per pupil. I will not attempt here to single out any state and analyze its statistics. That is an effort which courts in California, Minnesota, New Jersey, Texas, and New York (to name just a few) have undertaken as a result of a flood of lawsuits proposing to reduce the differences by judicial fiat.

Let me simply report that, as of this writing, the law of the land as propounded by the U.S. Supreme Court in *Rodriguez v. San Antonio Independent School District* (March 1973) is that Amendment Fourteen of the U.S. Constitution and its "equal protection" clause "does not require absolute equality or precisely equal advantages" from one school district to another, and further that "it has never been within the constitutional prerogatives of the Court to nullify statewide measures for financing public services merely because the burdens or benefits thereof fall unevenly depending upon the relative wealth of the political subdivisions in which citizens live." Translated from the judicialese, this means: (1) nobody's civil rights are violated because fewer dollars are spent upon his education than upon that of another student in another district, and (2) state-aid laws cannot be overturned merely because they don't fill all the gaps and level all the peaks of school spending among districts.

Sometimes I get the impression that other courts haven't read the *Rodriguez* decision, but inasmuch as it rules their own cases, I suppose (and I hope) that I am wrong about this.

How We Raise the Money for Our Schools

In the earlier days of the Republic, taxes were primarily of local origin for local purposes, including schools—and by far the most widely accepted and imposed local tax was that on *real property:* land and buildings. To the taxing authority, this type of levy offered two great advantages: it was virtually impossible to conceal real property or improvements to it, while the rates and revenue remain relatively stable from one year to the next, without regard to the financial fortunes of the owner or the community.

But what is advantageous to the tax gatherer is not always fair or helpful to the taxpayer, and there has been a movement away from property taxation for education.

The experts have developed their own way of classifying a tax, as either "progressive" or "regressive." They pin everything on income; if those in low income brackets pay proportionately more than those in high income brackets, a tax is "regressive"—which automatically carries with it the label of "unfair." To the extent to which a tax is not "regressive," it is "progressive" (and thus "fair"). To them, the highest form of fairness is the steeply graduated progressive income tax (used by most U.S. income-taxing jurisdictions), which grabs a greater percentage of one's income as that income increases. In the middle is the sales tax, a fixed-rate levy on purchases; they brand this "regressive" because the rate is the same for small and large dollar transactions. I am not sure that I agree with the label. You don't buy a Lincoln Continental unless you can afford one (including the taxes on it). At 5 percent or 7 percent or whatever, the sales tax on your Lincoln will come to more than if you had chosen a lower-priced Ford. While such a tax on what you buy does not necessarily reflect your overall *ability* to pay (wealthy people buy Fords, too), it does reflect what you *do* pay for your purchase, which more often than not is governed by your liquid wealth. So the sales tax is neither "regressive" nor "unfair" in my book.

The real property tax is. Paying taxes is a cash-up requirement, but real property is not a liquid asset. It may be worth a good deal if you sell it, but it may not produce one penny of income while you live in it. Taxes based upon its value without regard to the ability of the owner to come up with a given tax payment several times a year are "regressive" in the worst way—and that often happens. We've all had bad years and good years, but our property taxes remain the same (or go higher) regardless of our financial ups-and-downs. Young people just starting out in life and older folks on pensions and fixed incomes suffer most from constant escalations of property-tax rates.

Property Taxes Should Finance Property-Oriented Expenses

For the last ten years and more, I have been a maverick, in that I have opposed property taxation as a primary method of funding education. In a *Long Island Commercial Review* article appearing in November 1970, I suggested that taxes on property should logically be used to finance those governmental services which are *property-oriented*—police, fire, sanitation, water, roads, sidewalks, sewers, street lighting, and so on. Education is not one of these; it is a *human-oriented* service, not at all pinned to real property values. To tie the quality of a child's education directly and primarily to the static, nonliquid value of real estate in his or her town does not make sense to me, and it is unfair to the child. For that reason, I have consistently supported greater *state* efforts to assist those school districts with low per-pupil taxable wealth.

In this connection, we cannot ignore the impact of commercial and industrial property upon a district's ability to finance its schools through real-estate taxes. Where there is an abundance of such property, there is a high per-pupil base of taxable wealth; where there isn't, the per-pupil base will be low, and financing schools will be more difficult. In my own Long Island area, I note the advantages of the Long Island Lighting Company plant to the Glenwood schools, the Grumman installation to the Bethpage district, and the "Miracle Mile" shopping district to the Manhasset public schools—which also benefit from the presence of a complete elementary-through-secondary Catholic school system of excellent reputation, drawing families who will live in Manhasset and send their children to St. Mary's schools while they pay taxes to support the public schools they elect not to use.

What the People Think

The grading system I've mentioned is that of experts on taxation, whose criteria of values are not necessarily those of the people who pay the taxes. I have seen at least one recent, scientifically taken poll which tells us that taxpayer-voters in the polled area (the size of an average state, population-wise) rate, in the order of their acceptability, sales taxes (moderately "regressive" on the experts' scale), then property taxes (very "regressive"), and finally, in the most-objectionable category, federal income taxes (which the experts dub "most progressive" and thus "fairest").

This rather emphatic deviation from the experts' views on what is fair and unfair suggests that the people agree with a standard, uniform rate of taxation as preferable to graduated rates which increase with the dollar base to be taxed and thus give rise to a "bracket" system. That is the essential difference between sales and income taxes, in addition to the nature of the base.

I believe that the public's acceptance of a given tax is governed less by the way in which it is levied than by what it actually accomplishes when it is turned into government expenditures. If that were not the case, real property taxes for schools would have been junked years ago; they were not, as people were generally happy with the quality of education their schools displayed. It is only since the decline of confidence in the public schools that a rebellion against school budgets and the taxes to support them has grown.

In New York State, for example, the Gallup organization's announcement of their 1981 findings that public education continues to falter in popular esteem appeared in the same newspaper editions as the statistics on budget defeats, showing a single-year high of 19.9 percent during the 1969–74 period topped by a single-year high of 33.7 percent defeated in the 1975–81 period. The high years were 1969 and 1978; in

1981, 22.6 percent of New York's 656 budget-voting districts defeated their budgets at least once. My own informal soundings prior to the 1980 national elections convinced me that much public objection to the ever-higher rates of U.S. income taxation derived from a general conviction that too much federal revenue is wasted or used for purposes with which the individual taxpayer does not particularly agree. Objections to graduated rates were less of a factor than the nature of expenditures.

School-Budget Voting Is a Farce

While we're on the subject of property taxation and local school budgeting, let me confess that I have been beaten around the ears (verbally, that is) by some of my more conservative friends for my oft-repeated view that public voting on annual school and library operating budgets is a farce which should be eliminated forthwith (a proposal that has the survival odds of the proverbial snowball in hell).

Being Irish, I usually answer one question with another. To the query, "Why should budget voting be ended?" my response is "Why should we have it in the first place?" Why should our public schools and libraries be the *only* public bodies in the whole spectrum of federal, state, and local governments which must submit their annual operating budgets to a popular vote? And that is literally true; no other entity is required to do so. At every other level of government, in every other sort of public body, we elect the *people* who will run it and give them the responsibility for setting budgets and tax rates. If we don't like the way they do it, we boot them out at the next election. Why can't we extend the same temporary expression of confidence to our school and library boards which, in my estimation, attract top citizens with all sorts of talents to serve without pay for the betterment of our society?

Requiring public approval of school and library operating budgets is unfair to our schools and libraries. All of the anger and frustration and dissatisfaction which the voter may harbor against governments and taxes of all kinds comes to a head in the school and library budget votes, when the full brunt of voter hostility zeros in on these two public services.

I am a firm believer in representative government. We have adopted it officially as our basic constitutional system—distinct, as it were, from the king on the one hand and the mob on the other. But in some parts of the country we have allowed representative government to be eroded by substituting public referenda on specific proposals which would normally be decided by our legislatures. Get enough signatures on a petition, and the final decision on any subject can be shifted from the people's representatives directly to the people themselves.

If we're dealing with long-term bonding commitments or other arrangements which will be paid for by generations yet to come, I agree that the public should express themselves, just as they must have the last word on changes in their Constitution. But on legislative matters, involving the regular operations of government, direct democracy is not the best way to do things. Given the proclivity of citizens to vote *for* government goodies and *against* being taxed to pay for them, I can see public referenda becoming the most inflationary device since the helium tank was invented, aside from presenting a real danger to the orderly and sensible operations of government.

The "Mandated Expenses" Flap

When summarizing their objections to school-budget voting, the good folks who populate our nation's boards of education habitually complain that the votes are meaningless because more than 80 percent of their spending budget is "mandated" by the state or the U.S. government and therefore cannot be changed by local decision.

Let's take a closer look at that claim.

From the dawn of the Republic, the sovereign states have been and are held responsible for public education. I know of no state constitution which does not so indicate. One not-too-well-known but highly pertinent fact is that local governments, including school districts, are *subordinate agencies of the states,* sharing the states' powers only to the extent that state constitutions and legislatures authorize. The catch-phrase "local control of education" is often misinterpreted to mean that local school boards have powers not derived from the state; they don't. Most states give school boards wide latitude in handling their own affairs, but the state remains the ultimate boss—and that is as it should be, since the state bears the responsibility.

What are "mandates"? Loosely defined, they are things that the state or Uncle Sam tells the local board that it must do, or not do. In New York, for example, the state "mandates" the teaching of so many hours per week in the various required subjects which make up a good basic education. But are these subjects that the local schools would not offer unless they had been ordered by the state to do so? Of course not; these are courses that any self-respecting school system worthy of the name would include in its own curriculum. Why, then, must they be mandated by the state? That is done to prevent schools from cutting corners and shaving time from the minimum hours prescribed for these core subjects which serve the best interests of all the students in the state.

So, when your neighbor who serves on your local board of education tells you that most of the district's basic educational requirements are mandated by the state government, he is probably technically correct. But if he should try to leave the impression that things would be vastly different and less expensive if the state mandates did not exist, he would be leading you astray.

Let us be frank to concede that there *are* mandates which are extra costly. The most recent of these is the federal law which requires mainstreaming of handicapped children into the public schools, a tremendously expensive job if done properly but one for which little or no federal money is available to the schools. Judicial mandates don't carry any dollars with them, either. If a school is ordered to do something that it isn't doing, the theory is that it *should* have been doing it, and therefore that doing it now at the district's own expense is nothing more than deserved punishment. That's not much help. Until 1972, the New York Regents obtained from the legislature an annual fund to assist school districts in meeting desegregation orders. Thereafter, the solons refused to authorize such a fund, apparently in the belief that if no money were available, there would be no such judicial orders. They were wrong. They have since learned that judges don't really care how much it will cost someone else to do what their court has ordered—but to the best of my knowledge, there is still no New York State desegregation fund.

Then, of course, there are state-mandated subjects which the legislature orders taught in response to pressure from some lobbying group. New York youngsters must be told about the humane treatment of birds and animals, about the abuse of tobacco, drugs, and alcohol, about Communism, about the State Constitution (as a delegate to the 1967 Constitutional Convention, it took me six months to unravel that messy document), indeed, about any number of special subjects. Between the time that this is written and the time you read it, there may be more— cardiopulmonary resuscitation (CPR) and the Holocaust (Hitler's genocide against the Jews) are running strong at the moment in New York.

The fact that I mention these special mandates does not mean that I oppose their being taught in the schools. Far from it. I do feel, however, that most of them can and should be melded into the curriculum of an existing general field, like science or social studies, at the appropriate time when the students can glean the most from them.

Where the Big Money Goes

Eighty to 85 percent of the average public-school district's budget goes for *personal services:* teachers, specialists, administrators, clerical staff, grounds-and-buildings people, and so on. This is what your school board friend means when he tries to link expenditures with mandates. It costs money to pay teachers to instruct in those subject which must be taught.

But it is only the subjects and the time devoted to them that are mandated; the salaries of teachers and staff members, the terms of their employment (their job descriptions, how many hours they teach per week, how large their classes may be, what nonteaching duties are covered by their salaries, how long their contracts run, etc.), are *not* mandated by anybody, at least in New York. They are decided by boards of education after negotiations with teacher and staff representatives, and they are finalized in *formal contracts.*

Bringing all this into focus upon school budget voting, the 80+ percent of expenditures which are not subject to voter control are not removed from that control because they are state-mandated. They are removed from that control by virtue of being arrived at by legal, binding contracts with teachers' unions, building contractors, insurance carriers, etc., over which the voters have no say whatsoever. But whatever the case, *the 80+ percent of budgeted expenses are still not subject to voter control,* which is why I maintain that the annual popular vote "on the school budget" is a farce.

What happens when the voters turn down a budget? In New York, it's called "austerity," and it's a joke. The 80 percent is still paid out, under the terms of the contract. A few electives may be clipped from the course offerings; student extracurricular activities are curtailed (arousing the ire of the Booster Clubs, sports fans, PTAs and other partisans of the kids), some services (like buses) are put on restricted schedules—and the community has irritated itself, penalized its children and, in the end, trimmed damned little off the budget.

The one value of a budget defeat is not measurable in dollars and cents, but as a signal to the board of education and the professionals who run the system that something, somehow, is not right. Of course the same point can be made at open meetings, in letters to the editor, and in conversations with school board members. It should hardly be necessary to clobber the budget in order to register a gripe, but it happens. There is a nuisance factor in budget defeats.

I still maintain that annual voting on the school district's operating budget should be scrapped, but it won't be. Why not? Because our good friend and neighbor Joe Citizen still enjoys his annual moment of triumph (he has only one—or two, if we count the library budget vote) when he can pull a lever and vote against his own taxes, even if that vote is just about meaningless.

Incidentally, about half of New York's Joe Citizens *can't* vote for their school budget. They live in cities, where school expenditures are included in legislatively determined municipal budgets for all services. What's more, constitutional limitations set a fixed percentage of assessed valuation beyond which city spending cannot go, so Joe couldn't spend more money on his schools if he wanted to. Constitutional caps on spending bother me even more than operating-budget voting; in times of inflation or other upward pressures, schools are locked into increasingly inadequate spending limits which *must* sooner or later have a negative impact upon the quality of education in city districts. And a majority of the whole state's voters is required to change the constitution, which they are always reluctant to do when the change involves money. So Joe and his fellow-citizens of Strapped City are behind the eight-ball, and that's not right.

The New Drive for "Equity"

If you are beginning to understand that educational finance is a complex, tough business, wait awhile. It's going to get more complex, and tougher.

Until recently, educators had their hands full just trying to find enough money to guarantee the educational quality demanded of their schools by the voters of their districts. Now educators are faced with another problem: assurance of educational "equity," which means that a student in one school district in one part of a state won't get a worse (or better) education than another student in another district in another part of the state. This all started in California, where the state courts decided in the *Serrano* case that there were qualitative differences in educational services between one district and another which constituted a denial of equal protection of the laws. That decision touched off similar cases in other states, until the U.S. Supreme Court decided in *Rodriguez* that the equal protection guaranteed by the Fourteenth Amendment to the federal Constitution did not extend to public education.

As I hinted elsewhere in this chapter, *Rodriguez* has by no means dampened the ardor of the champions of equity, who continue to press the concept in legislatures, before state boards of education, and in the courts, where they usually rely upon state constitutions rather than the Fourteenth Amendment.

Such a case was brought in New York State by the Levittown school district and others, charging that the quality of education varied so widely from one New York district to another that an unconstitutional deprivation of rights resulted, and charging further that the state was not doing enough to close these qualitative gaps. Although the Regents had steadfastly recommended greater use of state funds to assist those districts with lower-than-average property wealth per student, the legislature had not agreed, but the judge in the *Levittown* case did, declaring the existing state-aid formula unconstitutional. At this writing, the case is in the Appellate Division, and in all likelihood will eventually be decided by New York's highest court.

Within a month of the *Levittown* decision in 1978, Governor Hugh Carey and I jointly appointed a Task Force on Equity and Excellence in Education, chaired by Max J. Rubin, Regent Emeritus and former head of the Great Neck and New York City school boards. I figured that if anyone could handle this hot potato, Max could—and the Governor agreed. In October of 1981, Justice Smith's decision was unanimously upheld by a four-judge panel of the Appellate Division; the fate of a possible appeal to the state's highest court, the Court of Appeals, is in doubt at this writing. The Rubin Task Force issued its report in February of 1982. It offered several combinations of solutions, all designed to help narrow the gap between the highest-spending and lowest-spending districts. No report of a forty-member group of experts will ever be unanimous, and this one wasn't. What it accomplished was to advise the legislature of various ways in which the mandates of the courts could be met, equitably and with minimal disruption. As always, Max had done his job superbly.

Levittown Could Be Pandora's Box

I cannot bring myself to think of my friends on the Levittown Board of Education and their allies as suburban Robespierres, hot after absolute equality even if it means the heads of the wealthier districts. They simply want a fairer shake from the state, a more effective way of using state funds to help the property-poor, student-rich districts, a cause which the Regents (before, during, and since my Chancellorship) have earnestly supported. I have not seen any demonstrations for complete dollar equality of spending, nor is that a requirement of the judge's decision. Nevertheless, *Levittown,* like *Serrano* before it, could have serious repercussions for the cause of educational excellence if the courts decide that "equity" means "equality" and that no district should be permitted to spend more per student than another.

We could be headed that way. "Equity" has favorable connotations; "equitable" means fair and honest and right and good. "Equality," on the other hand, is not so readily accepted. Equality for whom, with whom, on whose terms, and in what respects? Equality of opportunity, of results, of what? Equality connotes a leveling, a sameness, a repression of efforts to improve—all of which are anathema to many Americans. And . . . *equality is not necessarily compatible with quality,* which is the goal of all in education. But if the courts, lacking any other measuring rod, decide that equity cannot be achieved short of equal spending on each student, *Levittown* could turn out to be the Pandora's Box of modern schooling, loosing a new force which can doom public education to permanent mediocrity, which in a pluralistic society is fatal.

Justice Hopkins Dissents

Although he concurred in the New York appellate finding that lack of a true system invalidated the state's school-financing laws, presiding Justice James D. Hopkins dissented sharply from the *Levittown* majority's view that New York's educational funding arrangements violated "equal protection" in that the same amount of money was not made available for each child's schooling.

Observing that "it is doubtful whether cost alone is decisive of the quality of education" and that "it is not at all clear, and, indeed, what material is available is to the contrary, that more expenditures results in increasing learning skills," Justice Hopkins pointed out that in the *Levittown* case "there is neither proof nor finding that any of the individual plaintiffs suffered an absolute deprivation of educational opportunity or even a substantial diminution of educational opportunity." In other words, the less wealthy districts can and do provide a satisfactory level of education in spite of unequal funding capabilities.

Recalling that New York has historically delegated functions to local governments of varying resources without any claims of constitutional violation, Justice Hopkins cited as examples welfare, public health, "the care of persons suffering from natural disorders" and public housing, all directed by the state constitution. To this list, one might add various essential services performed by local entities under state law, such as police and fire protection, sanitation, parks, and the like. Does the constitution require, after all these years, that there be a statewide formula mandating a specific number of policemen, firemen, or sanitation men for each thousand citizens, regardless of where they live? Or for each thousand dwelling units? Must identical amounts per citizen be spent by Town A and Town B for parks and beaches? The impact is mind-boggling.

Justice Hopkins summed up the case against defining "equal protection" in terms of equal spending: ". . . the argument of the plaintiffs underpinning their claims of constitutional discrimination on the ground of disparity of wealth proves too much and would, if accepted, effectively destroy the long-established governmental principle that the municipality can be expected to deal competently with State functions delegated to it."

Justice Hopkins's conclusion that relatively low district wealth and expenditures need not mean poor educational quality has received support from an unexpected source: the plaintiff Levittown School District itself. *Newsday* reported on February 19, 1982 that while this gap in property wealth and school spending between Levittown and richer districts still remained, Levittown's board president, James Ward, and its superintendent, Gerald Lauber, insisted that Levittown's educational performance was excellent: "Lauber and . . . Ward . . . both defend the quality of education in the district. 'I don't think there is any district with a particularly better education, especially in the elementary schools,' said Ward, whose children go to Levittown schools."

How, then, can it be seriously contended that the low level of district wealth per pupil has denied equal educational opportunity or an excellent education to Levittown's children?

Al Shanker Warns the Courts

In an August 1981 column headed "Courts Must Weigh the Consequences," American Federation of Teachers' President Albert Shanker warned of the "unanticipated consequences" of court decisions which mandate complete equality of spending for public education. Said Shanker: ". . . a few years ago some clever lawyers argued that since most state constitutions oblige the *state* to provide a free public education for every child, it is unconstitutional to provide . . . unequal education. These lawyers hoped that as the courts threw out existing school finance schemes, legislatures would not dare demand that rich districts reduce spending to make them the same as the poor ones. Rather, they expected, the state legislatures would come up with additional funds to bring the poor districts up. Meanwhile, the rich districts would be told to stop spending more . . . to wait until the poor caught up.

". . . asking rich districts to stand still during years of double-digit inflation was really asking them to take a reduction. But now, with . . . taxpayer rebellions . . . a court-ordered move which demands complete equality of spending, or even near-equality, could lead to disastrous consequences.

"We have had a long tradition in our country of local control and largely local support of schools. Many parents sell their homes and move from one school district to another because they want the better education provided in the second district. If the courts now rule that the better schools they moved for and are paying for are unconstitutional . . . that they will have to reduce the quality of education in their district either by actual budget cuts or by standing still while inflation cuts them back . . . there will be a price to pay. It will certainly add to the numbers who want to get the government off their backs. It may also add to the numbers who will decide that [their present residence] is not for them—

they'll move to a state where they can still buy a home in a better district. . . .

"Court decisions designed to promote greater equality could lead to greater inequality . . . the abandonment of public schools by huge numbers. . . . The courts must take the consequences of their actions into consideration. Judges must be more aware than they have been that their decisions usually set in motion a chain of events the end of which may be extremely destructive. . . .

"[The court] could order substantial help for poor districts and those with burdensome special problems. It could order special help for the poor and the handicapped . . . and it should. But it must stop short of trying to impose equality of spending or effort on all districts."

Al Shanker's fear, developed more fully in his column, is that court-mandated equality will impel those who demand educational excellence for their children to forsake the public schools for the independents. He has a point; the shortcomings of the public schools now account for a good part of the move away from them, and court-decreed stagnation in one district while money is pumped into others could speed up the exodus.

Although my own devotion to educational pluralism (and my faith in the survival of the public schools, *if* we start doing what is right for them) makes me somewhat more confident than Al, I am not one whit less troubled than he is about the adverse effects of court-ordered mediocrity—the inevitable result of court-ordered spending equalization—upon the quality of an American public-school education.

My Lonely Fight Against "Capping"

When I first stood up as a brand-new Regent to speak against forced transportation of children to schools far beyond those they would normally attend, nobody took my part, and I was dubbed the Lone Regent. Years passed before others began to agree and we eventually relegated busing to a last-resort status—and then usable only if children's rights were protected.

In the final months of my eleven-year tenure on the board, I became the Lone Regent once again. Capping local spending for the public schools was the issue and, once more, nobody took my part. I was heard politely, but when the showdown came, there was one Regent voting against capping: me.

So be it. Majority rule never determines what is right and what is wrong. It is merely one acceptable way of reaching a decision to act or not to act.

What is capping, as applied to school finance, and why have I gone on record as opposing it—in 1973, 1978, 1979, and now?

A quick definition of capping might be this: an equalizing device whereby a legal limitation is placed upon per-pupil spending by a school district with greater-than-average taxable wealth per pupil, designed to restrain that district's efforts while tax-poorer districts catch up in per-pupil spending.

I have never been bashful about my opposition to capping. At the first meeting of the Rubin Task Force in 1978, I concluded my introductory remarks by saying:

"Our legitimate and overdue effort to find a more equitable system of distributing funds to our schools must not be allowed to impede or override our primary mission—*the attainment of excellence* in our schools, both in teaching and in academic performance. Nor, in our zeal for greater equality, should we stifle or otherwise discourage the willingness of our citizens to dig deep into their own pockets for better schools for their children in their local districts.

"Former Commissioner Joe Nyquist put it this way: 'We should not fill the valleys by chopping off the mountain tops'—and I agree. If you cannot improve the quality of education for some children without diminishing it for others, you will not have answered the challenge at all.

"Each of the 700+ school districts in our state, according to its means and ingenuity, has been a testing ground in our . . . search for better education. They must not be reduced to a dull, unproductive level of sameness, even in the name of equity."

Four years later, in the final Rubin Report, we learned that the Task Force had split down the middle on capping: "While about half the Task Force members believed that the goal of reducing expenditure gaps required mechanisms (such as limits in state aid increases) to discourage such high spending, the other half believed that an overriding issue was the freedom of local districts to support the best education they could afford, if they so wished."

In 1979, however, the Regents were caught up in the rush to equity; they proposed a capping system which would have eventually meant that the Empire State's more than seven hundred educational laboratories, each developing its own answers to rugged challenges, would close up shop and slip easily into a pattern of uniformity which would be dictated by a single dollar amount which was permitted for the schooling of each child in every district. None could be different.

I demurred. Of course I was concerned about those districts which were resource-poor; of course I was convinced that the real property tax was an inequitable and inadequate way to fund public education; of course I acknowledged that the state has a responsibility to help those districts which, despite their best efforts, were unable to provide a decent education for their children. But to me, quality was and is *absolute*, not relative. I asked: "What is the new ideology, the modern rationale, which now commands us to abandon the solid principles upon which we and our predecessors built a fine system of public education . . . ? What do the advocates of 'capping' local spending want and expect to accomplish?

"We live in an egalitarian age, wherein it is more important, more fashionably correct, that things be *equal* than that things be good.

"Our traditional goal of *excellence* for everyone, an absolute, qualitative goal, is now subordinated to the new goal of *equality* for everyone, a relative and quantitative goal.

"By the populist standards of our times, when excellence and equality are incompatible (as they sometimes are), *equality* must prevail. Only in this context can 'capping' be understood."

The proponents of capping argue that it would not really lower educational quality in those districts whose efforts were to be halted, even if (as Al Shanker has stressed) inflation actually reduces the value of per-child dollar spending. But the whole thrust of the *Levittown* rationale upon which they base their argument is that dollar spending, or the lack of it, *does* affect the quality of education, because spending and quality *are* directly related. To inhibit or reduce our dollar commitment to a child's education is to inhibit or reduce the quality of that child's schooling. More money does not always produce better schools, but less money or inflated money won't improve anything.

And there is another consideration—one that goes right to the heart of the way we Americans think, and do things. "I am convinced," I told the Regents, "that it is wrong for the Board . . . the state's educational policy-making body, dedicated to the promotion and maintenance of excellence in our schools, to restrain, inhibit, penalize or otherwise discourage local citizens from using their own resources to improve the quality of their own children's education in their own public schools."

For two hundred years, we have been free to dig as deeply as we chose into our own pockets, in order to build, staff, maintain, and operate the finest schools our money can buy. Is that great tradition about to come to an end, because somebody orders that there will be no new commitments, no improvement, until such time as every other district is willing and able to spend exactly as much per child as we do? Senator Joe McCarthy may have made "un-American" a bad word, but if anything can be called "un-American" these days, it is educational capping—alien not only to our goal of scholastic excellence but to our American dream as well.

If you agree, you will not be happy about the final decision of the Regents on capping. Three good friends on the board voted with me to delay any decision; when we lost that one, I became the Lone Regent once again. A wistful small-type note in the Regents' *Journal* wrapped it up: "Chancellor Black voted in the negative. He wished the record to show that he voted in the negative solely because of his opposition to the proposal for 'capping' local efforts; he joins his colleagues in unanimous support of the [state-aid] plan." Maybe I'll frame that one.

Capping: Not a Big Hit in the Garden State

About the same time that the New York Regents were debating capping, an article appeared in the *New York Times* headed: "Jersey Funding Caps: More Becomes Less." New Jersey had already tried capping, and the experience was not a happy one. Describing some of the problems that capping had brought to the Garden State's schools, the reporter found, among other things, that caps in many cases forced the abandonment or reduction of essential local services. For example, the costs of heat, utilities, etc., rose higher than the capped budgets could cover.

I called the Regents' attention to the article. They smiled, and voted for capping anyway. Equity, which no one could oppose, had been effectively transmuted into equality, which required that some districts must stand still until others become equal. It was too sweet-smelling to resist. It took a long time for the truth to penetrate my thick Irish cranium: being against capping was like being against motherhood, apple pie, the flag, and God.

I still don't like it. And neither did the New York State Legislature, which rejected the Regents' recommendation. Those who still believe that every citizen has a right to do all within his or her power to provide the best possible education for his or her children should applaud their representatives (not just in New York, but everywhere) when they kill off proposals to limit citizen efforts. And they might also say a silent prayer that their courts will be equally understanding of the principles involved.

The All-American Cap

I sometimes wonder if those who support capping (because they feel that school spending should be the same or almost the same for every child) have fully considered the ramifications of their position.

If, as they contend, it is unconstitutional or illegal or immoral or inequitable for one Texas district—or one California or Minnesota or New York district—to spend more per pupil than another district in the same state, why should one *state* and its combined local districts be permitted to spend more than another state? Why should we not cap *state* expenditures for schools?

The answer, I am afraid, is that if local districts are to be capped, logic dictates that *states* must be capped, too. When we talk of equity, the size of the entities involved is not material. Those twenty-five states which spend less than the national average must spend more, and (under the capping rule) the twenty-five states which spend more than the average must halt in their tracks until the lower-spending half manages to catch up, whenever that might be.

If we are going to have to wait until agricultural Arkansas (spending $1,301 per student, according to ECS figures) starts shelling out as much as oil-rich, sparsely populated Alaska (tops at $3,943 per pupil), or industrial New York ($2,800), the twenty-five "capped" states will be marking time for a long while — as inflation steadily lessens the quality of their children's education. *Cui bono?* To what good end? In my book, none at all.

And why do we stop there? Will the United Nations be next? Will Uncle Sam have to sit on American spending for schools until Zaire and Zambia catch up? It begins to sound silly . . . but it is a logical extension of the notion that equity will not be achieved until the same amount of money is spent on every child's education. If this becomes official policy for our own school districts and states, how can we take a different stance in the international community?

We must continue our ongoing efforts to improve the quality of education by committing additional resources to those districts which are least able to fund their own schools. That is what Joe Nyquist called "filling the valleys." Its purpose is clear and correct: better education.

But while the poorer districts certainly can and must be helped, it is folly to think that there will be sufficient state funds available to bring them all up to the spending levels of the most affluent, highest-effort districts. We do what we can with what we have.

Every dollar should go to the improvement of educational quality. Federal- and state-raised money must go where it is most needed. Locally raised money should be applied to the improvement of the local schools; no system is perfect. But there should be *no inhibition whatsoever* upon either of these efforts, other than the availability of funds and the willingness of taxpayers to commit them.

Most important, there must be no "chopping off the mountain tops." With state-aid funds being concentrated upon the poorer districts, the wealthier districts will have to rely more heavily upon their own resources. That being so, *they must not be impeded in their efforts to do so,* by caps or any other device. A policy of "if I can't have it, you can't have it" (which is what capping is) can lead only to reduction of excellence in the more well-to-do districts and the eventual elimination of local advantages which permit them to try new methods and new programs from which all may eventually profit.

When it comes to capping school spending, equality and quality meet head-on. I'll take quality every time.

Uncle Sam's Role in Financing Education

At the outset of this chapter, I promised not to prejudice either the work of the U.S. Advisory Panel upon which I serve or my own freedom to adjust my views on the basis of new data which the panel's research may produce. That being so, I will limit what I have to say here about federal financing to those elements upon which the panel has already commented publicly or which are needed to complete your understanding of my philosophy in general. My long-expressed views on the *abuse* of federal spending power (and how to eliminate it) are discussed in detail elsewhere in this book.

The panel recently issued two public statements. In one, we unanimously asked that the federal government reduce the vast and burdensome paperwork requirements imposed upon those who wish to qualify for federal-aid funding. Everyone seems to agree that there *is* much too much paperwork; the government itself has been making efforts to reduce it. So there is little to argue with on that score. Heavy reporting requirements are, however, involved in the second statement issued by the panel (I was not present for the vote) in which the members expressed their general preference for *categorical* grants rather than the so-called *block* grants proposed by the Reagan Administration.

Categorical Grants versus Block Grants

In the broadest sense, a categorical grant is one specifically pinpointed to a given purpose or set of purposes, with its permissible uses sharply defined and limited and the grantee required to spend it only in the prescribed manner. Most grants in recent years have been of the categorical variety, and it is because of the strict constraints upon their disposition by state and local authorities that paperwork has become so onerous.

Block grants, on the other hand, may be tagged for a specific educational purpose, but are not narrowly limited by requirements that the money be spent in exactly this way or that. State and local grantees have much more discretion in distributing block-grant funds than they do in spending categorical-grant money. Consistent with President Reagan's philosophy that the states should have more leeway in determining the best use of available funding, he has proposed the replacement of many categorical-grant programs by block grants.

I am not at all certain that I agree with the President in this case, although my reservations might be somewhat different from those of my colleagues on the panel.

A Politician's Dream

Block grants are a politician's dream.

What more delicious dish could be set before a governor facing re-election than a stack of fresh money—money which he did not have to extract from his constituents in taxes but is free to distribute to them as he sees fit?

It is or should be a fundamental principle of government that the authority which dispenses funds has a right to set the standards and terms upon which those funds will be made available. Governments do not generate money or wealth. It belongs to the taxpayers and is extracted from them to serve accepted public purposes. Although the excessive paperwork required by categorical grants is undoubtedly overkill on the side of caution, and although it may in some cases cost the recipient entity more to administer than the grants are worth, there is at least some assurance that the taxpayers' money—what's left of it—is spent upon that for which it is targeted. Such assurance is not possible if the government hands out a block of money for a broad, general purpose and gives the recipient plenty of leeway in spending it.

Perhaps the core of my problem with block grants is my problem with "revenue-sharing," wherein the federal government simply hands back a wad of tax money to the states and local governments. Revenue-sharing is not too different from block grants, except that grants are more specifically directed to a stated goal.

But if the United States is going to collect tax revenue only to pass it back to the states and localities, why should Uncle Sam collect it in the first place? All it does is take a round trip to Washington, with processing costs subtracted along the route. In my view, it could have been better left in the taxpayer's pocket. If his state or city or school district needs it, they can obtain it directly from him.

In passing, I should confess that I consider revenue-sharing to be a delusion, if the generous government which is sharing its revenue is operating on a deficit basis (as the U.S. has been doing for too many years). In that case, there is no leftover federal money to be "shared" with the states and local governments. The commitment to federal purposes is greater than federal taxes can pay for; how can there be anything left for others? Even if Uncle Sam were to operate on a balanced-budget, break-even basis, there would still be a monumental federal debt to retire—and debt retirement should certainly take precedence over revenue-sharing in any intelligent fiscal program.

What the Federal Government Can Do

There is a role for the U.S. government in education. For one thing, Washington can and does commission and analyze statistics across the country, statistics which can be tremendously helpful to all who labor in the educational vineyards, and which might not be obtainable by a state government, at least not as easily. I have referred to a state's school districts as so many educational laboratories where experiments are constantly being conducted for later sharing with others. The states should be thought of in the same way, and the wide variations in their ways of dealing with schools can be of great value to their sister states and to educators in general, when gathered, analyzed, and published by the United States.

We have already discussed the mutual value of U.S. contracts with higher-education institutions for research and development, particularly in the field of defense. The country can and should fulfill its obligations to veterans by helping to pay for their college education; such assistance also helps the colleges themselves.

Uncle Sam can offer financial help where it is needed most. The ESEA program begun in 1965 pinpointed underprivileged and educationally deprived students (in their districts) for special help, and we know from new reports by the National Assessment of Educational Progress that federal help is working to enhance the quality of education for those who have been shortchanged. Because we are devoted to the raising of levels of academic performance, particularly among these youngsters, we should applaud the contribution of ESEA to the cause of excellence.

But, in so doing, we must not forget that the extra effort which ESEA funds made possible *might* have been provided by *state* and *local* governments. Funds are funds, and their use is what it is, without regard to the source. Are the states and the cities and the school districts making a *maximum effort* in the financing of their schools? I anticipate that we will learn the answer from our panel's research. And I suspect that the answer will be that some states are doing their best, and some are not.

Recent ECS statistics covering the ten states which spend least per pupil are not encouraging. Their spending is 27 percent off the national average; their state-local revenue for $1,000 of personal income is 13 percent below the average, indicating a subpar effort. Even so, their per-capita (not per-student) school spending as a proportion of all expenditures is 3 percentage points *above* the national norm. It appears that (1) they don't tax as much as they might, but (2) education takes an above-average chunk of what they do collect, although (3) it still doesn't provide enough money per pupil. Perhaps the fact that their U.S. funds as a percentage of all education expenses runs *71* percent over the national average has something to do with the effort, or lack of it, in these ten states.

Human nature being what it is, dollars from Washington usually tend to *supplant,* not supplement, local and state dollars in support of a given program. Unless we make certain (categorically) that the federal money is intended and is used as *additional* help toward the solution of a problem, not as a substitute for state or local funds, we will be contributing very little to the whole solution, while allowing the states and localities to divert their resources elsewhere. Education is their responsibility, and they should not be offered a free ride for which generous Uncle Sam has bought the ticket. On the reverse side of the coin, Uncle Sam should not order the states to do things without the help of U.S. funds. You may be sure that the federal Advisory Panel will give these aspects of federal funding very careful scrutiny.

One final cautionary word is important. There has been a tendency for the dishers-out of federal money to bypass state educational agencies and hand the funds directly to local authorities. This is a dangerous game. When someone writes the history of the Department of Agriculture's dismally failed summer feeding program for New York City children (which eventually had to be rescued by the State Education Department), it will reveal the shocking waste of money and goods which can ensue when there is overreliance upon community agencies at the local level. The state has the basic responsibility for education; proper disposition of federal funds should be a part of that responsibility, as should enforcement of federal rules.

Summing Up

I believe that the states and localities, being best suited to provide public educational services, should not only run the schools but shoulder the major burden of financing them.

I believe that the differences among states and among school districts in the way their educational systems are governed, operated, and financed provide useful examples and information which can benefit all of education.

I believe that the decline in the percentage of state-local revenues which is devoted to education is unfortunate and counterproductive, and should be reversed.

I believe that the public's view of what constitutes a "fair" tax differs from the experts' view and is weighted more heavily in terms of public acceptance of the use to which the money is put, which explains why property taxes for education have survived as long as they have.

I believe that property taxes should be devoted primarily to property-oriented government services, and should not be relied upon as the main source of public-school funds—in other words, that a child's education should not be tied to the real-estate wealth of his community.

I believe that public voting on school operating budgets, public referenda on school issues, and constitutional tax limitations upon spending for schools can be and often are hurtful to the quality of education in a school system and should therefore be abolished.

I believe that state mandates governing the basic curriculum common to all schools provide necessary legal safeguards against cost cutting which reduces educational quality. I further believe that some other mandates are not needed, and I believe that those U.S.- or state-mandated programs which require significant expenditures that a district might not otherwise make, and may be hard-pressed to make, should be funded in whole or part by the mandating agency.

I believe that school district authorities should stop placing the onus for "mandated costs" upon the state when those costs are for regular curriculum programs and when more than 80 percent of a school district's budget is determined not by mandate but by negotiated contracts between the district and its staff.

I believe that quality and equality in educational services are not always compatible—and that quality must always take precedence over equality.

I believe that the citizens of a school district should not be prevented, inhibited, or discouraged from, or penalized for, committing as much of their own resources as they choose for the improvement of the quality of their children's education in their own public schools.

I believe that our colleges and universities should be able to accept research and development grants from the U.S. government, and veterans and qualified but underprivileged students should be able to accept U.S. help toward their college education, without such assistance being used to impose federal authority on the higher-education community.

I believe that the proper role of the federal government in school finance is in research and in the provision of supplementary financial assistance to those states and local districts which need it but which cannot themselves provide it, even with maximum effort, and I further believe that such assistance should be administered with adequate safeguards guaranteeing the proper use of the funds, but with minimal paperwork requirements.

I believe, finally, that whatever U.S. dollar aid is provided to education should be transmitted through the state education agencies, which must be responsible for proper disposition of the funds to local districts and, where required, to individual children. I believe that this method of distribution is the only one compatible with the state's basic responsibility for education.

9.

Heavy-Handed Uncle Sam

Federal Dollars — America's Newest Narcotic

JOSEPH R. BONGIORNO, M.D., New York State Regent for Brooklyn and Staten Island, was a tall, handsome, articulate, intelligent, deeply religious man who devoted his life to the health care of children and young people. Cancer claimed Joe early in 1980; I will always remember him as one of the finest human beings I have ever known.

And on June 24, 1977, Joe Bongiorno hit the ceiling.

What prompted an outburst of anger from this normally quiet, gentle, and compassionate medical man?

On the final morning of the Regents' June meeting at Albany, the Education Department proposed what appeared to be a routine amendment to clause (c) of subparagraph (ii) of paragraph 7 of subdivision (c) of Section 135.4 of the Regulations of the Commissioner of Education, designed to remove a "disparity" between the Commissioner's Regulations and Title IX of the Educational Amendments of 1972, bringing state rules into conformity with federal rules.

The subject was female participation with men on secondary-school interscholastic athletic teams in certain sports.

New York State had always been a leader in promoting coed sports of the noncontact sort. In fact, an April 1971 rules change further liberalizing the state's already liberal policy in the field drew complaints from women athletic directors that the best women athletes might be drained away from girls' sports to play on boys' teams, thus ruining interscholastic competition among girls.

In 1977, however, the question was different.

191

Both Uncle Sam and New York State agreed that physiological differences between young men and young women of high-school age warranted barring coed participation in certain contact sports. New York had always included baseball and softball on the prohibited list; now the government had told New York to allow girls to play on men's varsity teams in these sports or face charges of violating U.S. laws against sex discrimination.

That's what led Dr. Bongiorno to protest. His years of observing young people's athletics and treating injuries to players had convinced him that interscholastic baseball and softball could be very dangerous for young women playing on men's teams. Heatedly denouncing the federal order as "idiocy," he described situations in which girls could be badly hurt in boys' baseball games. "We're not talking about the Little League . . . we're talking about varsity high school baseball . . . boys better than six feet tall and over two hundred pounds." He concluded that: "The responsibility of the Regents is to protect children. Do you allow a free choice when, in good conscience, you feel that it's against [the children's] own best interest?"

The national public high-school athletic association (and New York's) agreed with Dr. Joe; so did I, having played grownup hardball myself (with a bent finger to show for it) and having seen Bobby Reese, pitcher for the Port Washington, New York, Fire Department softball team, suffer a nose broken in six places by a hard line drive. Other Regents (including the three women on the board) saw the whole thing as a male chauvinist rear-guard action. One Regent feared that state defiance of federal terms would create a dilemma for local school boards: facing a conflict between a U.S. order to let girls play in the disputed sports and a state regulation forbidding them to do so, the local boards could not get insurance for their teams, and risked loss of their federal aid. Even so, Dr. Bongiorno won a short-lived victory, 6–5. The Regents later agreed to let the girls play, if they passed a preschedule physical examination; the school boards' worries were over.

But what was the real significance of all this?

Everybody Missed the Point

The point was not that the young women athletes were risking limb, if not life, by playing on boys' contact-sports teams. The point was not that men were trying to keep women in a protected and therefore second-class role. The point was not that the school boards had to be spared embarrassment. The point, which I tried to make although no one was in a mood to listen, was this: In the name of the Founding Fathers, by what right does the United States government presume to tell local public high-school athletic directors which students must be allowed to play on their varsity sports teams?

The answer was, and is: *by no right at all.*

And the point was lost in the smoke of the battle about the specific matter at issue, just as the same point has been lost in so many other battles about sex discrimination, racial integration, energy conservation, air pollution, and similar popular causes. By diverting the attention of the public to the *particular issue* involved in each case, the federal bureaucracy has stepped up, steadily and relentlessly, its invasion of the prerogatives, rights, and responsibilities of the fifty states and their local governments. The carefully constructed constitutional separation of powers has been all but erased, particularly in the field of education, while we have fixed our eyes and ears upon the merits of specific issues rather than basic concerns about who should be doing what.

Back to the U.S. Constitution, One More Time

When you want to know which level of government should be doing what, go back to the source: the United States Constitution. In it, the Founding Fathers spelled out clearly the powers delegated to the federal government by the states, and added, in the Tenth Amendment of the Bill of Rights, this unmistakable rule:

"The powers not delegated to the United States by the Constitution, nor prohibited by it to the States, are reserved to the States respectively, or to the people."

In more than 190 years, this language has not changed. Now, as then, the federal authorities have only those powers which the Constitution specifically awards to them, *and education is not mentioned anywhere in the entire text of the Constitution.* For that reason, and because education has traditionally been that function of government most jealously kept in the hands of the people themselves, federal legislation has always refrained from interfering in the governance of America's schools and colleges. Congress has spoken out in that vein; for example, Section 404(b) of Public Law 94–482, the Education Amendments of 1976, defines the barriers to U.S. involvement in these words:

"No provision of any applicable program shall be construed to authorize any department, agency, or officer, or employee of the United States to exercise any direction, supervision or control over the curriculum, program of instruction, administration or personnel of any educational institution, school or school system . . ."

Could any instructions to the executive branch be clearer than these? I doubt it. They were so clear, in fact, that a succession of Congresses, secure in the feeling that such explicit limitations and prohibitions upon federal power could not and therefore would not be ignored, neglected to monitor the federal-state relationship.

The Courts Agree: Hands Off Education

Perhaps the overconfidence of the Congresses was abetted by a succession of Supreme Court decisions reaffirming the reserved powers of the states in the field of public education, which the New York State Regents annually cited in their messages to Congress on "Federal Legislation and Education."

In the historic *Brown* decision (1954), the Court stated that "education is perhaps the most important function of state and local governments," a position reinforced in *Wisconsin v. Yoder* (1972), which said that "providing public schools ranks at the very apex of the function of a state."

The Court said of the Tenth Amendment (in *U.S. v. Darby*, 1941): "The Amendment states but a 'truism' that all is retained (by the states and the people) which has not been surrendered"; the later *Fry v. U.S.* decision recognized that "the [Tenth] Amendment expressly declares the Constitutional policy that Congress may not exercise power in a fashion that impairs the states' integrity or their ability to function effectively in a federal system."

While it is clear that Congress may use its spending powers under Article I, Section 8 and Amendment XIV for aid to education, a use supported by the Court in *Oklahoma v. Civil Service Commission* (1947), the states and localities are not required to participate; they do so voluntarily, entering into a contractual agreement if they accept the conditions upon which U.S. grants are based.

Perhaps the most conclusive judicial confirmation of the fifty states' retained sovereignty in those fields not ceded by them to the U.S. government in the Constitution is to be found in *National League of Cities v. Usery* (1976). There the Court said it had "repeatedly recognized that there are attributes of sovereignty attaching to every state government that may not be impaired by Congress, not because Congress may lack an affirmative grant of legislative authority to reach the matter, but because the Constitution prohibits it from exercising the authority in that matter." The Court warned: "If Congress may withdraw from the states the authority to make those ... decisions upon which [public service] functions must rest, we think there would be little left of the states' 'separable and independent existence,'" adding that "Congress may not exercise that power so as to force directly upon the states its choices as to how essential decisions regarding the conduct of integral government functions are to be made," concluding that "such assertions of power, if unchecked, would indeed . . . allow 'the national government [to] devour the essentials of state sovereignty.' "

Yet, despite the unmistakably clear instructions of the Congress and the equally positive warnings of the U.S. Supreme Court over the years, the New York Regents found it necessary to remind the Congress in February 1978: "Recent Federal legislation in education . . . includes provisions that displace state choices in structuring governmental operations and in requirements of educational service. *The Federal partner appears to have stepped beyond constitutional bounds.*" (Italics supplied.)

Uncle Sam: Extortionist

In the long debate which preceded the adoption of the Elementary and Secondary Education Act of 1965, skeptics insisted (1) that U.S. aid must be extended to *all* children who qualify for it, regardless of the type of school they attend; (2) that the taxpayers of those states which make a conscientious effort to deal on their own with the problems addressed by U.S. aid must not be soaked to provide dollars for states which do little or nothing to help themselves, and (3) above all, that the acceptance of U.S. money would not lead to federal intervention into the governance and operation of the schools.

When ESEA became law (four years before I was elected a Regent and plopped into the middle of the controversy), I, too, harbored these reservations, but I had no doubt at all about the intention and the capability of the Congress to see that they were dealt with properly. Everything would surely come out just fine.

How wrong I was! How wrong millions of us were! The nonpublic schools have had to scream and scratch to get their kids' share of ESEA funds. States like New York, paying for their own programs for disadvantaged children long before ESEA came on the scene, seldom if ever got back all the money their taxpayers shelled out to cover ESEA programs. And, as Congress looked the other way, federal authorities have moved in to exercise practical control over the everyday management and operation of our schools and colleges. How do they get away with it?

Simple. They do it by *extortion.*

Here's how it works. School districts make their budgetary plans on the basis of certain assumptions about what will be forthcoming from Uncle Sam under the various formulas outlined in federal-aid regulations. Because much of the aid is destined for disadvantaged youngsters, the poorer school districts are likely to be more heavily dependent upon federal funds for the running of their schools. They can least afford to lose those funds.

The budgetary process in public education is a very delicate affair, matching anticipated revenue against necessary expenses while attempting to hold down tax rates and thus avoid the taxpayers' wrath. Much of what will be spent is determined by negotiations with teachers' associations, often arrived at after formal budgeting has been completed. Some costs are fixed (interest on bonds, for example); others (the cost of gasoline for school buses, heating oil or gas for school furnaces, insurance premiums, snow removal, vandalism repairs, and the like) must be predicted. Against total expected requirements, the local district calculates how much it may expect from the state and U.S. governments based upon aid formulas which, at local budget lock-in time, may still not be fixed. Local property tax rates are then proposed, debated, and eventually adopted.

Then along comes Uncle Sam, in the form of HEW (now the Department of Education) bureaucrats, threatening to yank the rug out from under the district *by withholding all U.S. funds* unless the school board or the state immediately complies with some just-arrived-at administrative decree which may be wholly unrelated to the purposes of the laws providing such aid.

That is extortion: Do what we tell you to do, or we will not give you the money you were promised.

Federal education officials are not stupid. They are well aware that most local school districts cannot cope with sudden and severe slashes in their operating budgets. They know that school districts have contracted for services in the expectation that, having qualified for U.S. funds by meeting the terms of aid legislation, those funds will be forthcoming. They realize that local tax rates cannot be quickly and arbitrarily raised to offset the unplanned loss of federal dollars. The U.S. government has unlimited resources (which we have given it) to hire legal counsel, but our districts do not; indeed, those districts which have most to lose by withdrawal of U.S. aid are usually the poorest districts. Working without expected and budgeted U.S. assistance while fighting a long, costly lawsuit to regain that assistance presents a difficult choice to the local school board—and the federal power-brokers know it.

Thus, in almost every case, the local board will knuckle under to federal authority without a court battle, complying with whatever ukase the government imposes, simply to assure the uninterrupted flow of federal money into the district's bank account . . . and their school system has become "hooked" on the narcotic of federal dollars.

The power to withhold U.S. aid if an institution does not comply with federal laws has been specifically granted by such legislation as the Education Amendments of 1972, and at this writing is being considered by the U.S. Supreme Court. But the point at issue here is not obedience to law, a matter for the courts; it is the propriety of enforcing administrative interpretations of a law upon other governments under threat of withholding funds, despite the Tenth Amendment and Section 404(b) of P.L. 94–482 (1976), instructing the executive department not to "exercise any direction, supervision or control" over the states and local school districts.

The last thing the federal bureaucracy wants to confront is a court challenge to its decrees by state or local systems. Thus far, they seem to have guessed right, gambling that their threats to withhold U.S. aid funds will keep potential challengers from filing suit to get the money they have qualified for. The net result is that the federal government has been using the power of the purse—using our own tax money—to force our compliance with their orders. By so doing, they usurp the traditional and constitutional authority over education from the states and the local communities, where that authority rightly resides.

And Uncle Sam has been getting away with it.

Horrible Examples Abound

We have already noted how federal extortion worked in the Title IX sex-discrimination flap about which varsity interscholastic teams must be coeducational. That's not the end of the story, however. A couple of years later, in November 1979, a Title IX complaint muscled Long Island public-school superintendents into establishing three seasons of high-school sports for girls instead of the traditional four, because boys' sports are played on a three-season basis. The complaint (by an enthusiastic paralegal) alleged that the difference meant that girls received less practice, less conditioning, and less instructional time than boys, while shorter seasons meant less pay for girls' sports coaches than for their boys' sports counterparts. With the Office of Civil Rights of the U.S. Department of Health, Education and Welfare poised in the wings (having told the Illinois High School Athletic Association in 1977 that they were in violation of Title IX because their boys' and girls' sports seasons were unequal in time), the Long Island superintendents knew the ball game was over before it began. The girls got their three seasons.

But the "equal rights require equal seasons" rule did not meet with universal acceptance and acclaim. Compacting four girls' sports seasons into three meant that more sports must be played simultaneously in each season, thus limiting the variety of opportunities for individual girls. Coach Joan Smith of Valley Stream North complained that the adjustment was itself discriminatory in that "it curtails girls from a variety of activities during the year"; Joan Case of Clark commented that smaller schools could suffer because there might not be enough girl athletes to field all the teams at one time.

Some of the kids didn't care much for their new freedom, either. Two sixteen-year-old Jericho High School students, Lori Friedman and Elyse Lichtman, organized a campaign to restore four-season sports. Miss Friedman, who had to give up volleyball under the new calendar, said of the three-season plan, "It stinks"; she claimed that it meant fewer choices for girls and possible cancellations of some sports for lack of players. Miss Lichtman, who had to give up field hockey, commented; "No one consulted us, the girls who play sports. Sometimes equal is not equal."

Equal Treatment May Not Have Equitable Effects

These young women have apparently learned what too many Washington "doubledomes" can't seem to realize: that treating two people in exactly the same manner may not be equitable at all, and that there's a difference between identical and equal.

What will you give Aunt Madge and Aunt Agnes for Christmas? Steering-wheel covers? Aunt Madge drives; Aunt Agnes does not. Red handbags? Aunt Agnes would love one; Aunt Madge is a carrot-top who never wears red. Five-pound boxes of chocolates? Aunt Madge has a sweet tooth; Aunt Agnes is a diabetic to whom such temptation might be lethal. Checks for $25 each? Aunt Agnes, on a pension, would be grateful; Aunt Madge, who owns three apartment houses, would raise her eyebrows. Identical gifts may be useful and welcome to one, useless— even harmful—to the other.

The "Animal Farm" Concept of Equality

At the risk of belaboring this one aspect of the subject yet once more, I refer to the blue paper-bound document before me as I write: *Digest of Significant Case-Related Memoranda* issued by the Office of Civil Rights of HEW in 1979. One case deals with a sports program which provides freshman, JV, and varsity teams for boys in various sports but only varsity teams for girls. There is no evidence that the OCR has asked whether the greater number of boys' teams might result from greater demand for participation on the boys' part, or that the five different sports available for boys (as opposed to three for girls) might also be attributable to student choice. In determining discrimination, demand does not seem to be a factor, nor does any attention seem to be paid to the readiness of a school to provide additional teams if youngsters want to participate on them. The federal criterion is stern: If there *are* more sports teams for boys than for girls, the girls are being discriminated against, period.

The "remedy" in this case was even more curious:

"The greater number of teams and sports available for males shows that overall athletic opportunities for females are limited. [Wrong. It shows nothing of the sort, unless certain sports requested for girls have been arbitrarily rejected by school authorities, which is not the case here.] Therefore . . . the school district must open participation on its 'boys' baseball and track teams to female students who wish to try out for them. (*There is no requirement that boys must be permitted to try out for the girls' volleyball team because, although there is no volleyball team for boys, overall athletic opportunities for boys have been greater than those for girls.*)" [Italics supplied.]

There it is: equality is a class action, not an individual right. The boys who might want to play volleyball rather than something else are out of luck, because they belong to the class called boys which, *as a class,* fields more different teams than girls do.

George Orwell said it in *Animal Farm:* "All animals are equal, but some are more equal than others."

Local Situations Should Be Resolved Locally

The girls from Jericho also learned that practical questions about local policies and procedures can be more sensibly resolved locally, where conditions are known and possible effects can be easily predicted, than in the concrete theory-factories of Washington, D.C., where it is standard practice to cast one mold into which every school district in the land must be stuffable.

But that is not the plan of the federal bureaucracy. Although Misses Lichtman and Friedman were supported by the Jericho school district's Title IX coordinator, Louis Fusaro, on the ground that the three-season sports plan for girls may actually have violated the spirit of Title IX, he conceded defeat (according to *Newsday*):

". . . the vote [of the superintendents, to reduce girls' sports seasons from four to three] had been taken 'under duress' because the civil rights office had threatened to take away federal money if the group [of Long Island school districts] did not comply."

Walther von der Vogelweide put it this way in his poem, *Millenium:* "Might is right, and justice there is none."

Uncle Sam: Fashion Arbiter

On November 19, 1979, the federal government announced that it would "enforce provisions against sex discrimination that prohibit schools from setting different dress codes for males and females." The announcement was made with a straight face by Patricia Roberts Harris, Secretary of Health, Education and Welfare in the Carter Administration, overturning the ruling of her predecessor, Joseph A. Califano, Jr., who would have stripped the U.S. government of any authority to review and decide complaints about dress codes under Title IX. Secretary Califano may have had some trouble swallowing the notion that because boys don't have to wear bras to school, girls need not wear them either, or (again) he may have read the law which prevents federal administrators from exercising "any direction, supervision or control" over the operations of schools. In any case, his views no longer counted.

In a reverse twist so unusual that it inspired a "man-bites-dog" story by the Associated Press, the Thorndike (Maine) board of education ruled in 1979 that James Bean, the only male member of the school's varsity field hockey team, must wear the standard team uniform, a skirt or kilt; had Bean been allowed to wear male attire, the girls could have worn it, too. How did he get on the team? Although Thorndike's eligibility rules barred seniors as first-year varsity players, Coach Margaret Prior allowed Bean to join because she "didn't want a hassle" about sex discrimination. Bean himself commented sensibly: "What I wear isn't important. I just want to be left alone and play hockey." The Associated Press does not tell us whether Bean was permitted to wear a protective supporter.

So Uncle Sam became the fashion arbiter of our educational system, dictating what will and won't be worn by whom in the schools. And educators, fearful of losing their federal aid, meekly accepted U.S. decrees—while the Congress, having legislated against this type of intrusion into a field reserved to the states and local governments, turned its eyes elsewhere.

Ferndale, Michigan: One of a Kind

The chilling effectiveness of federal dollar power as a weapon for enforcing unchallenged compliance with U.S. orders by states, localities, and institutions was brought home by Gene I. Maeroff in a *New York Times* story dated March 4, 1980.

According to Maeroff's report, more than a quarter-century after *Brown* and eight years after Title IX, only one—*one*—school system in the entire country had resisted federal pressure long enough and with sufficient determination to have a fund-termination order now in effect against it. Everyone else who had been fingered by the feds had capitulated or made a deal; no new orders had been issued since 1972, when the Ferndale, Michigan, system (about which Maeroff wrote) lost its

U.S. funds for failing to end what Washington considered "deliberate segregation" by race in the district's schools.

Ferndale, just north of Detroit, had 5,368 students in 1980, of whom 11.1 percent were black. Maeroff comments: "All of the youngsters, black and white, attend the same high school, and the two junior high schools have about the same number of blacks. Each of the eight elementary schools has some blacks, and the school district's faculty is 16 percent black. . . . In contrast, four of the five elementary schools, which are organized on a neighborhood basis, remain less than 5 percent black, despite an open-enrollment program *allowing black families to select any elementary school.*" Federal ire fixed upon the Ulysses S. Grant School in the neighborhood where most blacks live; Grant had been virtually all black from its opening in 1926 until 1974 (after the fund cutoff) when efforts were made to integrate it by offering an informal, open-classroom program in addition to traditional studies. Grant now has almost as many whites as blacks, but the feds are still unhappy because "all 184 students in the traditional program are black; 184 of the 199 in the open-classroom program are white." Washington will not be satisfied until the entire system (already integrated except at the elementary level) has an 11.1 percent black student body in every building, even if that can only be accomplished by busing around younger pupils, mainly blacks, *despite their parents' obvious wish to have them move through the system in the way they had always moved.*

Ferndale's situation simply illustrates once again the federal obsession with statistical mixing as an absolute requirement which ignores both the *bona fide* efforts of school authorities to integrate their systems and the wishes of parents both black and white to keep their kids in the schools where they feel a good education is already provided. I cite Ferndale to emphasize that it is the *only* respondent among many which (according to news accounts) has not knuckled under to we-are-cutting-off-your-federal-funds extortion. If only *one* among thousands of state and local governments is willing to accept the loss of federal funds by standing up to Washington's administrative decrees, the federal system is in serious trouble.

The Irony of Ferndale

There is a sad irony in the Ferndale problem. Desegregation is intended to provide equal educational opportunity for blacks—to give them a better shot at a quality education. At Ferndale, the school authorities have tried their best to desegregate their system without resorting to elementary-grade busing which is unacceptable to black and white families alike. Because the federal people are not satisfied with Ferndale's solution, they have withheld U.S. dollar assistance since 1972, at the rate of $400,000 per year. And whose education is hurt most by that action? That of Ferndale's *black children.*

As Maeroff points out, the withheld federal money was and is intended for remedial education for disadvantaged students. "Much of that money," he adds, "would have been spent on the black youngsters said to have been the victims of discrimination." Improvement of the *quality of education* available to Ferndale's black pupils has been sacrificed to force a racial mix unrelated to the question of educational excellence. If this is federal caring imposed upon local intransigence, our educational system is better off without it.

There is a further irony at Ferndale. In "an apparent contradiction that neither side can explain fully," the U.S. government still gives the Ferndale district $535,000 per year to run adult education, Head Start, and job-training programs, according to Maeroff's account. While there are no U.S. dollars to help Ferndale's disadvantaged youngsters in their regular studies, there is federal money available for pre- and postschool-age and nonbasic extension programs. Ferndale's people had trouble making sense out of this anomaly, and so do I.

Some Other Federal Fantasies

Elsewhere I alluded to a 1970 Syracuse University finding that there is less disruption in predominantly black secondary schools when the faculty is mainly black as well. Disruption being defined as an interruption of the educational process, the cause of educational quality would seem well served if black teachers were encouraged (or at least permitted) to serve in black neighborhood and community schools.

But that isn't the way the feds want things to work. They are less concerned with quality than with racial mixing. You and I might suggest that teachers be assigned to schools where they *want* to teach, or where they seem *best suited* and *most needed.* But not the federal authorities. In an action later supported by the U.S. Supreme Court, the U.S. Department of Health, Education and Welfare withheld $3.5 million in special school aid from the New York City system because "black teachers were assigned in disproportionately high numbers to schools with largely black enrollments and in low numbers to mostly white schools," according to a *New York Times* account in 1979.

This federal action was not based upon any charge that New York City discriminated against minority teachers in its hiring and promotion practices; indeed, the city schools had come under criticism for bypassing their own Board of Examiners' teacher-testing requirements by hiring numbers of untested teachers on an emergency basis, presumably to meet the need for more minority faculty. The federal flap involved *assignments,* yet a system had been devised whereby minority teachers drew their school assignments from one box (containing predominantly white school names) while others drew theirs from a second box, in which the predominantly minority school names had been placed. This "federal roulette" touched off such a public uproar that another arrangement was substituted, in the hope that it was proof against federal charges of discrimination: all teachers picked their assignments at random from one box.

But the federal authorities insisted upon racial mixing of the faculty as well as the student bodies of New York's schools. The city did its best to oblige, so that their U.S. aid would not continue to be withheld. And the courts? They differed over the question of whether the determining factor should be the *intent* of New York's school authorities (which certainly was not to discriminate) or the *impact* of their actions (which the federal people denounced as discriminatory, whether by intention or not). To the majority, impact seemed sufficient; to the three-Justice minority, the concept of discrimination demanded proof of intent, which Congress had mandated in another part of the law.

But throughout all this, nobody—at least, nobody whose thoughts I have seen recorded—asked the one question which to me should be paramount. *In assigning teachers to schools, what factors are most important in assuring high-quality education for the children?* Must the statistical mixing of races be the one-and-only, overriding determinant? Must we ignore considerations of a teacher's training, qualifications, experience, past record, and personal choice? Is role-modeling, ability to control behavior, and the understanding which comes of a common ethnic heritage of no value in the teacher-student relationship?

In the same context, U.S. authorities in 1978 charged New York City with "segregation by classroom," targeting certain "racially isolated" classes for elimination. City Chancellor Irving Anker replied that 45 percent of the classes were bilingual sessions ordered in 1974 by a federal court to help non- and limited-English-speaking youngsters to learn English, while another 41 percent were special classes grouped by ability for remedial or honors work. The original complaint had alleged that such ability-grouping was intended to perpetuate racial segregation, but someone looked up the law (Title VI of the Civil Rights Act of 1964), which permits the practice if there are both remedial and honors classes.

To their credit, the feds backed off and okayed the city's program, but the point is that they saw nothing amiss about reaching right into the classroom and becoming involved in the day-to-day administration of the local schools, despite the clear rule of Congress that they were *not* to do so. Federal zealots had become obsessed with the idea that racial integration "by the numbers" was more important than questions of educational excellence. They may have the last word (and, with court support, they often do), *but they are wrong.* My worry is that too many generations of youngsters will have been condemned to inferior education before these people see the light or retire to other fields of endeavor.

Parlez-Vous H'mong?

No, that's not a typographical error. If you happen to be a young Laotian refugee in the Chicago school system, and if you understand only the H'mong mountain language, Chicago must find and pay someone who speaks both English and H'mong to help you master your class work. So said the Department of Education in an October 1980 set of proposed regulations governing bilingual education in the states. In Chicago, the new rules would mean "creating questionnaires and training interviewers in 139 languages just to find out which youngsters are entitled to such instruction," according to a *New York Times* dispatch. Every district in the nation would have to instruct children in their native languages, providing teachers and facilities, until the kids had learned English well enough to join regular school sessions. The English as a second language (ESL) plan, whereby non-English-speakers studied in regular classes while getting intensive schooling in English every day, would become illegal under the new federal rules, which have since been modified drastically by the Reagan administration.

Regent Emlyn I. Griffith of Rome, New York, who was serving at the time as President of the National Association of State Boards of Education (NASBE), pointed out that the U.S. proposal "seeks to tell schools everywhere how and what they must teach students." Griffith added, "We can scarcely imagine a more serious threat to our diverse educational system."

The Colleges Too: Hillsdale and Grove City

The public schools were not the only educational institutions to feel the heavy hand of the federal bureaucracy.

In 1975, the U.S. Department of Health, Education and Welfare promulgated its Title IX regulations against sex discrimination; every college receiving federal funds would have to hire without regard to race, creed, color, or sex.

Along with all other colleges and universities, little Hillsdale College in Michigan (with about a thousand students and seventy instructors in 1980) was advised that it had ninety days to comply with the law. Hillsdale didn't need government threats; founded in 1844, it had been graduating blacks and women since before the Civil War. So the administration politely informed the Department that it would not comply with the paperwork dumped upon it. Okay, responded the feds, comply, or you lose your federal aid money. Hillsdale had an answer to that, too: We do not receive any federal aid.

But the ingenuity of the Washington power-wielders was not yet exhausted. As in the case of every college, some of Hillsdale's *students* received U.S. aid, such as veterans' benefits. HEW ruled that if Hillsdale continued to refuse formal compliance with Title IX (although it was not charged with violation of IX), its federally assisted students would lose their U.S. aid. Hillsdale considered this dodge unfair to its students and brought a suit against HEW; at this writing, it has not been finally resolved.

In 1977, a 101-year-old western Pennsylvania institution, Presbyterian-oriented Grove City College (with 2,186 students and ninety-five teachers in 1980) was also given the word about Title IX. Like Hillsdale, Grove City had never discriminated against women or blacks; not only did it not accept federal funds, but it regularly rejected *state* financial assistance. President Charles S. MacKenzie, supported by his trustees, followed Hillsdale's lead in refusing to sign HEW's "assurance of compliance." Writing in the *Reader's Digest* (August 1980), William J. Miller reports that: ". . . MacKenzie received a series of increasingly stern phone calls from HEW officials in Washington. 'The callers kept telling me that we had better sign, that they had ways of making us sign,' [said] MacKenzie. 'When I asked the callers to put their statements—some of which were threatening to the point of intimidation—in writing, all refused.' "

When Grove City remained adamant, HEW's muscle-persons took the same tack they had taken with Hillsdale: punish the students: About seven hundred (one-third) of Grove City's undergraduates were receiving guaranteed student loans, Basic Educational Opportunity Grants (BEOGs) or other aid. That aid would be withdrawn.

Many citizens are unaware that U.S. departments employ *their own* administrative law courts to rule on disputes, including those in which the department itself may be a party. Grove City was hauled before one of these and lost, when the administrative judge ruled that the grants to students indirectly aided the college, and that such funds could therefore be denied to the students by the judge's boss, the Secretary of HEW. In fairness, it should be added that the administrative judge found that: (1) Grove City had not failed in any way to comply with the antidiscrimination provisions of the law, but merely with the demand that the HEW form be signed; (2) that this "refusal is obviously a matter of conscience and belief," and (3) that he had no power to find *any* HEW regulation illegal, because ". . . there is very clearly given to the director [of HEW's Office of Civil Rights] a total and unbridled discretion to require any certificate of compliance that he may desire, reasonable or unreasonable. There are no guidelines."

Grove City then took its case to the federal courts, where U.S. District Court Judge Paul A. Simmons ruled that Grove City did *not* have to sign the HEW form, that HEW could *not* cut off student loans because "the law creating them specifically exempts them from such action," and that (although BEOGs did amount to U.S. aid to the college) HEW could not deny them to students unless it could prove the college guilty of discrimination. This decision has mixed effects: while it holds that aid for which the individual qualifies and which is paid to him or her becomes aid to a college when it is paid over for tuition, room, or board, an actual finding of lawbreaking must be made to warrant imposition of such penalties. It does, however, point up the problem—poorly drafted legislation which extends extraordinary powers to administrative officials.

Who Runs Higher Education?

The increasing influence of the federal government in higher education was analyzed by Senator Pat Moynihan in the December 1980 issue of *Harper's*:

"Federal influence has gone from encouraging the development of curricula, which was the main theme of the National Defense Education Act, to much more pervasive setting of standards as to student enrollment and faculty selection. . . .

"The federal government has acquired the power to shut down any university it chooses. The more important the university, the greater the power. And the greater the concentration of federal power in one place, the greater the danger."

Quoting David Riesman, Moynihan added:

". . . education is . . . vulnerable to attack because something done in one of the three thousand accredited institutions by somebody may offend somebody or get in the papers. . . . Education is best served by decentralization, not only in this huge and diverse country but also within the federal government and its many agencies."

Certainly the record of U.S. intervention in the internal workings of higher-education institutions is not reassuring to those who place a premium upon educational independence from political domination. Couple it with the sorry story of federal extortion tactics at the elementary-secondary level, and the pattern is clear enough to impart a severe case of the jitters to those who worry about the future of American freedom.

The Road to Bankruptcy

Given our overriding concern for the quality of education offered to our young people, we are not likely to be happy with the paperwork blizzard generated by federal bureaucratic requirements—a growing storm of forms and questionnaires with which schools and colleges must cope at considerable expense in time and in money which could have been spent on the teaching-learning process. The *Readers' Digest* reports, for example, that Grove City College "received a 50-page government request to count the number of students (by sex, race and major) who received degrees the previous year (including degrees the college doesn't even offer). Another wanted Grove City to measure the square footage of every room on campus."

Completion of required government paperwork at school and college expense has become so burdensome that the federal Advisory Panel of which I am a member asked (in 1981) that these costly procedures be reduced to a reasonable minimum.

But that's not all. A 1980 study for the Joint Economic Committee of Congress found that six federally mandated programs (clean water, unemployment coverage for state and local employees, free public education for all handicapped children, making mass transit accessible to the handicapped, bilingual education, and the Davis-Bacon minimum wage scales for federally subsidized projects) cost state and local governments an amount equal to their receipts from U.S. revenue-sharing for all purposes, which theoretically should be theirs to use as they choose. The mandates have wiped out that option, and now revenue-sharing itself seems on the way out. As the *New York Times* reported:

"Estimating the cost of complying with mandates is difficult, and just doing so would cost up to $800,000 in the first year, according to estimates by the Congressional Budget Office. But sponsors of [reform] legislation said that amount is dwarfed by the total waste involved in carrying out the current mandates.

" 'Because many grants come with regulatory strings attached, such assistance can end up, at least in raw dollars, costing more than it brings in,' Thomas Miller and Michael Fix of the Urban Institute wrote. . . ."

Meeting federal mandates would cost New York City $711 million in capital expenditures and $6.25 billion in operating expenses in the 1981–84 period, in the view of Mayor Edward Koch, who illustrated the effect by citing one area: in order to receive a particular federal grant for mass transit, the city would have to spend $1.3 billion to make subways accessible to the handicapped. At an estimated $38 per ride, the Mayor observed, it would be cheaper to provide the handicapped with taxicab fare.

Blindsided by the Treasury Department

While the public schools and colleges were struggling with administrative decrees imposed under threat of withholding U.S. aid, while independent colleges were getting their share of federal harassment by HEW's Office of Civil Rights—and while everyone was trying to cope with the rising tide of government forms and questionnaires—some private schools and colleges were hit unexpectedly by a new adversary, the U.S. Treasury Department. Theirs was a new threat: removal of tax-exempt status.

Columnist James J. Kilpatrick, an articulate foe of the use of money power to gain federal domination over American institutions, cited in a 1981 article the case of Bob Jones University in Greenville, South Carolina. Bob Jones is a fundamentalist religious college of 6,300 students, about half of whom are preparing for the ministry or teaching positions in the mushrooming Christian schools.

A trial court found (and the Fourth U.S. Circuit Court of Appeals did not dispute) that at Bob Jones, "a primary fundamentalist conviction is that the Scriptures forbid interracial dating and marriage . . ." as a matter of genuine religious belief. But the Internal Revenue Service of the Treasury Department disagrees, taking the position that unless Bob Jones U. abolishes its doctrinal position against interracial marriage, it does not qualify as a tax-exempt religious institution under the tax code, a circumstance that would make Bob Jones U. liable for whopping back taxes and would dry up the college's sources of income through contributions. BJU does not accept government funds.

"Implicit in the government's position," said Kilpatrick, "is the government's power to abridge the freedom of religion. The Tax Code accords exemption and deductibility to organizations operated exclusively for 'religious, charitable, scientific, literary or educational purposes.' The IRS contends that the word 'charitable' applies to all the subject institutions; no institution is 'charitable' if its racial views violate public policy; the public policy of the government approves interracial marriage; therefore, Bob Jones is not charitable and does not qualify.

"That is incredible," Kilpatrick concluded. "The government is contending, in effect, that the First Amendment's guarantee of freedom of religion must yield to a bureaucratic determination of 'public policies.' "

Early in 1982, the Reagan Treasury and Justice departments announced that the tax-exempt status of Bob Jones and another fundamentalist institution would be restored, on the ground that administrative officials should not have the right to make such determinations on their own—an announcement that touched off a predictable firestorm from the liberal left. "Obscene," screamed Americans for Democratic Action; "Tax-Exempt Hate," howled the *New York Times.* "Nothing short of criminal," added the National Association for the Advancement of Colored People, and some black leaders darkly hinted that those who supported tax-exempt status for Bob Jones University would be forever branded "racists." The public outcry was so emphatic that President Reagan, correctly standing fast behind the principle that faceless bureaucrats should not be allowed to make decisions of this import on their own, nevertheless announced that he would ask Congress to remove tax-exempt status for any institution practicing "racial discrimination."

Meanwhile, the Bob Jones matter continues to move through the courts. By the time this book is published, the U.S. Supreme Court may have announced whether it will hear the university's appeal from the adverse decision of the circuit court, which sided with the IRS. But a question has been raised that is fundamental to our American system: In order to qualify for official treatment on an equal basis with other institutions of its kind, must a school or college accept all aspects of what stands at the moment for "public policy"? Must that be the case even if the particular public policy is incompatible with the religious beliefs of the organization operating the school or college?

Suppose the question were not racial discrimination. Suppose that during the 1960s and 1970s, when "public policy" was to fight an undeclared war against Communist North Vietnam, tax exemption had been denied to colleges that refused to support that war—colleges that, for example, threw out ROTC and declined to accept defense research contracts. Would the ADA and the *New York Times* have supported denial of tax-exempt status to those colleges? Certainly not; and they would have been right, although this example would have involved no questions of religious beliefs.

Governments sometimes pay for abortions for poor women, as a matter of public policy. But suppose that a hospital operated by a religious group that rejects abortion on moral grounds refuses to permit such surgery within its facilities? Should the hospital's tax-exempt status be lost because it will not go along with "public policy"? There must be many similar situations.

Educational and religious freedom from various forms of taxation has been public policy for years. Nobody argues that Bob Jones University does not serve these purposes; the college was targeted for penalties not for that reason but because racial discrimination, wherever it may be practiced, is anathema in today's scheme of things. And who is prepared to predict what positions, held by which colleges, will be anathema tomorrow?

Regardless of the particular policy in question, freedom is freedom. It would be hard to find any action more dangerous to our freedom than the use of governmental power to deny normal tax-exempt status to an institution that declines to concur in some facet of current "public policy." Such denial flies in the face of the very idea of a university as an arena in which competing and contradictory ideas have full freedom to contend with each other.

What we, with a few courageous exceptions, have failed to note is that the central issue here is not discrimination but *academic freedom.*

Some critics of the Reagan Administration's decision would have us believe that it confers some special privileges upon Bob Jones University. Not so. It simply would restore to BJU the exemptions and deductibility shared by all colleges and universities, of which BJU is undeniably one. In 1819, Chief Justice John Marshall opined that "the power to tax involves the power to destroy"; in a highly competitive field like higher education, loss of tax advantages available to competitors could be fatal. If the colleges and universities of these United States were not so damnably protective of their liberal image, and were more concerned about their survival as free institutions, they would be yelling like stuck pigs about what is happening to Bob Jones University, just as they should be (but aren't) yelling about the jailing of a University of Georgia professor in 1980 for refusal to reveal how he voted in a faculty decision about academic tenure. Ted Fiske of the *New York Times* has referred to the Georgia case as "another sign of the growing willingness of courts and Federal officials to involve themselves in matters of academic decision-making that were once considered beyond judges' expertise."

In his *Devotions,* written in 1623, John Donne said it all: "No man is an island, entire of itself . . . any man's death diminishes me, because I am involved in mankind; and therefore never send to know for whom the bell tolls; it tolls for thee."

I Hear the Bell

It is difficult to recall when I heard the first faint tolling of the bell that seemed to intone the impending demise of education's freedom from political domination. When I became a New York Regent in 1969, the colleges were in a state of open rebellion against government over Vietnam, civil rights, ecology, women's lib, and all sorts of perceived injustices. The higher-education community had never, to my knowledge, been more at loggerheads with Washington; indeed, President Richard Nixon, like President Lyndon Johnson before him, was unwelcome on almost every American campus other than those of the U.S. service academies. A government takeover of education? No way.

But I soon learned that while all this noisy confrontation was making headlines, other developments were taking place.

First, money. The Great Society buildup of U.S. funds for states, localities, and institutions, originated by Johnson with the Elementary and Secondary Education Act (ESEA) in 1965 and continued by Nixon, Ford, and Carter, made all of education, public and private, higher and elementary-secondary, more dependent upon federal largesse, more willing to accept whatever terms and conditions accompanied that largesse, and more hesitant to challenge the potential denial of that largesse in order to extort compliance with extra demands thrown in by the federal bureaucracy out of the blue, changing the rules after the U.S. commitment had been made.

Second, attitude. The great majority of American educators consider themselves liberals; I have commented on that condition elsewhere in this book. That being so, the established belief of our more left-leaning liberals that the national government can do almost any job better, more fairly, and more effectively than anyone else, public or private, meant that most educators were delighted to accept U.S. funds, with no misgivings and regardless of the strings attached, during the wine-and-roses glow of the Great Society years.

But things are different now. I sense hard second-thinking among educators about the impact and depth of federal involvement in education. This uneasiness may have begun on the fringes of the issue, expressed as resentment against excessive paperwork requirements or unhappiness about the cost (both in dollars and in independent judgment) of compliance with federal orders which accompany federal grants— especially when such costs eat away the grant funds. Sooner or later, however, the educational community will realize that some modus operandi must be found whereby the federal government can help states and localities without running the show.

There is a way. The louder the bell rang in my ears, the more thought I gave to the developing problem of federal encroachment and how to stop it without stifling the legitimate assistance which the United States can provide to its member components. And, best of all, others had heard the bell and had begun working on answers just as I had.

The Regents' Proposal to NASBE

After repeated warnings to the Congress that the federal government was overstepping its constitutional bounds and violating Congress's own legislative limitations against U.S. intervention into "the curriculum, program of instruction, administration or personnel of any educational institution," the New York State Board of Regents decided early in 1979 that a parallel line of attack might provoke some action. They therefore asked NASBE, of which New York is a member, to adopt among its national resolutions one which I had authored, proposing seven guidelines for federal aid-to-education legislation.

The Regents suggested:

(1) All laws should specify the Congress's intent that federal-aid funds *must* be used affirmatively to improve education, not negatively or punitively to enforce compliance with federal orders;

(2) All laws should continue specifically to prohibit federal control of education;

(3) All laws authorizing federal grants should be written as *contractual* arrangements, with states willing and able to qualify under their terms being entitled to aid funds as a *contractual right,* regardless of extraneous matters not directly pertinent to the purpose of the laws;

(4) All laws should exclude from qualifying and performance requirements any considerations not directly relevant to the specific educational purpose of the laws;

(5) All laws should specifically prohibit the practice of withholding or threatening to withhold federal aid funds, for which a state or local agency has otherwise qualified, as an instrument to enforce compliance with any other federal order;

(6) All laws should specify that complaints against states or local agencies about noncompliance with any federal order (exclusive of the contractual requirements of the aid legislation itself) should be pursued *through the courts* for final determination; and

(7) The Congress should establish and maintain its own monitoring system whereby federal administrative compliance with the legislative mandates of the first six guidelines can be observed and enforced.

NASBE's response to our proposal was gratifying. For the first time in its twenty years' existence, the national organization representing virtually every state board of education stood up on its hind legs at its 1979 convention at Williamsburg, Virginia, and unanimously adopted Resolution 79-5-B:

"Although federal funding of state and local education is properly contingent upon compliance with the requirements of the authorizing legislation, the threat of or actual withholding of federal funding should not be used to force compliance with other, unrelated programs because it creates discontinuity and instability in all educational planning."

While NASBE's choice of a reason (discontinuity and instability in planning) was less important to me than the creeping takeover of education by the federal government, it was still a perfectly valid reason and one familiar enough to be acceptable to all the states' representatives.

There have been other encouraging signs that the states have had enough of federal dictation; the New York State School Boards Association reported in March 1981 that "California schools will forfeit $79 million in federal funds rather than submit 'compliance plans' required by the U.S. Department of Education [to enforce federal prohibition against] segregating handicapped children from other children," a practice which still is hotly debated in educational circles.

The "Black Boycott" of Federal Aid

Meanwhile, in April 1979, I had added some fuel to the mounting fire of discontent about federal encroachment by announcing to the Regents that I would no longer vote for any measure involving acceptance of U.S. funds by New York State. I expressed the point of the "Black Boycott" in these words:

"I need not reiterate my deep conviction that increasing U.S. intervention into education's policy-making, governance, and daily operations, using the threat of withholding U.S. aid funds to force compliance with federal orders, will eventually lead to *federal control of education.*

"Until such time as the Congress puts an end to the practice of federal extortion, I shall henceforth *abstain* from voting on any motion involving requests for or acceptance of U.S. funds. I cannot vote *against* federal funding, because it so often serves useful and necessary purposes—but I cannot conscientiously vote *for* it, knowing that greater state and local reliance upon U.S. dollars will increase federal authority over education."

I deliberately made this declaration part of the Chancellor's annual "State of the Regents" message read at our public meeting; reaction from the press and the educational community provided me with what one of my favorite Presidents, Theodore Roosevelt, would have called "a bully pulpit"—which I used to good advantage.

One Congressional Reaction

My objective, of course, was to catch the ear of the Congress. It was and is the Congress—and only the Congress—which has power to plug the loopholes whereby unelected federal bureaucrats use our tax money to extort our compliance with their own notions of how education should be governed and conducted. I therefore distributed both my "Black Boycott" pledge and my seven-point legislative proposal to members of the New York Congressional delegation.

In an extension of remarks on May 16, 1979, Representative Jack F. Kemp, of Hamburg, New York, read my proposal into the *Congressional Record,* prefacing it (on page E2373) with these comments:

"Mr. Speaker, our country is witnessing greater and greater intrusion by the Federal Government into our daily lives. With increasing regularity we are experiencing the relentless narrowing of the areas in which we are still master of our own actions and decisions.

"In the field of education, this is particularly alarming. The Constitution has been stretched by the Federal Government in numerous instances to assume authority over education which the Constitution clearly prohibited.

"I recently received a letter from an eminent educator, Chancellor Theodore M. Black, of the board of regents of the State of New York, in which he states his determination 'to abstain from voting at Regents' meetings on any motion to seek or accept Federal aid funds until the Congress acts to monitor enforcement of the Constitution and its own laws in order to curb the use of threats to withhold such funds as levers to force compliance with administrative orders. . . .'

"As Dr. Black states, 'Increasing federal intervention into the operations of educational institutions could eventually lead to the nationalization of America's schools and colleges.' I urge my colleagues to give serious consideration to the erudite assessment and suggestions he has made. What a pleasure to see this type of leadership exhibited at a time when so few are willing to be heard, much less stand up."

As recounted earlier in these pages, the ugly specter of nationalized education also drew the ire of New York's Senator Moynihan in his *Harper's* article entitled: "State versus Academe: How the Government Nationalized American Universities." He concluded: "If the private institutions of America are to be preserved, we are going to have to learn to defend them."

The most effective way for Americans to prevent U.S. government preemption of education, public and private, state and local, elementary/secondary and higher/professional, is for Congress to enact and monitor legislation which *forbids* federal intrusion.

A New Bell Tolls — on a Brighter Note

When President Ronald Reagan took office in 1981, he named Terrel H. Bell of Utah to be Secretary of Education—the top job in a department which Republican candidate Reagan in 1980 had vowed to dismantle.

Secretary Bell, an undauntable man who served as a U.S. Marine, has a long record of professionalism in education. He taught high-school chemistry and physics and was a superintendent of schools in his native

Idaho; later he became U.S. Commissioner of Education (1974–76), after which he returned west to take the job of Education Commissioner in Utah, where he was serving when tapped for the Reagan cabinet. He took with him to Washington some ideas which are as fresh as they are fundamental, the proof of their validity being the horror that they have struck among the surviving Jacobins of the federal educational bureaucracy which has imposed its own notions upon the country's schools and colleges for too long.

On July 8, 1981, Secretary Bell addressed the national convention of the American Federation of Teachers, at Denver, Colorado. His speech was short and to the point. Among his thoughts are these, which are also mine—and perhaps yours as well:

"What we're talking about here is less governmental interference for more people—local and state control. Strengthening State and local control is what this administration is about. . . . We think, and rightly, I believe, that you and your fellow citizens know your problems and needs a heck of a lot better than a bureaucrat, sitting in Washington away from your locale, what's best for you and your city or state.

"As we have created more and more Federal programs in education, each has come with its own funding authority. . . . Each has required school officials to comply with its own planning, monitoring and reporting procedures and all of the other attendant paperwork.

"Education must be given the flexibility to provide better services to students. We can no longer afford the waste of dollars and human resources on recordkeeping and excessive rules and regulations—requirements that deprive us of valuable time we could be spending on more pressing educational matters.

"Under a conservative philosophy, we will not be trying to tell you how to teach, nor will we engage in radical stretching of the law—as has happened all too frequently in the past. . . . There is nothing in our American laws or the Constitution which anoints the Department of Education with the power of 'National School Teacher,' 'National School Superintendent' or 'National School Board.' *The rules that Congress and the courts have mandated for education are meant for orderly guidance in the use of the taxpayers' money. They were not made for the enhancement of Federal power.*" [Italics supplied.]

Secretary Bell cited examples of regulations which have been scrapped by his orders:

The proposed bilingual education rules (discussed elsewhere in this book) "were not only inflexible, burdensome and incredibly costly; they went so far that they actually prescribed the teaching method. . . . If I had allowed the prescription of how to teach in this area, the next step would be telling you how to teach math and reading . . . as a teacher in America, you have your own teaching methods; you are not a puppet to be controlled by Federal strings formed by the over-stretching of the law.

"Washington is not going to tell your students how to dress or how to wear their hair. The Department of Education will not press for dress code regulations under a tortured interpretation of the meaning of Title IX. . . . Recently, I put a stop to consideration of regulations that would have impacted on school recordkeeping in regard to discipline. [That proposal is noted in Chapter 3 on discipline.] These records would have been used to determine whether or not discipline had been applied in a discriminatory way in the schools. I think it ridiculous to become involved in picky fights over how many females versus males got spanked in a particular school.

"You can have white commencement gowns for the girls in your schools and blue for the boys. You can have a separate boys' glee club and a girls' glee club. Your school can even sponsor a banquet for mothers and daughters or a fathers and sons outing. You can do any of these things and the Feds in this Administration will not come after you for violation of Title IX. It is absurd to even think that such matters should be a serious concern, but Federal rules in the past have been stretched that far."

And, the Secretary added, "You will not see us leading the parade into the Federal courtroom to press for busing across town to attain racial balance. At the very least, you can bet that we won't be monitoring and preaching for new reforms . . . and we won't be meddling in new social schemes to make people more equal and less distinguished and different. If the judge orders it—then we must carry out our duties. But we will not be taking the initiative. . . . We will not be constantly on your backs and looking over your shoulder."

Why have the American people, through the Reagan Administration, finally turned their backs upon the liberal consensus which for two decades and under Presidents of both parties governed the federal approach to education?

Checker Finn, writing in *Change* (September 1981), assigns a number of reasons, the first of which is the undeniable fact that after twenty years of growing federal influence, "our schools and colleges are snarled in red tape *and their educational performance is deteriorating.*" Further, Finn adds, the position of President Reagan and Secretary Bell

". . . has to do with the perception that a government program may do more harm than good; that a regulation may stifle creativity and autonomy on the part of those regulated, even as it eases some other problem; that federal funds produce federal junkies—institutions and individuals that cannot survive without ever larger injections of the resources they have become habituated to; that being told what to do and how to behave brings another, subtler form of dependency in the reluctance of institutions and their leaders to make difficult decisions for themselves; that entanglement with government means entanglement with politics, the inevitable result being politicization of the institutions so entangled; that the evenhandedness and 'public' values necessarily embodied in federal agencies cannot but squeeze, level and homogenize the clients of those agencies, thereby eroding the idiosyncrasies, singular value structures, and qualitative differences that made them worthy and special institutions in the first place."

Finn concludes, as do I, that "the issue, of course, is the erosion of excellence in American education and the need to improve the quality of teaching and learning from first grade through graduate school."

The War Isn't Over

It would be greatly reassuring to think that, with Secretary Bell in charge, all will be right with the educational world. He is, in my view, the right man in the right place at the right time—a new and effective champion of individual freedom and the Constitution.

But as Presidents come, so they go, taking with them their philosophies and their cabinet members. Secretary Bell is not a lifetime appointee, as are the hundreds of U.S. judges appointed by a previous President who allowed his administration to be misused, in the ways we have cataloged here, by an army of unelected professional bureaucrats devoted to the aggrandizement of federal authority by every means possible—bureaucrats who may be temporarily powerless or jobless at this writing but who are still around, awaiting another chance to run the government.

And, as Secretary Bell reminded us, the judges are still in charge. Regardless of a cabinet member's own philosophy or his President's policies, court orders must be obeyed.

Our course, I think, is clear.

Abuses that occurred once can occur again, unless we take appropriate steps to prevent their recurrence.

The Congress is the key. The executive branch, in applying and enforcing laws enacted by Congress, can do only what Congress has authorized and within the limitations specified in the law. Even the judiciary's decisions are (or should be) governed to an extent by what Congress intended to say and did say in writing a piece of legislation.

And the Congress has a clear right to monitor the administration's performance.

While it may not be the last word in security against a repetition of the abuse of federal power to which we have been subjected in recent years, the seven-point set of guidelines I proposed to the Congress in 1979 for the drafting of U.S. aid-to-education legislation is at least a good start. Secretary Bell's refreshing attitude should not lull our lawmakers into thinking that nothing now need be done. On the contrary, this is the time for the Congress to protect the integrity of its own policies and laws *for the future* against misinterpretation and misapplication by administrators of any political stripe.

The juggernaut of federal aggrandizement which, if allowed to proceed, could have crushed the whole federal system conceived and created by the Constitution, seems to have been stopped. It is up to the Congress to see that it does not start again.

Summing Up

I believe that federal administrators, using popular causes as a cover, have unconstitutionally and often illegally invaded the prerogatives, rights, and responsibilities of the states and the people with respect to the governance and operation of our educational institutions.

I believe that federal authorities, against the expressed will of the Congress, have used the threat of withholding U.S. aid funds as a lever to extort compliance with administrative decrees without risking court challenge.

I believe that federal invasion of the rights reserved to the states and their people in the field of education has been largely motivated by questions of the perceived rights of various special classes within our population, not by considerations of improving the overall quality of education, and I further believe that educational excellence has not been well served by such federal intrusion.

I believe that the Congress has been guilty of imprecise draftsmanship and omission of monitoring provisions from its aid-to-education legislation, and that these defects have enabled administrators to impose their own views upon schools and colleges by threatening to withhold U.S. funds or by other devices, including threats to withdraw tax-exempt status and deductibility of contributions.

I believe that the Congress can correct the situation by adopting appropriate legislative language assuring that U.S. aid will be granted on a *contractual* basis between consenting coequal parties, not subject to withholding because of some extraneous provision unrelated to the specific terms of the contract, and I further believe that Congress should set up a monitor to see that this procedure is observed.

I believe that the attitude expressed by Secretary of Education Terrel Bell, pledging to end federal intrusion into the governance and day-to-day workings of schools and colleges, is wise and salutary, but I also believe that *permanent* safeguards are needed to prevent a renewal of federal encroachment in the future, and that these safeguards should be set in place by the Congress without delay.

I believe that if such corrective measures are taken, the danger of nationalized American education will diminish and the freedom of our schools and colleges to pursue their quest for educational excellence will be restored and enhanced.

10.

Teaching and Testing

The Two Indispensable Elements of Good Education

SOCIETY's heaviest responsibility is borne by educators. We have entrusted them, as partners, with the monumental task of building America's future by molding today's children into the citizens of tomorrow. If there is any single occupational group which deserves the title of America's MIPs (most important people), it is those who are charged with the education of our younger generation.

They should be treated accordingly.

And they should act accordingly.

We haven't always been fair to our teachers. While we have acknowledged their importance and instructed our children (until recently, at least) to obey them, we have not (again, until recently) paid them well. Outside of their own academic circles, they have not been extended the prestige given to, say, doctors, lawyers, bankers, and business leaders. While we have afforded special protection for their jobs in terms of tenure rules, and have established retirement funds for them, we have not been able to shield them from negative economic, fiscal, and demographic developments which impact upon education as a whole and especially upon their individual careers. What job security they have is fine, but only as long as their jobs are there.

As a consequence of their natural desire to better their lot—a distinctly American drive which has enabled this country to become as strong as it is—teachers have followed the example of others by banding together in associations, which in turn have become parts of teachers' unions, under the umbrella leadership of the independent National Education Association and the American Federation of Teachers, an AFL-CIO affiliate. To the extent that the unionization of teaching has made the teacher's life more rewarding and more secure, it has been good for education, drawing into the field many who might otherwise not have cared or dared to enter. In other ways, unionization has had less happy results which will be discussed later in this chapter. But my personal impression is that unionization has been and is a net plus for education.

One caveat, however: Even the advantages of unionization have not produced enough able, qualified candidates for teaching jobs. This troublesome development deserves to be examined.

They're Not Exactly Beating Down the Doors

Fred M. Hechinger of the *New York Times,* in June 1981, cited comments by J. Myron Atkin, Dean of Education at Stanford University, and Lawrence A. Cremin, President of Teachers College at Columbia University, on the "decline of quality in teacher training"—which help to explain why the pool of new teachers is so shallow. Atkin suggests several reasons why qualified graduates now turn away from teaching:

Education was once one of the few professions open to talented women; now, a wide range of careers competes for them. Teaching still ranks near the bottom among careers requiring college degrees, both in starting salaries and opportunities for advancement. Declining enrollments and economic austerity weaken job security for teachers. Because their duties remain so constant, teachers become bored (here I differ with Dr. Atkin; for the teachers I knew and admired, each new class was a new challenge). The brightest students are discouraged from taking jobs below the college level. Teacher-training schools are too easy; they do not offer stimulation for the more able students.

To these turnoffs, I add a few of my own.

Earlier I focused attention upon today's teachers' problems in maintaining discipline. Too much milksoppery in court decisions involving disruption, too much kowtowing to "students' rights" (except the fundamental right of every student to an uninterrupted education), too much administrative unwillingness to apply discipline "in loco parentis" and too much student disinterest in being educated—all these often combine to make the classroom a hell for the teacher. There was a time when elderly Miss Grimshaw could tongue-lash an exuberant football player and make it stick, but no more. Both teacher and student know that Miss Grimshaw has no backup, no authority. So she and other older teachers shrug their shoulders, take their pensions, and leave as quickly as they can, while their potential replacements decide they want no part of life in the new jungles we have grown for them.

This crisis in teaching is made worse by the current tendency of local bleeding-hearts and doting mommies and daddies to descend at the drop of a ruler upon the classroom teacher who has dared to wave a finger at obstreperous little Cathcart. Where once parents would have given the school a free hand to keep him in line and keep him studying, too many of them now demand discipline *of the teacher,* not Cathcart. What is worse, some gutless administrators do not stand up for their teaching staffs in such confrontations. Some of these will not act because they know they will not be supported by their equally timid school boards. My observation, however, is that the better administrators will back their staff right down the line—and local pressure be damned.

Does Togetherness Make Good Education?

We have also touched briefly upon another development which can cause serious daily problems for the teacher: the mandated priority of *social* objectives over tested educational principles.

Commissioner Joe Nyquist was fond of saying that the essential purpose of education is to help each child to become all that he or she is capable of being. I agree, and I think that most teachers would agree. But that isn't the principle upon which schools and teachers are allowed to operate today. It has been scrapped in favor of *heterogeneity:* the theory, jointly imposed by educational-bureaucratic elites and activist judges, that the most important element of schooling is to expose each child to the greatest possible variety of other children. By so doing, we further brotherhood, peace, and the mutual-assistance spirit of the Little Red Schoolhouse, or so the rationale goes.

In practical terms, however, the teacher finds herself or himself having to cope with a classroom populated with gifted children capable of advanced work, average youngsters eager to move through the system at the expected pace, and slow learners whose need for special attention is obvious. All these children are entitled to the teacher's simultaneous ministrations for the entire school day—an impossible assignment. The gifted will be bored most of the time; the underachievers won't know what's going on, and the average kids may—*may*—move along, albeit at a slower pace than they can and should maintain. Throw in the disciplinary problem-children who are kept in or returned to the classroom under present policies, add the newly acquired "mainstreamed" handicapped pupils, some of whose handicaps involve disruptive behavior and most of whom need and deserve extra attention from special-education teachers who may not be available, and you have some idea of what today's public-school teacher faces as a matter of daily routine.

Each successive survey reports a rising rate of teacher burnout—loss of both the will and the capacity to cope, not only with the classroom situations I have described but also with an overload of paperwork, general decline of discipline in the entire school setting and, in some areas, the danger of vandalism or theft of one's property and possible physical harm to one's person. What surprises me is not that so many experienced but burned-out teachers are packing it in before their normal retirement time, or that so few qualified candidates are accepting teaching assignments, but that so many dedicated teachers continue to stay at their posts day after day, year after year.

Teaching Quality: On the Skids?

Dr. Cremin and Dean Atkin have expressed serious concern about the *quality* of today's teachers.

Atkin points out that "the aptitude of high school seniors choosing teacher training is at the bottom of entering college classes." Why should that be? He cites a number of reasons we have already cataloged, plus what he sees as a society whose optimism is dwindling and whose faith in education "seems to have been abandoned." Let me suggest this possibility: nobody knows better than a high-school senior how little respect and authority today's teachers enjoy, and how difficult their jobs have become. Is that senior likely to choose teaching as a career? Possibly (particularly if he or she doesn't qualify for much else), but today's bright young people are less inclined to follow in the footsteps of their own instructors than the students who looked up to the role-models of my youth and yours.

In any event, the facts are there: in recent Scholastic Aptitude Tests (scored from a bottom of 200 to a top of 800), verbal scores of high-school seniors intending to teach averaged 392, compared to 498 for those considering a career in the physical sciences and 505 for English majors. W. Timothy Weaver, Associate Professor of Education at Boston University, refers to those high-schoolers headed for teaching jobs as "academic weaklings"; his analysis shows them 34 points below average on verbal tests and 43 below average in math; they scored worse in English than did majors in any other field

And they don't do much better when they emerge from college courses in education. Why? Teacher-education curricula are not demanding enough. Dean Atkin places part of the blame on the fact that "the smattering of educational psychology, history and philosophy given to most prospective teachers does not prepare them for professional analysis of the schools' condition. Many get little more than 'helpful hints about effective classroom procedure' and scant intellectual preparation." He believes that "among the 1,200 teacher training institutions there are at most two dozen with programs bright students would find demanding."

Dr. Cremin points out that "serious shortages of good teachers in such fields as mathematics, computer science, telecommunications and the sciences make it imperative for salaries in those areas to be made competitive with those in other careers competing for the same talent." In other words, people trained in these specialties command good salaries in business and industry, but unless we pay equally well to attract capable *teachers* in these subjects, the schools will not be able to produce enough qualified specialists for business and industry—an argument which makes a lot of sense. The trouble is that the idea of differentiated salaries (science teachers getting more than humanities teachers with the same credentials) might cause the unions to balk, but, says Dr. Cremin, "Why not assume that the unions can act in statesmanlike fashion?" I am ready to make that assumption, but I will feel happier about it when I see some concrete examples.

Professor Weaver's contention that English is a weak spot in the preparation of new teachers is borne out on all sides. *Newsweek,* as far back as 1975, reported a finding by the National Council of Teachers of English that a candidate for a job teaching high-school English can go all the way through high school, college, and advanced-education degrees *without taking a single course in English composition.* It has been estimated that more than half of our secondary-school English teachers did not specialize in English at college. *Newsweek* reported that half the applicants for positions as English teachers in Montgomery County, Maryland, were unable to pass a basic test of grammar, punctuation, and spelling, and that the Stamford, Connecticut, Board of Education required all teachers to pass a test in written and spoken English, after having received "incomprehensible communications" from some English teachers in the Stamford system.

Citing a report in the *San Francisco Examiner,* William Randolph Hearst, Jr., quotes an editorial:

"Not too long ago the Lemon Grove School District in San Diego County [California] administered a literacy test, scaled at the eighth-grade level, to prospective teachers and teachers' aides. It must be assumed that the results proved a shocker to trustees and parents alike, for 55 percent of the aides and 35 percent of the prospective teachers failed one or more parts."

The district, says Mr. Hearst, "tried again by downgrading the tests to the seventh-grade level in reading and writing and to the sixth-grade level in arithmetic"; he reports:

"Given such gracious latitude, only 35 percent of the aides failed this time, as did 20 percent of the proud teachers, possessors of bachelor of arts degrees and owners of state teaching credentials."

Why do the schools of education seem to be failing us so badly? The answer takes two forms: (1) many of the schools are doing well, but (2) some are between a rock and a hard place. With the recent downgrading of teaching in the public mind, and the relatively low competitive opportunity for budding teachers in a declining market, it is very difficult to attract young people into education careers. Those who are so attracted seem less able to cope with academic subjects than those who are not, so the colleges reason that they will have to lower their standards for teacher education, or close down completely. That's tough to take, but one hopes that our fine system of teachers' colleges can be kept afloat until we manage to reestablish the dignity and authority of teaching in the United States.

No Wonder They Can't Write

Many of our children's difficulties with the mother tongue stem directly from inadequacies in teacher preparation—and our kids *do* have difficulties.

The late James Knapton, who resigned as supervisor of remedial English at Berkeley, California, when the university's essay requirement for admission was dropped, expressed his concern about the deficiencies in high-school English programs: "Diagraming sentences is out, no one teaches Shakespeare any more, and there are all those kids talking and rapping with each other, not knowing how to examine what they think in one discursive sentence." The essential requirement, said Knapton, was that English teachers must be taught how to write. "If *they* don't know," he asked, "how on earth are they supposed to teach the children?" Jacques Barzun added: "We have ceased to think with words. We have stopped teaching our children that the truth cannot be told apart from the right words."

What has happened? Mario Pei, the world-famous philologist, explained it this way: Much of education is controlled by "a school preaching that one form of language is as good as another; that at the age of five anyone who is not deaf or idiotic has gained a full mastery of his language; that we must not try to correct or improve language, but must leave it alone; that the only language activity worthy of the name is speech on the colloquial, slangy, even illiterate plane; that writing is a secondary, unimportant activity." In short, Pei contends that the acceptance of bad, incorrect English writing and composition is *deliberate* on the part of those in education who feel that insistence upon saying things the right way is too confining, too repressive of the child's freedom.

The result is a national disaster. Students reach college and graduate into life with inadequate training in English, *because they have not been properly taught in elementary and secondary schools*—and they have not been properly taught because their teachers either didn't know the rules of spelling, grammar, and composition, or didn't consider them important.

Examples? They are legion. All of our children attended (one still attends) what is considered one of the better suburban public-school systems in the New York metropolitan area, with a very high ratio of college-going graduates. Shortly after she was married, one of my daughters was still including "letus" on her supermarket shopping list. One of my sons won a junior-high biology prize with his report on the extended stay of several white rats in our cellar while he made experiments exposing them to hexachlorophene soap. His "A" paper spelled hexachlorophene perfectly, but spelled "making" m-a-k-e-i-n-g. After a decade of exposure to the mother tongue, he still had not been taught the basic rules of spelling.

I wince in recalling one stressful Regents' meeting with the Commissioner's Student Advisory Committee at Albany during the bad period of Vietnam. Asked her views on one of the topics of the day, one high-school senior managed to blurt out something like this:

"Well . . . like . . . I mean . . . well . . . you know . . . it's kind of . . . like . . . well . . . I mean . . . you know . . ."

We never really found out what it was she was trying to say, although we tried our best to help her say it.

That's Not My Job

Our local schools have developed the excellent practice of sending children's papers home for parents to review, sign, and return. In exercising this responsibility, however, I have noted with puzzlement that many of my youngsters' papers in science, social studies, or subjects other than English *are not corrected for mistakes in spelling, grammar, or composition.* The teacher seems to comment and grade only on the basis of the subject matter of the paper, not its execution.

In pondering the possible reasons for this omission, I have come up with one possible explanation: today's teachers are not *supposed* to deal with any subject other than that which they are hired to teach. That is far less hair-raising than another possible explanation: the teachers don't know English errors when they see them. I prefer to believe in the division-of-labor theory, which is explainable, if not justifiable, in the context of unionized teaching. The one bad effect, however, is that if nobody tells the youngster that he or she has spelled a word wrong or used incorrect grammar, *he or she will presume that it has been written correctly,* and will make exactly the same mistakes next time.

Given the prevalence of the "that's-not-my-job" syndrome, I will not try to suggest any perfect solution beyond making it plain to teachers that *any* error left uncorrected is a disservice to the child and a hindrance to educational achievement. Dedication is not dead among teachers (I hope and believe); this situation offers an opportunity to prove it.

A Vicious Circle

It is important to see the decline of written and spoken English in our schools and colleges for what it is—a vicious circle that has already begun and is all too apparent. Where spelling, grammar, and composition are inadequately taught in the elementary grades, performance in the secondary grades suffers. College English is the next victim, even with remediation of the failures of earlier instruction. We have already noted that those collegians who intend to teach seem to have lower-than-average English scores and these, becoming teachers, are inadequately prepared when they move into the schools and are responsible for instructing elementary pupils in the basics of the language and its use. The circle is completed, and begins again.

It must be broken. But where? Surely we can agree with Dr. Cremin and Dean Atkin that schools of education could stand some improvement. We can remedy the situation discovered by the National Council of Teachers of English by *requiring* would-be teachers (in particular teachers of English) to take and pass courses in English grammar and composition—and we can test every teacher before certification. We can rely less upon credentials and more upon *performance* in qualifying teachers for promotion, salary increases, and tenure, a movement which has been stirring in various states, including New York. We can do a better job of identifying youngsters with special problems in English by assigning more composition and essay work, with less reliance upon true-and-false and multiple-choice questions which are easy to grade but which do not reflect the degree of a student's mastery of the language. We can *guarantee* greater effort on the part of both teachers and students by making high-school (and college) diplomas contingent upon passage of appropriate tests of pupil proficiency in the use of English.

And we must do more than that.

It is all well and good to demand that teachers act to improve their students' performance in English (and indeed in every subject), but that is just one side of the coin. It is equally important that *we make it easier and simpler for teachers to do their jobs.* Somehow, and probably without thinking through the consequences of what we do and don't do, we have managed to make teaching more, not less, difficult.

How We Make It Tough on Teachers

In some cases, we do not pay teachers what they might earn in other jobs, which leaves us with those who could not qualify for the other jobs. Many parents no longer inculcate in their children a respect for teachers and teaching, nor do they extend to school administrators reasonable authority to deal with disciplinary infractions by their youngsters. We (and here "we" means courts, legislatures, and upper-echelon school nabobs) cater to student rights without stressing student responsibilities; classroom discipline declines so badly that education is disrupted, and even the kids themselves demand the return of authority.

In my view, we ask teachers to do too much that is unrelated to their students' affirmative school experience and academic improvement. True, teachers have always supervised extracurricular activities (sports clubs, the school newspaper and yearbook, dramatic and musical presentations, the marching band, hobby societies, and the like), which once was included in their salary but is now compensated specially. That is not what I call "too much"; it remains voluntary. James J. Kilpatrick reported in 1975 the comments of two teachers directly on the point:

A Greenville, South Carolina, teacher gave one example: ". . . the school has been mandated to provide adequate nutrition for all students. This means having the necessary facilities and serving a hot lunch which meets government specifications. At grade school level, this also means teacher time spent in supervision rather than in teaching or planning. This year, we are also mandated to serve a nutritious breakfast when students arrive by bus before they get to their classes."

And an upstate New York teacher complained: "I am supposed to be mother, father, minister and probation officer. On a single day recently, I had to cope with a 14-year-old girl who was pregnant and with another girl, also 14, who was still strung out on whatever drugs she had been taking the night before. I had to have a long talk with a boy out on probation for assault. We had a committee meeting on study halls. After the last period, the principal met with several senior teachers to discuss 'due process' procedures for suspension hearings."

A recently retired teacher in Akron, Ohio, who wrote disdainfully of the fads, innovations, restrictions, and extraneous demands loaded upon the school, summed it up: "Older teachers take the new ideas and teach in spite of them. Young teachers aren't aware of what is missing, mainly discipline, order and facts. You [Mr. Kilpatrick] are correct when you say that standards will steadily diminish. And there is no one more horrified than I."

That is the sort of thing I call "too much," and it *is* too much. Yet many schools cannot afford all the specialists who are trained to handle such matters as nutrition, drug abuse, psychological and disciplinary problems—so the teachers get the job. They shouldn't. They should be left free to do what they are expected to do and what they are trained, hired, and paid to do: *teach academic subjects.* Before you start screaming at your school board about heavy expenditures for nonteaching personnel, consider their dilemma: These extra academic responsibilities have been imposed upon the schools; they must be met, and they can be met only by (1) hiring qualified people to meet them, or (2) diverting regular teachers from their duties to meet them. To me, it is infinitely preferable to pay a bit more and let the teachers teach.

Traditional versus "Permissive" Schooling

James Kilpatrick reported as far back as 1977 on what he characterized as a "massive" study of teaching techniques: the Abt Associates' survey for the United States Office of Education, in which 9,200 third-graders were divided into two groups, one of which "received what might be termed an old-fashioned education; the other received what might be termed a new-fangled education." Kilpatrick cites the report:

"Pupils in the first group were taught by the book. They learned reading with heavy emphasis on phonics; they learned arithmetic by memorizing number combinations. They had homework every night, even in kindergarten. . . .

"Pupils in the second group were taught the fun way. Here the emphasis was on freedom of choice for both teachers and pupils. The teaching was 'informal' and 'innovative.' These were 'open classrooms.' Teachers experimented with a variety of techniques in reading and arithmetic.

"After three years, the Abt Associates analyzed standardized tests given to the 9,200 children. Would you believe the old-fashioned pupils did better? Of course they did better. The differences were striking. In nearly all of the 100 participating cities, children who were taught by the basics far outscored those who were taught the fun way. And this was true even though the per-pupil costs were much higher for the free-

and-easy group, who were showered with teaching aids, audio-visual gadgets and other devices intended to make the children feel better about school."

Kilpatrick's conclusion was briefly stated: "Perhaps the Abt findings will have a shock effect upon educators everywhere—but don't hold your breath."

Innovation Can Be Teaching's Own Worst Enemy

Innovation for the sake of innovation is the byword of the educational establishment. Students suffer through epidemics of miracle solutions, which are either solutions to problems that do not exist or solutions which create new problems.

How about the New Math? Suddenly parents were told that the traditional way of teaching mathematics wasn't good enough; now the kids would learn better and faster with a system based on bases: base 10, whatever. While I have always been willing to help my own children learn any subject, my ability to assist came to an abrupt end with the New Math. I see no evidence that our students are learning mathematics better or faster with this particular innovation.

How about spelling? One young lady from a local high school came to work as a file clerk in my office; her first day's record was so bad that her supervisor had to ask her whether she knew the alphabet. "Certainly," she replied, "I know all the letters—but their *order* is irrelevant, because it has nothing to do with the spelling of words." She might have had a point, but surely not as a file clerk or a telephone operator or in any other job where it is important to know that A precedes B. She is no longer with us.

In social studies (a combination of what once was history and civics and geography and anything else concerned with mankind—sorry, *hu*mankind—and its world), teachers' priorities show up in what their students seem to have learned best. In recent years, this has been a stress upon the environment, energy, women's and minority rights, the problems of American Indians, consumer protection, etc., each of which is pounded home hour after hour, while a fundamental knowledge of our governments and how they work, how we managed to become the strongest nation on earth, and the meaning of concepts and trends in American and world history are given short shrift.

My junior-high son was recently required to take several weeks of cooking instruction; he loved the course. I do not consider culinary training for boys to be in any way "sissified"; it can be very practical, if the student becomes a chef. But I do have reservations about cooking as a *required* course on two grounds: (1) although cooking is essential to any-one who is to become a homemaker, it is a specialized subject for anyone else; (2) time spent in required cooking classes might be better spent in shoring up the student's proficiencies in those basic academic subjects where he or she is weakest. Does this mean that I am anti women's lib? Certainly not. I have the same objections to required shop courses.

And what happened to penmanship? The Palmer method, with its gracious curves, has given way to the harsh imitation of typewriter let-ters called manuscript. Mine, as I mentioned earlier, is a virtually un-readable combination of both, as I was a guinea pig in a failed elemen-tary-school experiment with manuscript during the 1920s. The Palmer method, albeit old-fashioned, has one great virtue: you can read it.

Phonics versus Gimmicks

One of the longest internecine conflicts since the Hundred Years' War is that between the advocates of teaching reading by phonics (learning letters and their sounds singly and in combination, and applying that knowledge to vocabulary) and those who prefer the "look-say" method, in which entire words are read as they are seen.

Rudolf Flesch, whose *Why Johnny Can't Read* (1955) was followed in 1981 by his *Why Johnny Still Can't Read,* holds that the phonics system is by far the better way. Reviewing the second book in the *New York Times,* Joseph Featherstone, headmaster of the Commonwealth School, said: ". . . Mr. Flesch certainly has a point. Children need to learn to decode letters. Readers whose grip on phonics is shaky are less likely to stray from basal readers into real books. . . . An emphasis on specific skills is a good corrective to the aimlessness of so much education. . . . Test scores in elementary schools have in fact improved over the past 10 years—perhaps because teachers employ more phonics than they used to."

To Mr. Featherstone, the real problem is that children don't do much with the skills they have; in the later grades, he says, "Their prob-lem seems to be that they aren't learning to think and to read and write (in other words, to use their skills) *for a purpose."* In his view, motivation and direction are as important as methodology; as for the latter, how-ever, he sees much that is good in the phonics method of teaching read-ing.

Early in the 1970s, the New York State Regents teetered on the brink of a red-hot battle about the teaching of reading. Many of us felt that on the record phonics had proved to be the better way. The profes-sional staff of the State Education Department leaned toward look-say. With so many other controversial issues on the front burner, we decided (and I agreed to the decision) that *both* methods should be used; whichever seemed to help the individual child learn best should be the way he or she learned reading.

In retrospect, the Regents were both right and wrong: right about the superiority of phonics, wrong in allowing the teacher a choice between phonics and look-say. The teacher is going to use the method in which he or she believes, and try to make it work for the child. Teaching by *both* methods simultaneously will lead to nothing but confusion. The best way, then, is the simplest: use phonics. It worked for years, and it can work now.

I will spare you a lengthy summary of several decades of argument on the subject, observing simply that lots of youngsters learned to read very well under the discipline of phonics, and that reading scores began to decline *after* we began to substitute look-say or an indigestible succotash of theories for the teaching of reading by phonics.

There is an old adage: "Don't quarrel with success." For some reason, educators pay too little attention to that advice, preferring to jump upon each passing bandwagon festooned with the banners of the latest fad. If we can jump on, why can't we jump off just as easily? In the case of look-say, we should.

While we're on the subject of gimmicks, it is reassuring to note that the dollar crunch has begun to eliminate the Mickey Mouse electives that distracted secondary-school kids during the bad period (my son took "Flying," but dropped it; he preferred to stoke up at a local doughnut shop during open-campus free periods, another Vietnam-era mistake). Considering that excellence in regular subjects can result in portable credits that might help complete college requirements (his three biology credits did), concentration on those subjects is extremely important for college-bound youngsters.

Latin: A Tree Can't Grow Without Roots

No educator in his or her right mind would try to teach a student physics or chemistry unless that student was solidly grounded in mathematics. What teacher of American history would lead into the New Deal or World War II if his or her students had not already been taught about the origins of our country? Teaching doesn't work that way; you start with the fundamentals and work up to the refinements.

At least, that's what you do in every subject except the teaching of language skills: reading and writing in English.

English has three roots—Latin, Greek, and Anglo-Saxon. My father was required to study Greek at Fordham Prep in the first decade of this century. I never was offered a chance to take Greek; not enough students were interested. Anglo-Saxon? That has become a descriptive term for "dirty word," the kind that one finds scrawled on the boys'-room partitions.

And Latin? I took four years of it in public high school and one year in college, just about the same exposure my father had before me. Then something happened to Latin; it was stigmatized as a "dead language" and declared irrelevant because nobody spoke it anymore. Nobody even wrote it, except for Vatican scholars and assorted antiquarians. The demand for Latin classes sagged, and this basic root of our language seemed headed for the same fate as Greek.

The worst part of all this was that we played "The Emperor's New Clothes" with Latin. Nobody dared to speak out against the trendiness of the times. After all, if a child knows what a word means by looking at it and saying it, who cares where it came from? Many of us believed in Latin, but declined to defend it, while English comprehension and skills continued to decline in our schools and colleges.

Happily, Latin is on its way back. And who is bringing it back? The kids! Observing how well their Latin-trained contemporaries and older siblings do in English vocabulary tests for college entrance, high-schoolers are requesting Latin courses in sufficient numbers to warrant the reinstitution of such curricula. In the *New York Times,* in August 1981, Gene Maeroff reported:

"The decline in Latin enrollments in secondary schools seems to have bottomed out, and as many as 170,000 students may enroll in courses this year. . . . Latin enrollments in colleges also have apparently stopped falling, and the annual enrollment is holding at about 24,-000. . . . The new stress in Latin is, in part, a reaction to the relaxation of standards that critics of education have perceived at all levels. . . . Studying Latin has usually been thought to reinforce a student's foundation in English. That function now seems especially valuable to educators who are trying to restore respect for language."

Maeroff quotes Edward Phinney, Chairman of the Classics Department at the University of Massachusetts, as saying, "There is a turn-around, and Latin is not dying"; he cites a comment by Floyd L. Moreland, Classics Professor at the City University of New York: "The 1970's proved that the experiments of the 1960's really didn't work. Statistics show that those with a background in Latin do better on standardized tests."

Bravo! (Webster says the word originated with the Latin *barbarus,* meaning fierce.) If Latin is coming back, can Greek be far behind? I hope not: the teaching of the English language needs all the help we can give it.

Speaking of Language . . .

While we're on the subject of language, the teaching of *other* languages to American students is a national disgrace. Virtually every other civilized nation makes a point of seeing to it that their future citizens know at least one language other than their own—but not the United States.

U.S. Representative Paul Simon, in "The Tongue-Tied Americans," pointed out that "the United States continues to be the only country where you can graduate from college without having had one year of a foreign language prior to and during the university years." This is, in part, the fault of the campus revolts; Stanford University, for example, reinstituted in 1981 a language requirement dropped in 1969 "at the height of the student rebellion against all requirements," as Fred Hechinger reported in the *New York Times.* Even so, Hechinger says, fewer than 4 percent of current public-school graduates have had more than two years of a foreign language. Our government service is starving for qualified linguists; other sources reported, for example, that (1) only one officer in the U.S. Embassy in Kenya is required to speak Swahili; (2) when a Russian sought asylum in the American Embassy in Kabul, Afghanistan, nobody there spoke Russian; (3) no one in the U.S. Embassy in India speaks Hindi; (4) none of the more than seventy staffers of the European Division of the Office of the Secretary of Defense speaks either German or French.

Concluding that "one reason students rebelled against the language requirement in the first place was that the teaching often was so poor that the time spent on it seemed wasted," Hechinger stresses the need for fluent linguists in American government and industry, on the sound theory that we will be left behind in the competitive world of today if we cannot communicate with other nations and their people.

Should Teachers Be Treated as Professionals?

If teachers have had an unreasonably low status in our society because of the many problems that we have discussed, can that status and the self-respect and self-confidence which must be present to assure good teaching be acquired or reacquired if teachers are recognized as a *professional* group, rather than simply practitioners of a career?

Some way must be found to improve the public image and the self-image of teachers; lacking that, good recruits will be hard to find and early retirements will continue. The motivation to *be* a teacher, and (once a teacher) to do a professional job, may be at least in part contingent upon public acceptance of teaching *as a profession,* whose practitioners enjoy the same legal standing as doctors, lawyers, engineers, accountants, and other professionals. The professionalization of teaching is a subject of widespread current discussion in the United States.

As far as I am concerned, teaching *is* a profession. It is as important, and as specialized, as medicine, law, accountancy, and engineering. Indeed, no one can enter those professions unless he or she has been properly *taught* by a professional who knows both the subject and how to impart it to others—a teacher.

Some states have been making efforts to establish teaching as one of the accepted professions, whose members would be subject when charged with unprofessional conduct to first-instance trial and judgment by their peers—other teachers—and not by a government body at the local level. Final decisions would be made and punishment (if any) meted out by a state agency, such as New York's Board of Regents.

This application of the trappings of professionalism to the teaching profession is not as simple as it sounds. There are many and significant differences between teachers and (to take one example) doctors. Most teachers work for governmental units; most doctors work for themselves. The clients of public-school teachers are far less free than those of doctors to give their "business" to someone else. Teachers have ongoing contact with their clients day after day, 180 days a year; doctors administer their preventive and curative expertise only when their clients require it. Teachers deal with impressionable young minds on a hour-after-hour basis for nine to ten months a year; they are a much greater part of their clients' lives and development than are doctors with their occasional contacts.

Further, teachers are protected by law to a much greater extent than doctors. Once a teacher has earned tenured status, it is extremely difficult (certainly in New York and probably in most states) to remove him or her from professional practice; doctors can be effectively hobbled in their work by professional discipline or malpractice suits. A doctor who has been accused of deficiencies in his performance inevitably loses patients because of such charges; a questioned teacher either continues to teach or sits around in suspended but fully paid status, sometimes for years, pending a decision as to whether he can be fired or must be reinstated on a faculty.

And there is one more essential difference. Doctors don't belong to labor unions; teachers do.

Where I Draw the Line — and Why

During my tenure on the New York Board of Regents, we began to move toward competency-based (or performance-based) teacher evaluation, known as CBTE or PBTE, wherein the teacher's ability to *instruct* (as differentiated from his or her credentials, prowess in research, or skill in writing publishable articles) determined advancement and pay scales. That movement seems to have died a quiet death. Why? Neither the schools of education nor the unions liked it.

While I was Chancellor of the Board of Regents, Commissioner Gordon Ambach began to structure a plan for the establishment of teaching as a profession, which was finally (after several proposals and callbacks) advanced for the Regents' consideration shortly before I left the Board. It was a generally well-thought-out plan, with what seemed to me to be adequate protection for teachers and a degree of improvement in the system for removing not only the bad apples but the incompetents from the profession. But the Ambach plan had what I considered one fatal flaw: *it failed to say that the violation of a law or the deliberate ignoring of a court order was grounds for suspension or loss of professional status.*

Professionals Don't Strike

One of the factors that distinguishes true professionals from nonprofessionals (although the latter may call themselves professionals) is that professionals do not withhold services from clients, alone or in concert with others, in order to bring economic pressure upon them. *Professionals do not strike* or conduct "job actions" or "sickouts" or other semantic subterfuges which mean the same thing.

Professionals Don't Break Laws

A second distinguishing factor is that professionals do not break laws or codes applying to their profession. Those who do, and who are caught at it, are subject to professional discipline by both peers and the government, up to and including revocation of the right to practice, in addition to whatever penalities may be visited upon them by the courts.

Professionals Don't Defy Court Orders

One more distinction between professionals and nonprofessionals is that professionals do not refuse to obey orders of duly constituted courts. Here again, defiance can lead to suspension or revocation of the individual's right to practice his profession, plus whatever sentence may be imposed by the court for contempt.

Just before I left the Board of Regents, I told my colleagues that these reasons prevented me from recommending that teaching be made a profession under New York law. I reminded them that strikes against the public schools (where the great majority are employed) are illegal under the state's Taylor Law, which outlaws strikes by any public employee. I reminded them further that defiance of court orders was illegal in any event, and I suggested to them that conversion of teaching to one of New York's self-regulating, self-disciplining professions made no sense unless the leadership of the two teachers' unions publicly renounced the use of the strike weapon by whatever name.

The leadership of NYSUT (affiliated with the American Federation of Teachers, AFL-CIO) and the much smaller NYSEA (a member of the National Education Association) would make no such pledge in the spring of 1980, and at this writing have made no such pledge. I therefore urged that professional status not be granted to members of these organizations.

That is a matter of principle with me. What's more, the original New York proposal had the drawback of loading the disciplinary board of the proposed profession with union-affiliated teachers, who (if experience is any guide) could not be counted upon to administer appropriate disciplinary measures. Unions are by nature advocates, special pleaders for their members; there is nothing wrong with that, except that individuals thus oriented are not likely to be the most even-handed and unbiased judges of their union colleagues. It might be said that doctors, architects, accountants, and other professionals are equally protective of their colleagues, but that is not my observation — probably because *individual* responsibility means more in these professions.

Teachers' Strikes Are a National Problem

Because teachers' strikes are usually against a local school district or an individual college, we are inclined to think of them as small, isolated incidents, in comparison with a national walkout of air-traffic controllers or auto workers, for example. But teachers' stoppages are not confined to any locality; they take place all across the country, particularly in September as schools prepare to open. And they affect hundreds of thousands of students.

For example, on one particular day, September 22, 1980, 220,000 Philadelphia (Pennsylvania) pupils had been kept out of school for twenty-one days by a strike; Bellevue (Washington) was ending a three-week walkout affecting 20,000 youngsters; although twelve other Pennsylvania districts were out, Chambersburg's 8,700 students were ready to return; 3,000 kids in Wall Township (New Jersey) awaited a final settlement; 33,000 students in San Jose (California) were in the fourth day of a teachers' strike; Michigan reported eleven strikes in progress, involving 55,000 young people; two Ohio districts, with 9,400 pupils, were still out;

substitutes were teaching 5,000 kids in Sierra Vista (Arizona) on the fourteenth day of a strike, while Westerly (Rhode Island) strikers were keeping 3,500 pupils from class on the tenth day of their walkout.

No, teachers' strikes are not a minor matter, or a local one. They are nationwide, and their adverse effect impacts upon the education of the nation's young people.

What Happens When Teachers Strike?

The most obvious, most unfortunate result of a teachers' strike is the interruption of children's education. Whether their school is closed, or their classes are curtailed, or their regular instructors are replaced by less well prepared, mutually unfamiliar substitutes, the kids lose hours, days, weeks, sometimes months of learning which they can never recapture. By their very nature, teachers' strikes are detrimental to the overall quality of education, which alone is sufficient reason to oppose such strikes.

The American people concur. Through their elected representatives, they have made public employee strikes, including strikes by teachers in the public schools, illegal.

The second result of teachers' strikes, therefore, is that laws are openly and deliberately violated. When that occurs, and school authorities go to the courts for enforcement of the law, back-to-work orders and injunctions against striking are also deliberately defied—a third result of teachers' strikes.

Another negative result which sometimes follows in the wake of a strike is the outbreak of open hostility between striking teachers and school boards and administrators, as well as between teachers and substitutes who take their places to keep the schools running. Quite often parents and even children take active partisan roles in the dispute, creating still more hard feelings which long outlast the strike itself.

Then there is the spectacle of a school board squabbling in public with its teachers, the volleys of charges and countercharges flying back and forth, the angry letters to the editor in the local newspapers denouncing one side or the other — and the cold realization that the education for which the community has paid is dribbling away undelivered. All these are factors that erode public support for the local schools, an erosion which is bound to surface when the next budget vote rolls around.

The Ugly Side of Teachers' Strikes

In my view, the public defiance of law and legitimate authority, the loud animosity, and the frequent violence which mark teachers' strikes can be as damaging as the irretrievable loss of learning—because of their effects upon the children.

Press reports of strike-attendant troubles are many; an example will suffice. *Newsday* reported of the 1979 Levittown (New York) thirty-four-day strike: "There were grim confrontations between teachers and parents; buses were vandalized and tires slashed; substitute teachers received phone threats and were shoved and called obscene names; parents picketed the homes of school board members; angry students had a sleep-in at MacArthur High, and traces of anti-Semitism surfaced at community meetings."

This is bad news. Young Tommy and Tina are not stupid. They presumably have been taught to obey authority as represented by their teachers and their principals. Through daily contact, they have come to respect and often to admire their teachers. Then those teachers strike— and the youngsters see them and hear them screaming oaths and obscenities at their adversaries, thumping on the sides of buses with their fists, shattering windshields, cutting tires, harassing others by late-night phone calls . . . all acts which Tommy and Tina have been sternly told that *they* must never do. They learn that their striking teachers are deliberately disobeying the laws of their state, as well as back-to-work orders and injunctions against further law breaking. Finally, they may see their teacher role-models proudly and defiantly being marched off to jail in contempt of court.

What kind of example does this set for Tina and Tommy? A rotten one, in my estimation. The young people will be quick to ask: If teachers can forget the rules and defy the law and refuse to comply with a judge's orders, and if teachers can commit verbal and physical offenses against other citizens and their property, why should they—the children—act differently? If teachers can remain unrepentant for their misdeeds, why should Tina and Tommy refrain from misbehaving?

I can sympathize with those teachers who complain that lack of discipline in the schools keeps them from teaching properly. *But teachers who strike, defy legitimate authority, and indulge in actions which they would condemn if committed by students, will get no sympathy from me about their disciplinary problems with students.* Nor do they get much sympathy from the public at large, which, if I read the tea leaves correctly, has become more, not less, impatient with public-employee strikes.

One of the most important and necessary elements of the social contract whereby civilized people live in peace, harmony, and freedom together is this: If you do not like a law, you are at liberty to work, alone or in concert with others and by every legitimate means, to change that law. But as long as it *is* the law, you have no right to disobey it.

So far, striking teachers have not been severely punished for their defiance. They suffer loss of pay, to be sure, and some of their leaders may spend a few nights in jail, but there is usually an agreement not to prosecute in the terms of the final settlement, and the teachers return to their jobs without further penalty. The *Newsday* story of the end of the Levittown strike was accompanied by a photo of smiling teachers cutting an ice-cream cake at an end-of-the-strike celebration.

That could change if the temper of the American people is what it seems to be. There is no God-given or constitutional "right to strike," which is quite different from the right to quit one's job and go elsewhere. The people, through their legislators, determine who shall and who shall not be allowed to strike, and they are hardly likely to make it easier for teachers to deny their children the full measure of education to which they are entitled. With an overabundance of trained teachers in the job market, able to step in to keep schools running, the public is unlikely to be excessively tolerant of those who disrupt educational services. Who knows? We may even reach the point at which violations of the law are prosecuted to the fullest extent.

I issue no threats; I have neither the power nor the wish to do so. I cannot force anyone to obey the law, or to enforce it. But it should be manifest to any teacher who reads the newspapers and talks to other citizens that Americans are fed up with public-service strikes and stoppages and demonstrations, all of which add up to one thing: the disruption of essential services and consequent reduction of the quality of life.

We have entrusted to our teachers our own and our nation's most precious possession, America's children. What hurts the educational progress of those children is not likely to be tolerated by the parents of today, despite their traditional respect for the teaching profession. I therefore suggest to our teachers that when they are faced with a difficult decision, they carefully review their own personal dedication to their profession and their responsibilities to the young people they serve, before taking any action which reflects adversely upon both.

Are Teachers Overpaid?

Writing in the *Wall Street Journal* (October 1,1981) about the "Job of Controlling Public Sector Pay," Harvard economist Martin Feldstein has this to say: "The long waiting lists of qualified teachers who would like positions but cannot find work are a clear signal that teachers' salaries are too high.... The time has come to stop wasting taxpayers' money and scarce resources and to allow the real wages in these jobs to fall to a market clearing wage."

I cannot bring myself to agree with Professor Feldstein's purely quantitative, supply-and-demand approach to the question of compensation for teaching. Granted, we could reduce teachers' pay and fringe benefits to the point at which "market clearing" would occur—that is, when the number of those still willing to take teaching jobs at a greatly reduced wage level exactly equals the number of jobs available. But what would that do to the *quality* of the country's teaching corps?

Almost by definition, low wages will drive out of the profession those who are good enough to qualify for jobs in other fields. Those who would be left in teaching at the market-clearing point would be those at the bottom of the barrel professionally. As I have pointed out elsewhere, we are having more than enough trouble these days maintaining the quality of teacher-education graduates; various factors, including declining school enrollments and increasing opportunities for women in other fields, have depressed the academic achievement levels of those still in contention for teaching positions. Reducing teacher compensation would leave us with the worst of the worst, when what we need is the best of the best.

TESTING

I have deliberately coupled my thoughts on testing with those on teaching. Like love and marriage, you can't have one without the other.

Before school board members, administrators, and teachers start to howl that poor test results do not necessarily reflect inferior schooling, let me hasten to say that I agree (although many do not). There are other factors which can affect the individual pupil's ability to perform on tests and to understand the material upon which the tests are based.

Having said that, however, let me quickly add that *good* results on standardized tests *do* reflect good educational practices. Just as it is possible for first-rate teachers to propel educationally disadvantaged children into the ranks of the achievers, so it is possible for schools to take youngsters fully capable of scholastic excellence and so foul up their learning process with fads and gimmicks that they finish school undereducated, sometimes barely literate . . . and unable to cope with standardized tests.

But without testing we would never really *know* how well or how badly we are teaching the children, who are entitled to the best education we can provide, and who have but one chance to absorb that education. We cannot *know* where we are weak or where they are weak, or where remedies are needed and of what sort. *Testing is an absolute requirement of the educational process.* But does everyone accept that? No.

Who doesn't, and why not? The answers will become evident immediately when we recall that much of our educational system has fallen into the hands of liberal-modernists (or modernist-liberals—take your choice) to whom standards and competition are anathema.

Tests are based upon standards. They set standards. They establish goals to be met and exceeded. And in so doing, they inevitably invite comparisons between one challenger and the next. If you happen to believe, as I do, that the setting of standards and the encouragement of competition in reaching or surpassing them will inevitably produce better results—in education, in sports, in business, in almost every walk of life—you will understand and applaud the use of testing. But the liberal-modernists are schizophrenic on the subject; they like testing some things but they despise tests for others.

Americans Insist upon Testing

In most areas of American life, we demand thorough testing and we set high standards. When it comes to the products of industry, the liberals are always in the van, shouting the loudest for adequate testing. New drugs are kept under wraps until they pass the toughest of Food and Drug Administration tests. New car models are put through the most demanding tests on rugged proving grounds. Airplanes are regularly tested and retested for safety reasons. Test standards are so stringent for American ships that many lines sail under Liberian, Panamanian, or Norwegian registry. Electrical appliances must meet the stern tests of the underwriters' laboratory. And in all of this, I'm on the side of the liberals. Before I ingest something, or drive it, or fly in it, or sail on it, or flip its switch, I want to know that it has passed its tests.

We are pretty demanding about people, too. No general or admiral worthy of the rank would send his forces, tanks, ships, or planes into combat without extensive tests of not only weaponry but personnel; battle maneuvers are the traditional tests of the readiness level of soldiers, sailors, Marines, and airmen. We insist that those who want jobs as public safety officers pass rigid tests. The consumer protection movement (with the liberals leading the charge) demands that professionals requalify periodically, taking new courses and passing exams in them.

It is only when we come to the testing of *children* that the liberals do a 180-degree aboutface.

What's Wrong with Testing Children?

Any new proposal to test youngsters' academic proficiency inevitably meets with a barrage of objections. Looking at some of them tells us something of the liberal psyche: Testing, the liberals say, is traumatic. Putting the kids through the ordeal of having to *demonstrate* that they have indeed learned what they have presumably been taught can be harmful to the psychological well-being of children, according to this theory. It is particularly rough on kids who haven't studied or learned much.

Frankly, I can't recall that a great deal of traumatizing affected my generation, which grew up with quizzes, tests, and exams, accepting them as a normal part of the learning process. What's more, I've always thought that a primary goal of education is to prepare children for life—which is bound to be studded with all sorts of tests and traumas no matter how sheltered a child may be.

But, the liberals contend, testing cannot really prove with complete accuracy how well a child has learned. Perhaps not 100 percent; testing, like teaching, is a human function and thus imperfect. But as a measurement of the extent to which a youngster has retained what he or she has been taught, testing is way ahead of whatever is in second place.

But (another liberal "but") testing is sometimes biased. It can discriminate against those who are educationally disadvantaged. Some youngsters don't have a family setting conducive to learning; others don't understand English because another tongue is spoken at home; still others haven't received adequate preparation for the subject matter or testing on it; another group or groups have learning disabilities which prevent them from passing. These are questions of blame, and the notion is that if the child himself is not to blame for his relative lack of academic capability, he should not be tested, for he will fail. The fact that testing will show that he is having learning problems, and what the problem areas are, is disregarded; he should not be tested. The purpose of testing, which is not only to measure ability but to pinpoint weakness where remedial efforts may be applied, has no meaning for the liberal-modernist. The child is not to blame for the state of his education; somebody else is (society, his family, his teachers). To the liberal-modernist, it is far less important to find where he is deficient and help him to catch up than it is to protect him from the stigma of failure by not subjecting him to testing in the first place. This is the kind of twisted thinking that has brought so much of American education down to its mediocre level.

Robert J. Solomon of the Educational Testing Service summed up the liberal-modernist argument that poor test results prove that the test shouldn't have been given in the first place. To his own question, "What best describes the thinking of those who want to stop standardized testing rather than use the information (showing low student achievement) to help improve educational quality?" Solomon answers by citing the practice of early Mediterranean kings: "If you don't like the news, kill the messenger."

"Bias" in Testing?

The question of "biased" testing is not confined to children. Before me as I write is an August 1981 *Newsday* editorial entitled "Choosing Principals Without Biased Tests." It claims that examinations for the job of school principal in the New York City system discriminated against minority candidates. The proof? Why, in the latest round of these tests, the failure rate for blacks and Hispanics was *100 percent* (their italics). But the failure rate for *white* candidates was *close to 75 percent* (my italics). Even so, the 100 percent minority failure "proves" that the test was "biased" and "discriminates against minorities." *Newsday* suggests that the city return to the post-1969 practice of hiring on the basis of nontesting "job evaluations," which raised the number of minority principals from one to 25 percent. The question of ability is apparently immaterial, as is the fact that minorities are well represented on the New York City Board of Examiners which created the test in the first place.

The fundamental question here is: Do *results* prove bias? If, time after time, all the white candidates passed and all the others flunked, such tests could invite severe scrutiny of the questions they posed. But that isn't the case here. Strangely, I have seen no citation of anything specifically asked on this allegedly "biased" test which black and Hispanics, because they are blacks and Hispanics, probably could not answer correctly, although whites could. That should be the test for bias. If 100 percent of the male applicants had failed while 75 percent of the females didn't make it, or if 100 percent of the right-handed candidates flunked while 75 percent of the lefties did likewise, would those circumstances be proof of discrimination against men and right-handers?

Assessing bias on the basis of *results* is ridiculous on its face. But I have come to understand better and better as I move through the educational minefields that liberal-modernists don't really care whether their positions are ridiculous or not. If they did, they would have laughed themselves right out of the picture a long time ago.

"Teaching to the Test"

When the Regents were debating the survival of the statewide exams in secondary-school subjects which since 1865 have borne the name "Regents' Exams," we were constantly told that the use of tests which were uniform throughout the state (New York, in this case) would require the teacher to "teach to the test"—that is, to spend considerable time toward the end of the year in reviewing with his or her class the kinds of questions which are likely to appear on the actual exams.

This was supposed to be an evil practice, in that it *forced* the teacher to impart to the child not what he or she thought the child should learn but what "the state" thought the child should be taught in that particular subject. It apparently made no difference that the state tests were composed by committees of classroom teachers from across the state.

What's wrong with that? In my book, nothing. In the domain of her classroom, the teacher can spend plenty of time drilling the kids in what he or she considers important. This sometimes produces a raft of youngsters who are experts in nutrition (Punchy Duffy's Munchy Puffies are bad for your health because they're 95 percent air and 5 percent junk) and consumer protection (Mom is being ripped off when she buys a box of these Puffies, because it costs 79 cents and it is one-third empty—which is probably a blessing, considering their nutritional shortcomings). Yet the same kids may not have the slightest notion about what the U.S. Senate is, what it does, how it is organized and why, who their own Senators are or much of anything else about the government they will eventually be responsible for choosing.

Standardized, uniform tests—whether they are elementary-level tests of reading and math progress or secondary-school exams in essential subjects—stress to the child what the public generally considers important for him to know and understand, while pointing out to the teacher where individual pupils need help.

Perhaps even more important, the challenge of standardized tests offers the child an *incentive* to study and learn. Young people are sometimes unconvinced of the value of mastering this or that subject, or the value of knowing how to think logically and to draw correct conclusions from facts. They sometimes do not realize that Latin would help them with English, that geometry would sharpen their reasoning processes, that social studies would help them participate in governing themselves. They are not always attuned to education's multiplicity of purposes and by-effects.

If the matter is left there, up to the child to learn or not to learn as he or she sees fit, learning may not take place. But if the student must face an accounting (in the form of a test or tests) of how well he or she has mastered the subject, learning *will* take place. Whether as a competitive exercise or in isolation, standardized testing offers the carrot (the satisfaction of doing well) and the stick (the disappointment of doing badly) both at once.

In other words, *it is not the test itself, or passing the test, which is the ultimate rationale for testing.* It is to expand the learning and the knowledge and the grasp of reasoning of the young person who is to be tested, and to pinpoint the areas of weakness at which corrective and remedial help should be applied.

Aptitude Tests and College Entrance Exams

As youngsters approach college-going age, they are likely to take Scholastic Aptitude Tests (SATs), their preliminary versions (PSATs), and College Entrance Examinations. These are nationally standardized tests created and administered by private, professional testing services, and—as in the case of other standardized tests—there is a great deal of griping about them.

The most often heard protest is that such examinations do not accurately reflect all those characteristics which can contribute to a young person's success in mastering college life as well as college-level studies. *Of course they don't,* and they don't claim to. They simply provide some inkling of how an individual stands in relation to his entire national peer group in his grasp of the subjects tested. Colleges do not rely exclusively or even primarily upon test results when admitting applicants; other factors, such as local grades and secondary-school extracurricular activities, are always taken into account. Good marks on these tests won't assure anybody of admission to any college; on the other hand, however, very low grades can save an unqualified candidate lots of grief when, in evaluating them, the college authorities realize that he most likely cannot cope with college-level work at their institution.

More often than in past years, we now hear a new, economic argument against tests for college admission. A fee is usually charged those who wish to take the test; it is designed to cover the costs of conceiving, printing, delivering, securing, administering, and grading the tests, as well as making their results known to those colleges to which the test-taker has applied. Some hopefuls hire tutors to help them cram for the exams, which are given nationwide on specific dates, but the plus effect of tutoring is marginal; it is not a particularly decisive factor in ultimate acceptance. The antitest argument is predictable: it costs money to take these tests, so the tests discriminate against poor kids. Wrong—because that's not the way it works. I have yet to hear of any child not being able to take the tests because his or her family couldn't afford it; any school or district which would permit that to happen would be severely criticized and required to maintain a fund for such cases.

Who Could Vote Against Truth?

The art of legislative labeling is a great political game. Who will vote against a Clean Water Act or an Economic Recovery Act or a Full Employment Act or an Energy Conservation Act? No legislator facing a re-election campaign wants to be braced with a laundry list of his "no" votes on such obviously worthy bills. And the same thing applies to the newest twist: truth. We have "truth in packaging," "truth in banking," and, of course, "truth in testing." Who is going to vote against truth? That's why these bills, sometimes without much thought as to their need, usually become law.

The ever-present suggestion in a "truth-in-testing" law is that it is necessary because somebody (the testing agency) isn't being wholly truthful about something (the contents of the test), and somebody else (the test-taker) is somehow injured thereby. Evidence that this is actually so is sparse, if it exists at all, but . . . truth is truth, so no matter. These laws usually provide that the test-givers *must* allow the test-takers to see their corrected answers, and to challenge decisions which they think are unfair. It is contended that this right will be of special value to the disadvantaged and minority test-takers; although the rationale escapes me, it is not unexpected. Those who dislike testing per se have always contended that it is unfair to the "learning-deprived."

Of course, revelation of test answers to test-takers automatically compromises that particular test. It can never be used again, anywhere. The testing agency must then shoulder the cost of creating a new version, which in turn increases their costs and the costs to the test-takers—that is, if the testing firm is still willing to give the test at all. If the number of applicants taking it is small, it is sometimes uneconomical to have to prepare several versions of a single test; in such cases, the testing agency may well withdraw from that particular field. In this way, tests which are of value to those who must judge an individual's aptitudes for this or that career become unavailable—an unforeseen casualty of the quixotic search for dishonesty and deception.

What have the early results of new truth-in-testing laws told us? One thing, for sure: most of those who take the tests don't question the accuracy of the grading system. Of the 32,468 youngsters who took the Educational Testing Service's SATs in New York in the first year of the state's truth-in-testing law, only 7.6 percent asked to see their corrected answers. Were these the expected victims of testing trickery—the disadvantaged? No. According to *Newsday:*

". . . one-fourth of the students requesting test information come from families with annual income of $50,000. . . . One-sixth of the students asking for the information were from families earning less than $18,000 . . . those who asked for the test [results] were twice as likely as the non-requesting students to rank in the top 10 percent of their class, to have grade averages of 3.5 or higher, and to score 57 points higher on the verbal section of the SAT and 79 points higher on the math portion. The results also showed that white and Oriental students requested the data in far greater numbers than other racial or ethnic groups."

In other words, the better a student did on the tests, the more likely he or she was to ask why he or she hadn't done better.

Was any chicanery and deviousness discovered by the truth-in-testing requirements? One particularly intelligent youngster contended, correctly, that the prescribed answer to a multiple-choice question about the number of sides to a figure was wrong. The testing agency upgraded the answers, and that was that. This single instance was touted by the foes of standardized tests as a great setback for the whole concept of testing. But carelessness is not deception; one wrong answer should not nullify an entire test, much less all the tests. It is reasonable to expect that test-givers check their questions and answers carefully before testing, and to criticize them if they do not, but does this one slipup justify condemning all testing to the ash heap? Is it the horseshoe nail that will bring down the kingdom? It isn't, and it won't.

Competency Testing — the New Accountability

In recent years, Americans have become increasingly aware of and alarmed about the number of young citizens who have been handed high-school diplomas and pushed out into society with an inadequate grasp of learning fundamentals: reading, writing, and simple mathematics. They are concerned about the growing number of functional illiterates who are barely able to cope or survive, who cannot qualify for or hold jobs, who are totally unready for continuing education or the responsibilities of citizenship.

Through their governments, the worried public has responded to this unhappy development by prescribing *competency tests* for all secondary-school students—uniform statewide examinations in the basic skills, on which passing grades must be achieved to entitle the student to a high-school diploma. More and more states have adopted various styles of competency testing, but all are directed to the same end—*the reestablishment of standards.*

In early 1979, as the New York State Regents prepared to vote on the final refinements of the competency testing program we had been studying since 1973 and had initially promulgated in 1976, I outlined the situation in these words:

"... in too many places ... too many school boards have handed too many high-school diplomas to too many youngsters who have not achieved the scholastic standards to which those diplomas attest. For too many reasons, both within and beyond their control, local school authorities in too many cases have not been able to fulfill their responsibilities. It therefore becomes necessary for the state ... to take corrective action. ... Because I agree with Emerson that 'the less government we have, the better,' I personally regret the need for these state actions—but it has become inescapably evident that New York (like her sister states) can no longer depend upon the traditional principle of 'local control' to maintain proper standards of academic achievement at all times, in all schools, for all children. . . .

"*The diploma is the currency of education—and education has allowed its currency to be debased.* If we offer identical rewards to those who earn them and those who do not earn them, we destroy the motivation of both. There is a Gresham's Law of education: unearned diplomas make earned diplomas worthless."

If the state manages to reestablish the value of its high-school diplomas, I added, they will no longer be merely exit visas from the educational system, but real rewards for and thus incentives to genuine scholastic achievement. What's more, the schools, in their enthusiasm for consumer protection, could offer some protection to employers and higher-education institutions which look to diplomas as evidence of a satisfactory educational level (even open-admissions colleges require high-school diplomas for entrance). Finally, I posed, and answered, a rhetorical question:

"Can we honestly guarantee [today] that every individual whose name appears on a New York diploma is fit to enter the labor market, or college? Sad to say, we cannot. And we pay the price, as the flagging competencies of those entering the labor pool drive taxpaying business out of the state, while millions of dollars must be spent remediating our undereducated college freshmen."

Or, as James C. Enochs put it in *The Restoration of Standards,* "It is time to admit it: In the last dozen years, educators have made a mess of things. When we are clothing functional illiterates in caps and gowns the time has come to start plea bargaining. We are guilty."

Is Everybody for Competency Testing?

If any of us on the Board of Regents thought that our newly established competency-testing program would meet with universal acclaim, we were quickly disabused of that illusion. The wailing which greeted our action was worthy of the loudest banshee in my ancestral Ireland.

These were not difficult tests, either at the outset or in their stepped-up form. The first were so simple that they were widely ridiculed by everyone from Walter Cronkite and *Time* magazine on down, as being elementary rather than secondary in their required levels of attainment, because they were admittedly pitched to a seventh- or eighth-grade level. The media wiseacres immediately jumped to the conclusion that passage of these tests would guarantee a diploma for anyone and

that the Regents had actually *lowered* New York's high-school graduation standards to junior-high levels or below. Neither was true. The
pundits ignored the real explanation: that while a student could not receive a diploma *without* a 65 percent or better score on the competency
tests, he would also have to pass more difficult local requirements in
most schools, and that the Regents' targets were those schools which
handed out diplomas indiscriminately.

The low levels of the early tests were deliberately set so that early-
on discovery of weaknesses and remedial efforts could enable low
achievers to shape up before their senior year. Once such discovery-re-
mediation programs were in place, the tests could be (and were) raised
to higher levels of difficulty more appropriate for high schools. But there
were gripes. I responded:

"We hear anguished cries that the state must allow more time, provide more instructors, invest more money, to ready the children for these
new examinations. . . . Granted that the competency tests themselves are
something new—the subjects tested are as old as education itself: reading, writing, and mathematics. We are not asking the twelfth-graders to
solve problems in differential calculus, to write a Shakespearean sonnet
or to explain Plato's *Republic;* we are asking them to demonstrate 65 percent proficiency in the three 'R's—to show us how well their school has
prepared them for living in modern society."

Lots of careful thought went into making the competency tests fair
for everyone. The schools were authorized to use special methods of administering the tests to youngsters with language, hearing, eyesight, or
similar problems. Further, the tests were required only of those who (in
the opinion of competent professionals) were able to master them; those
considered uneducable by virtue of retardation were excluded from the
program. Finally, the practice of awarding local certificates to "handicapped" students was prohibited. This device had too often been used to
shirk a school's responsibility for identifying and providing remedial efforts to slow learners; it had enabled the school to dispose of its disruptive, chronically truant, and even educationally deprived youngsters by
branding them handicapped, handing them a certificate, and pushing
them out the schoolhouse door—a reverse twist on the Soviet trick of
branding troublemakers as mental cases and stowing them away in
prison hospitals.

But even with all these arrangements, including an adequate lead-
time notice permitting schools to discover and help those who might not
otherwise pass the basic tests, there were still complaints that they were
"unfair." I felt compelled to reply:

"We have been treated to hundreds of little moral lectures on what
is unfair about competency testing—99 percent of which ignore the fact

that the overriding unfairness, the ultimate immorality, is to have a youngster in one's charge for a dozen critical years without giving him even the rudiments of that education to which every American child is entitled."

The Failure-and-Dropout Bugaboo

There were other complaints, too. Loud teeth-gnashing was heard, particularly from the urban schools, to the effect that even the simple tests would result in so many failures and so many discouraging prospects that there would be a record number of dropouts—all of whom would become muggers, drug-pushers, or worse. When it was gently pointed out to these school people that it was their own schools that they were badmouthing and their own defaulted responsibilities that they were baring to the world, they quieted down a bit, but not entirely.

Did their dire predictions come to pass? No. The massive failure-followed-by-dropout exodus from the educational system never happened.

One of those responsible for the encouraging results that *did* happen was David Seeley, Director of the Public Education Association in New York City, where the calamity-howling was particularly high-pitched. Instead of joining the howlers, Dave Seeley said, in effect, "Let's not give up. I don't think the situation is as bad as it has been painted. Let's roll up our sleeves and put together some effective after-school remedial classes to help the slower kids catch up and learn. Let's stop complaining that there should be no tests. Let's give the children of New York a chance to pass them." He and his associates did just that, on a volunteer basis. And it worked. Dave Seeley, possibly more than any other individual, deserves credit for realizing that the Regents' competency-testing program was intended to *help* students by prodding their schools to give them the remediation they need, and for pitching in to make certain that they were helped.

The results were remarkable, in light of the predictions by the Cassandras of the city schools. Very few children failed the early tests in New York City, and Dena Kleiman reported in the *New York Times* in August 1981:

". . . [in 1980] 716 students were denied diplomas because they were found deficient in [reading, writing and mathematics skills.] . . . Last June, 42,363 students were to have graduated from public high schools in the city. Of these, 36,360 were granted diplomas and 6,003 were not. Only 1.7 percent [100+] of those who did not receive diplomas were denied them because they failed at least one of the three Regents' competency examinations.

"At the time that use of the examinations was being considered by the New York State Board of Regents, officials of the New York City Board of Education predicted that massive numbers would fail and therefore be unable to get a diploma."

Indeed, the competency-testing program has worked so well that city officials have instituted their own internal reading and mathematics tests for promotion to the fifth and eighth grades.

Competency Testing Produces Results

In October 1981, the College Entrance Examination Board released figures showing that New York State's college-bound seniors scored higher on their SATs in 1981 than in 1980. The average verbal test score rose from 424 to 427, and the math average from 465 to 471, *for the first time since the decline in scores began in the late 1960s.* National averages remained at the 1980 levels. Education Commissioner Gordon Ambach said: "I am convinced that the class of 1981 had better SAT scores because our state and the local districts and schools have been setting higher standards for academic performance. More was expected of 1981's seniors. As a result they worked harder to develop greater proficiency in reading, writing and mathematics. . . .

"For a long time there has been a deep concern about declining secondary school performance. I believe these results demonstrate we are turning the corner here in New York and will lead a national trend of increasing scores."

Ambach went on to praise teachers and school administrators for their positive response to the challenge of new state requirements and diploma standards, which became finally effective in 1981. He was echoed by John Bach, principal of Albany High School in New York's sixth largest city, where scores rose on both sets of tests:

"I think that the State Education Department's emphasis on minimum competency tests as a requirement for graduation from high school has heightened the emphasis on the basic skills—reading, writing and math, and that has permeated the instructional program all over the state."

While the foes of testing will contrive all sorts of reasons why the improvement in SAT scores is unrelated to the competency testing program in New York, even they must concede that competency testing as a diploma requirement hasn't hurt. The figures are there, and they are impressive. New York's seniors were 15 percent of the national total of SAT-takers, and a higher percentage of seniors took the SATs in 1981 than in 1980. What's more, a higher percentage of those who took the SATs scored better in 1981 than in 1980.

The turnaround in basic academic proficiencies—so long awaited by those concerned about the steady decline in national aptitude test scores—is, as far as I am concerned, a direct result of student and teacher responses to the new challenge of competency testing as a high-school diploma requirement.

The Revolt of the Bleeding-Hearts

It was too much to expect that competency testing would be unchallenged, despite its affirmative effect upon scholastic achievement.

Challenges have been mounted on different grounds in different states. In North Carolina, the suit against the competency testing system was dropped, because most of the pupils in the marginal category received remedial attention and passed. In Peoria, Illinois, a federal plaintiff charged that local competency tests for all kids (handicapped included) were unfair to the handicapped, who might not be able to pass them. In Florida, a federal judge enjoined the state's competency testing program for four years, contending that it did not provide adequate notice in advance of testing and that it continued the effects of past discrimination against blacks. In its amicus curiae brief against the Florida test, the Carter Department of Education said: "Because using the test as a graduation requirement deprives ten times more black students than white students of a high school diploma . . . this use of the test has a substantially disproportionate impact on black students." The feds also contended that the skills tested had not actually been taught to the students; one wonders how kids could reach the senior year of high school without ever having been exposed to any of the basics, in Florida or anywhere.

California's proficiency testing law has been challenged on different grounds, i.e., that the state's fundamental law and constitution specifically prohibit the superimposition of statewide minimum standards upon districts whose own standards differ.

In New York, the Regents' competency tests as a diploma requirement are being tested on behalf of two Northport students whose learning disabilities kept them from passing the tests, but who were nevertheless awarded high-school diplomas by the district. Local authorities said the tests were unfair to these students because they couldn't pass the exams "no matter how hard they try."

In State Supreme Court (which in the topsy-turvy world of New York terminology is the lowest of three levels of statewide courts), the judge rejected the argument that the rights of the handicapped students were violated by the testing program, but awarded them diplomas on the ground that longer advance notice should have been provided for their training. He indicated that the time between notification by the state in April 1976 and the administration of the tests in June 1979 was not sufficient, *although he declined to say how much time would have been adequate.*

The vagueness of this standard (if it could be called that) opened a figurative can of worms, as other districts reasoned that *their* handicapped kids who had been unable to pass competency tests might also win diplomas in court. The Plainview district, for example, announced that it would give diplomas to handicapped youngsters who complete their own Individual Education Plans (IEPs), whether they pass the state tests or not. In other words, the district will determine just how much each handicapped child is expected to absorb and retain according to his learning capacity (and without regard to how limited that might be), and will award him a high-school diploma if he seems to have absorbed and retained it (no matter how little real education it represents).

The chickens of the judge's "inadequate-preparation-time" doctrine in the Northport case have begun to come home to roost. In June 1981, Northport did it again, awarding diplomas to six mentally handicapped students (even though the district had by then been under state notice to train these youngsters since 1976), but the real shocker came from the Half Hollow Hills district, where many of the diplomas awarded to the handicapped went to residents of the Suffolk Developmental Center for the retarded. The reaction was reported in *Newsday:*

"At the age of 21, Lisa Gorelick cannot speak or dress herself, her family says; but, in June, she was one of 36 residents of Suffolk Development Center for the retarded awarded a high-school diploma.

" 'It's absolutely a travesty,' " her mother, Leila Gorelick, of Bethpage, said yesterday. "She isn't even toilet-trained, yet she is given a legitimate high-school diploma. I was appalled. . . .'

"At least 26 of the 36 developmental center residents getting the diplomas were severely retarded, district records show. Half Hollow Hills board members felt, however, those people should graduate because they completed individual BOCES training programs in basic skills, such as feeding oneself. . . .

". . . Lita Cohen, president of the Society for Goodwill to Retarded Children, representing families of more than 1,300 developmental center residents, disagreed. A diploma for such a child is meaningless, she said. 'They're not going out to work. They're not seeking higher education. . . .'

"Coleman Lyons, superintendent of the Half Hollow Hills School District, said his district decided to award the diplomas to developmental center residents because of Northport's court victory."

Events sometimes take unusual turns. Perhaps the judge should be thanked for encouraging local bleeding-hearts to demonstrate the ulti- mate nonsense of their position. Whether the state will now be permitted to get on with the business of reestablishing the high-school diploma as evidence of real scholastic achievement remains up in the air, however, as a flood of new complaints and appeals is bound to keep the courts busy for a few more years. All we can be sure of is this: When they start giving high-school diplomas to youngsters who aren't even toilet- trained, there's something wrong, somewhere.

What Is a Diploma?

The opponents of competency testing as a diploma requirement are not concerned about the inconsistency of their arguments. On one hand, they argue that even severely handicapped children should receive, sim- ply for "working up to their own potential" (like feeding themselves, in Half Hollow Hills), the very same credential that is awarded to an A+ student headed for college or a job. On that basis, the diploma is an award for effort; it certainly is not testimony to competence. On the other hand, however, they will simultaneously argue that handicapped children who cannot pass minimum competency tests should get di- plomas so that they can get jobs—an argument which depends for its va- lidity upon the employer's acceptance of the diploma as *assurance of the applicant's competence.*

Half Hollow Hills Superintendent Lyons defended the award of di- plomas rather than certificates to the retarded youngsters by saying that certificates "are of no use in the job market." Even the judge in the Northport case bought this specious reasoning: "The denial of a diploma could . . . have severe consequences on [the handicapped child's] future employability and ultimate success in life."

A high-school diploma should tell an employer that the person named on it has satisfactorily completed courses of study at the high- school level. That is what it says, that is what the employer or college admissions officer interprets it to mean, and that is what it should mean. If it does not in truth attest to that level of competence, then it is a handsomely printed, elaborately worded, carefully countersigned *lie.*

A diploma is not a certificate of attendance. A diploma is not an award for effort. A diploma is an official testament by a legitimate edu- cational authority that its named holder has successfully mastered his academic studies at the performance level of the institution issuing the credential.

To demean and debase the diploma by awarding it for any lesser accomplishment or for virtually no accomplishment at all is not only fraudulent and deceptive but a crime against the quality of education, no matter how pure the motives of those who commit it may be.

One cannot fault the defenders of handicapped children for their compassion or their dedication, and I do not. What I *do* fault them for is allowing their compassion and dedication so to becloud their thinking that they are willing to bring down in ruins what we are trying to rebuild in this country: an educational system based upon quality, upon excellence, and upon genuine achievement.

The Testing of Teachers

The new demands for ongoing demonstrations of professional competence, in terms of refresher courses and requalifying exams for lawyers, doctors, accountants, engineers, and other members of the recognized professions, coupled with the new drive by teachers for official recognition and treatment as professionals, has inevitably led to a controversy about testing teachers.

Those pointers of the finger of blame who contend that it is the teachers' fault, not the kids', when competency tests are failed, will insist that teachers be subjected to competency tests of their own.

This is not a universally popular proposition among teachers. Arguments wax hot and heavy as the New York Regents attempt to jell their long-bubbling plan to license teachers as professionals. Of course, entry-level tests for certification and employment are fairly common devices, although they differ in the degree of difficulty from one state or district to another. What is primarily at issue is the need for refresher tests and requalification.

I will not review all the arguments pro and con. Let me simply associate myself with Albert Shanker, AFT President, in his 1980 assessment of the question:

"The American Federation of Teachers . . . strongly supports testing. We—and, we believe, a majority of all teachers—do not want to get rid of anything except ignorance. We believe that tests tell us things that are important for students, parents, teachers, colleges, government and the society at large to know. We also believe the public unquestionably has a right to know what we are doing in the schools—how well or how badly.

"Moreover, we would *like* to see the testing of all new teachers before they are hired, a far from universal practice at present. And when the society decides that it is necessary to retest doctors and lawyers and other professionals after they have been practicing for fifteen or twenty-five years, then we will go along with retesting veteran teachers as well.

"Like any other statistics, of course, test scores are open to misinterpretation and misuse, and the tests themselves aren't perfect. But that calls for better tests (and perhaps even *more* tests) together with a campaign to educate the public on what they mean—not an end to testing."

He adds: "As for the charge that tests are biased against minorities and the poor, that's like blaming the thermometer for the fever—and just about as effective in treating the illness. . . . Math tests are biased against those who can't answer math questions, and reading tests are biased against those who can't read. . . . Opponents of teacher testing . . . note that a good grade on a math or English or social studies exam won't tell you if a person will make a good teacher. . . . True enough. But you can find out if an aspiring English teacher can spell or if a math teacher can do math. If they can't, there's no point looking at other qualities."

Testing of children or of teachers will never be popular in educational circles, because poor results can be embarrassing to teachers in both cases. But isn't that the way life works? And doesn't it work that way for everybody? Life is a rough proving ground. You can make all the claims you want about the quality of your product, but the world, particularly the skeptical world of today, says "Show me." If you've done your job right, testing your product will prove it to the world. And if you know that you will be tested, you'll do your job right.

Summing Up

I believe that America's educators, to whom we have entrusted responsibility for the training of our children, need and are entitled to all the respect and support we can give them.

I believe that teachers' unions have had a generally beneficial effect upon education, but that strikes, defiance of court orders, and some work rules have had a negative countereffect.

I believe that the terms and conditions of teachers' employment should be those that are best for the children, not for the teachers or the taxpayers.

I believe that declining enrollment, official retrenchment, loss of classroom authority, the overloading of extra duties, and other factors have weakened the demand for teaching positions; I believe that in the shrinking pool of applicants for these positions, many are underqualified, and that schools of education have lowered their standards to meet that factor, with the result that a vicious circle of declining academic quality has been set in motion.

I believe that we have permitted a frightening drop in the quality of English-language instruction, and that the abandonment of phonics as a method of teaching reading, the decline of Latin as a foundation for English vocabulary, and the seeming unconcern of teachers for correct spelling, grammar, and construction are producing too many semi-literates.

I believe that our failure to require students to learn at least one language in addition to English is a tragic error.

I believe that experiments with educational gimmickry and permissive quackery, using the children as guinea pigs, has been detrimental to educational quality.

I believe that teachers should not be treated as professionals unless they renounce strikes and the defiance of court orders.

I believe that testing (of teachers and of students) serves two valid educational purposes, by providing an incentive for teachers and their pupils to mount their best efforts to master the tested subjects and by revealing how strong or how weak a system or school or student might be, thereby indicating where remediation should be applied to make teaching and learning better.

I believe that widespread instances of inferior performance justify standardized statewide testing to ensure that all schools and districts are fulfilling their responsibilities to all of their students, not merely the most advanced.

I believe that the integrity of diplomas, having been allowed to deteriorate by their being awarded regardless of scholastic achievement, must now be restored by the imposition of strictly enforced minimal diploma standards, determined by state tests.

Finally, I continue to believe that the fundamental question to be answered when making decisions about teaching and testing is this: Will the quality of education be improved, and will standards of excellence be raised? No other considerations, no matter how superficially compassionate they may seem, no matter how politically attractive they may be, can be allowed to interfere with the attainment of academic excellence.

11.

Selected Short Subjects

Things We Should Keep
in Mind

HAVING come with me this far (and I thank you for that!), you may be wondering, "Why didn't he mention X, or Y, or Z, in which I am particularly interested?"

Perhaps this chapter will answer your concerns.

In the preceding chapters, I tried to address the major problems of education—those broadest in scope and deepest in impact. That does not mean that those are the only important elements of our educational system; it means simply that they, by virtue of their generality, required a full chapter in each case. Others, equally important, are less complex and can be discussed briefly.

Why did I head this chapter "Selected Short Subjects"? A confession, if you don't mind. When I was young, and used to spend Saturdays from 10 A.M. to 4 P.M. in the now-defunct Mineola Theater (I met my girl inside, beyond the ticket booth) the program included not only two feature films plus Free Chinaware for the Ladies and Bingo, but also "Selected Short Subjects"—a Martin Johnson Travelogue, a Pete Smith sports specialty, Movietone News (we started booing Hitler in 1933, because his posturing was so damned ridiculous), a couple of Looneytunes and Merry Melodies, and my favorite, the thirteen-episode serial, *The Phantom of the West* (wherein, to my utter disappointment, the killer was revealed in the thirteenth chapter to be the ranch foreman, whose name was Black). To me, the "Selected Short Subjects" were as interesting as the main features. I commend them to you.

GOVERNANCE

Who should govern education? Who should make educational policy? Who should do the legislating for the educational system?

Lay people

Professional educators have two important functions in the governance of education. Their voices should be heard when educational policy is being initiated, planned, and debated; indeed, they should take the initiative in suggesting policies, rules, and regulations. And once those policies, rules, and regulations have been duly enacted, the professionals should be entrusted with their operation and enforcement.

But the policies should be *decided,* and the rules and regulations *legislated,* by boards composed of lay people, preferably unpaid, who have a concern for education and perhaps some past experience in the field but who are in no way committed for their livelihood, either full-time or part-time, to any specific element of the educational community for which they make the rules.

It is painful for me to say this, because I know many fine members of governing boards who do have a degree of personal dependence upon this or that school, college, or organization which may be interested in what the boards will do. Good as they are, valuable as their contributions may be, *they shouldn't be there*—as long as that attachment, and that unspoken allegiance, is still effective.

Examples? I will give you none. I will not embarrass anyone. If you are not willing to take what I say on logic and on faith, that's up to you. But I am aware of instances—none of them illegal—which, if I chose to divulge them, would hammer the point home beyond any further question.

Why should this be a matter of concern? For one good reason: In more and more cases, those who have the power to designate individuals to governing boards of educational systems are tending to treat those boards as if they were constituent assemblies to which men and women should be named *as representatives* of this or that segment of the educational world.

That is precisely how it should *not* be done. Governing bodies should be composed insofar as possible of disinterested people who are knowledgeable and devoted to the concerns of education *as a whole,* leaders who have earned a reputation as being intelligent and fair and decisive, ready to listen to all viewpoints but owing prior commitment to none. The only representative factor should be geographical, so that all parts of the governed area have spokesmen who can express regional considerations.

In the same vein, we hear of attempts being made to exact from potential appointees to educational governing bodies a promise that they will vote in a given way when a certain subject is being decided. That is an unconscionable interference with the independence of a member of an official agency. It is quite correct to ask a candidate's *views* on any subject—but to insist in advance that if appointed he or she must *vote* in a given way is to negate the whole purpose of a deliberative body. If every member is committed at the time he or she joins the group, votes could just as well be taken by mail. In our Regents discussions and debates, my mind has been changed (and sometimes changed back) often enough for me to understand that members of independent boards must have complete freedom to make up their minds when the talking is ended, the facts are in, and it is time to decide. In the case of education, this means freedom from pressure—either by organizations or institutions to which one owes one's livelihood or by political power-brokers.

Why should educational governing boards be *unpaid?* They work hard; they take time from their families and their occupations; they undergo election campaigns or stern official scrutiny or both before they can take office; they are bombarded and badgered by all sorts of special-interest groups wanting this or that. Surely anyone who voluntarily undergoes all this should be compensated, right?

Wrong. Putting a monetary price tag on a job not only can demean it among the governmental functions of which it is one, but also can and does attract people who want the job for the money. It's as simple as that. Members of educational governing boards should want to serve for service itself, for the chance to do something for the young people of their institution, community, or state. That should be the *only* motivation for participating in educational governance. If boards at any level are paid (anything above expenses, that is), their motivation and with it their quality will be diluted.

These principles apply to all governing boards: state or local boards of education, college or private-school boards of directors or trustees, any top-level entity which makes decisions for the educational institution involved. Sometimes the law or bylaws which establish such boards and delineate their powers will contain specific safeguards against conflicts of interest. If so, fine. If not, they should. At the very least, the people who choose members of such boards should observe these cautions as a matter of common sense.

Finally, governance over *all* levels of education, from pre-K through professional school, should be exercised by a *single* body whose decisions are predicated upon one philosophy. Is there any logical reason why one group of officials should oversee a child's schooling for twelve or thirteen years in the elementary-secondary phase, and then be required to turn him over to a higher-education group for the next four-plus years? Of course not, but that's the way it's done in more states than not, and often the two bodies are at loggerheads with each other, which does nobody any good. Articulation, mutual credit-earning arrangements between high schools and colleges, is weak or faulty under a divided-governance system. And if two different philosophies of education prevail, the student suffers.

Both levels of education exert their influence upon the other. That influence should be measured and guided and monitored by *one* body, at the state level, where the ultimate responsibility for education resides.

LOCAL CONTROL IS NOT A MYTH

We frequently hear that local control of public education does not exist anymore—if it ever did.

That is not the case. It did exist, and it does—except in Hawaii, where our fiftieth state chose to rely upon state authorities, without local school districts.

More than anything else, two factors have combined to fuel premature reports of the death of local control of the schools. The first of these is the constant complaining by local boards of education and their representatives about "state mandates" which govern the spending of local tax money; the lament that 80 percent of local school expenditures are decreed by the state certainly gives the impression that local people and their boards really don't run anything. The second factor is just as bad: When the people rise in their wrath to defeat "the school budget," they often find that they've knocked out only the band, the football team, the school newspaper, and a few buses. Spending for everything else goes on as usual, and the local citizenry feel that they actually have very little say in what happens.

But local control and direction of the schools remains a very important fact of life. Who hires (and sometimes fires) the superintendent of schools? The peoples' representatives on the local school board. And make no mistake about it; the superintendent, as the top executive officer of the district (like the headmaster of a nonpublic school) can set the tone for the entire system. The "super's" choices for major administrative posts, particularly for building principals, will determine how education is to be conducted throughout the system. Local schools which have developed a modernist-liberal tilt or a traditionalist or back-to-basics thrust usually have done so under the influence of a strong superintendent who has convinced his board to move in that direction. The fact that he is the employee and the servant of the people through their elected board of education does not tell the full story. Some board members are only too ready to defer to the "professionals' professional," the superintendent of schools.

Local Choices, Locally Made

State mandates usually confine themselves to spelling out what subjects must be taught at what levels, and how much time is minimally required for each. In fact, most state regulations impose *minimum* standards, leaving it to the district to exceed them if it chooses and to attain them in whatever way it chooses. States will certify teachers (by examination), but it is the local authority which selects them, promotes them and, if necessary, disciplines them. Nor does the state determine how much teachers are paid and what their fringe benefits will be; local boards do that, in the negotiating process. How a subject is to be taught is the prerogative of the teacher, who is supposed to know her or his trade. Local examinations are composed by local teachers, and graded by them. While some states provide a list of textbooks from which their schools must choose, others (including New York) do not limit local choices strictly. The local board approves elective course offerings, over which the state exercises no control. The board also has full freedom to organize its district's schools as it sees fit: some like the straight 8–4 elementary-secondary arrangement, others prefer a 6–3–3 setup with a junior high and still others opt for the newer "middle school" concept, using another combination of numbers. Each district governs its own extracurricular programs and sets its own disciplinary rules. Each district determines how many buildings it needs and how they are to be financed. Each district decides what plant facilities will be available to its students: swimming pools, athletic fields, air conditioning, computers, and so on.

These and many other elements of public education are the prerogatives (and responsibilities) of the *local* authorities, not the state. Although there may be more or less state control in some parts of the country than in others, the general pattern is clear: the state sets minimum standards, and the localities take it from there. Further, the local boards always have (and usually exercise) the right to impose *tougher* requirements than the state's minima.

The State Is Still the Boss

Having pointed out many of the rights and privileges which constitute "local control" of education, we should constantly reemphasize the fact that in our American federal system, *the states are sovereign,* and all governmental power stems from them.

The federal government is a union created by the states; its authority is limited to that granted by the states and their people through the U.S. Constitution, which cannot be changed without the concurrence of at least two-thirds of the states. The term "United States" is not empty of meaning; it is what we are: states, united in a common bond for common purposes.

Local entities—counties (or, in Louisiana, parishes), cities, towns, villages, and special districts, including school districts—are all *subordinate agencies of the state* in which they are located. The powers which they have are theirs because the state has chosen to *share* its power with them to that extent. That shared power can be extended or curtailed as the state and its people see fit. Insofar as education is concerned, responsibility for public education has (in all cases with which I am familiar) been given to the state governments by their people—and in any organization worthy of the name, authority must accompany responsibility.

Sometimes local boards of education forget that they are arms of the state, and that they can no more disobey state laws or defy state regulations than the hand can defy the head. In exercising their responsibilities to provide a proper education for all children within their boundaries, the states have often found it necessary to impose minimum performance standards upon students and schools, in response to growing popular concern about the decline in scholastic achievement evident across the country. The states are accountable, and are held accountable; it is their responsibility to take remedial measures, but those measures have in many cases been greeted by howls of resentment and rashes of lawsuits "to keep the state's nose out of our local schools." The truth of the matter, of course, is that all public schools are *state* schools, run by local people whose authority is granted to them by the state. Minimum competency testing, certification and recertification of high schools, performance standards of all kinds are simply various means to enable the state to do what it is required to do: provide a proper education for its children.

Why does state law forbid strikes or work stoppages by public employees, including public-school teachers and staffs? Why does state law leave so little to be affected by refusal of local voters to pass their school budgets? For one and the same reason: It is the responsibility of the *state* to see that its future citizens have the full benefit of educational opportunities which, if they are lost for a day or a week or a month or are reduced in quantity or quality, can never be recaptured for or by the affected children.

School Decentralization in New York City

Students of the effects of fragmented authority in education will be watching for an evaluation of the more-than-ten-year-old school decentralization program in New York City. Set in place shortly before I became a Regent, the new arrangement responded to community pressures (not all of them peaceful) by increasing local power over (and presumably also local interest in) the city's public schools, which had hitherto been ruled by what was described as an omnipotent but not particularly effective headquarters at 110 Livingston Street. The city was divided into thirty-one (now thirty-two) "community school districts" (any one of which includes more pupils than virtually any other school district in the state) which elect their own boards. These in turn are responsible for the designation of their own chief school officers and management of their own affairs.

The verdict is still not in on New York's decentralization. I have urged the Board of Regents to mount an evaluation of the program as an early priority. We do know that achievement levels were such (in the city, as in the rest of the country) that the Regents felt compelled to initiate preparations several years later for the competency testing program set in place in 1979, and to enact stiffer requirements for the recertification of high schools (which are still under Livingston Street control). Although we do not hear too much about the decentralization program these days, the newspapers did report that much of the money intended for the schools with the lowest reading performance had, as of 1981, gone to the schools with the highest reading levels ... which doesn't make such sense for a remediation program, and doesn't attest to the effectiveness of community control.

I would suggest that we not pass judgment on the decentralization of New York City's public schools until the results are in—but that no time be wasted in determining and assessing those results. The quality of education for a good many children depends upon it.

In Education as in Politics, There Ain't No Gratitude

Speaking of the New York City schools, those who remember the first announcement of the Regents' minimum (or basic) competency testing program (BCTs) in 1976, during my Chancellorship although preparation had begun in 1973, will recall that the city school people and the liberal media indulged in an orgy of hand-wringing, forecasting that thousands would fail and take to the streets, complaining that the simple (to *Time* magazine, laughable) state tests were too tough, too unfair, placing the onus for inferior education on the students rather than the schools, and on and on, ad nauseam.

Then the first tests were given. As we have noted elsewhere, only a handful failed, and many of those passed on later tries. What's more, the extra efforts which the system and organized parents devoted to helping learning-deprived youngsters master the basics began to pay off in terms of better marks in standardized statewide performance tests. Having seen that the imposition of higher standards as a requirement for advancement actually worked, New York City Schools Chancellor Frank Macchiarola (a good educator and an even better politician) installed an achievement testing program for promotion from one grade to the next at certain levels—a requirement that would not have been considered before the state competency-testing experience.

Macchiarola deserved, and received, high praise from the pundits and editorialists of the metropolitan media for his tough new policy of testing as a criterion for moving ahead—and I would be the last to begrudge Frank his earned laurels.

But what provokes an ironic chuckle from me is the fact that not one of those now bestowing kudos upon New York City's schools for their academic improvement has recalled (certainly not for the public record) that it all started with the Regents and their much-maligned state-imposed competency testing programs—programs which were alternately damned and pooh-poohed all along the airwaves and up and down the newspaper columns when they were first suggested. I am still waiting for the first editorial thanking the Regents for having shown the initiative and leadership to do what the city schools still would not dare to do had the state not shown that it could be done successfully.

But I won't hold my breath. In education, as in politics, there ain't no gratitude.

Is Local Control Doomed?

Even as educators point to federal and state legislative and administrative mandates as the main dangers to local control of the public schools, the *real* peril looms from another quarter: the courts.

The judiciary, by its orders respecting busing, discipline, bilingualism, mainstreaming, faculty hiring, book selection, and other educational matters, has already intervened deeply and drastically in the management of local public schools.

But if court decisions in pending "equity" cases decree that the same dollar amount—no more, no less—be spent upon the schooling of each child in a state system, local control would be condemned to death, for its essence is the freedom of a community to draw upon its own resources to the extent it chooses, in order to provide the best educational opportunities for its own children. When that freedom is killed, local control dies with it.

PARENTAL RESPONSIBILITY

One of education's greatest problems today is that two very powerful centrifugal forces are working simultaneously on young people.

On one hand, the schools and colleges are inclined to shrug off their traditional responsibilities *in loco parentis*—that is, to discard their role as surrogate parents of children in their charge, a role primarily as disciplinarian but also as adviser about personal matters and instiller of values and standards. On the other hand, parents often tend to leave everything to the schools, neglecting or simply refusing to shoulder their own age-old responsibilities as parents. When I see those late-evening quickie TV commercials asking "Do You Know Where Your Children Are?" I think of so many families to whom the question should be posed: "Do You *Care?*"

In the golden days of the 1950s, when education and educators were riding high, there was a tendency to suggest that parents "butt out" of the educational picture, and leave schooling to the schools. Don't try to help your children with their work; we, the schools, will take care of that. Just see to it that the kids are in school—and if you can't do that, we have truant officers who can. This all-too-frequent attitude took its toll; parents became conditioned to thinking that schools were capable of handling all aspects of a child's growth and life, and that the schools wanted this role. That being so, why not let them do the job? The generation gap widened, with parental consent. After all, the kids were getting all they needed in school, weren't they?

This mutual misunderstanding of the complementary roles which home and school must play has served the children badly. At the time in life when kids most need (and want, although they may not admit it) guidance and counsel, discipline and direction, respect and love, they often cannot find it—whether they look to their parents or their teachers.

That women should enjoy equal status with men is a perfectly valid principle, but the child's confidence in and reliance upon Mom does not mean that she is somehow inferior to Dad. To the child, it is the other way around: Mom runs the show. We must recapture the realization that *fulfillment of responsibility as parents demeans neither woman nor man.* Being a good parent is just as vital, just as gratifying, as being a good executive or a good professional. Those who think that providing one's family with all the material advantages is the sole mark of a good parent should be asked to explain why the boy or girl who has everything so often goes "off the deep end." The answer is that the young person really does *not* have everything. He or she probably lacks the one most important advantage of all: the love and understanding and help of parents who take the time to care.

Today's economic constraints aggravate the problems of parents. More and more, Mom must find some way of contributing a second income, even when the children are quite young. Kindergarten helps to provide free time for her; prekindergarten and nursery school help, too, and both can serve legitimate educational purposes. However, the novel notion of *early* prekindergarten (at ages two and three) cannot be truly educational. It is custodial, and not a function of the schools.

We must guard against relinquishing basic responsibility for child-rearing to society (that is, to government, including school districts). Being a parent is an *individual* matter, accomplished in concert with the other parent if he or she is present, alone if not. It is a responsibility which can be *shared* with others—schools, day-care centers—but should never be abandoned to them.

COST-AND-QUALITY FACTORS: CLASS SIZE, PROMOTION, SENIORITY, TENURE, AND DISMISSAL

It is my dubious distinction to live in what has been labeled the highest-taxed area of the highest-taxed county of the highest-taxed state in these United States. If I don't, you couldn't prove that by my tax bills, which friends from other parts of the nation call unbelievable.

For the money, we get what I consider to be darned good public services: schools, police and fire protection, roads, and all the other local-government functions. For the price, we should. And the price keeps going up. And up. And up.

The deep concern of Joe Citizen about his whopping tax bills centers on his schools, which are, collectively, the pride and joy of our region, but are, at the same time, the one public service that eats up most of Joe's property taxes. This concern is reflected in the public-opinion research conducted for a Long Island task force on school costs, of which I am currently chairman. Nobody wants to reduce the *quality* of public education, but everyone is anxious to hold down, and if possible reduce, its cost.

Can that be done? The assignment is a tough one. Naturally, a good starting point is in the area of *personnel* services, which constitute better than 80 percent of all school operating costs. These services are almost universally the subject of contractual negotiations between school authorities (most schools now have business managers) and the union or unions representing school employees. Five of the elements of employment terms which seem always to be in the forefront are class size, promotion, seniority, tenure, and dismissal practices.

How one views the many facets of teacher-student-school relationships varies depending upon where one sits. That which seems best to a teacher may not seem best to a taxpayer, and a parent's conclusions may be somewhere in between. For my part, I must apply the single standard which has been my criterion throughout my association with education: *does it help or hinder the quality of educational service?*

Much has been made of the size of the class a teacher must try to control and teach. While it is certainly easier for an instructor to give individual attention to the members of a class of fifteen as opposed to a class of thirty, there is (in my view) very little plus-or-minus effect when there is a change from twenty-five kids to twenty-seven, or from fifteen to fourteen.

Far more important in its bearing upon educational quality is the makeup of the class and the concentration that the teacher is able to bring to bear upon her or his teaching task. As I have said, if the young faces looking at him or her belong variously to the very talented, the average, and the way-behind, it is tough to arrange a simultaneous meeting of the minds with all of them. If a disruptive or a handicapped child requires even a momentary breaking-off of the teaching-learning process, the other students lose. If the teacher must divert instruction from the essential skills and subjects to address mandated gimmickry, it hurts the overall education of the youngsters.

As for the teacher's movement through the system, there is a dichotomy created by the in-place existence of traditional protective devices upon which unionized status has been imposed. Are the teachers to be treated as professionals or as union workers? In their view, of course, the safeguards of both should be maintained, but we cannot always be certain that this hybrid system guarantees the retention of the best teachers or the optimum educational opportunities for the students.

Promotion seems to be a hard-and-fast rule-book process. The teacher works for a master's degree which, together with continuation in the school system for a set period, qualifies him or her for advancement and eventual tenure—a special status that guarantees additional job security. I don't particularly care for credentialism as the sole criterion for advancement, just as I don't believe that publication of one's writings makes one a great teacher. I have observed that some colleges offer masters' courses that are flimsy and frothy, knowing that teachers must acquire the degree to advance themselves. I would prefer a system whereby the degree is coupled with some performance criteria, evaluating the teacher *as a teacher in the classroom.*

Seniority can be troublesome as a hard-and-fast guideline for promotion or layoffs; for example, a district forced to cut its staff may find itself with three senior German-language teachers for fifteen students and only two teachers certified in required-for-everyone math specialties. Is there an alternative to seniority status as a pecking order in advancement or dismissal? Other than rules or laws interrupting seniority to prevent skewing of the curriculum, I can think of none.

Tenure (job security) was a good idea when it was established in the early 1900s, in New Jersey; in those days, the teacher had no champion but the law. Today, it seems to me that unionized teachers have more than adequate contract protections, without a further need for legal roadblocks barring dismissal of incompetent teachers. In an April 1981 WCBS-TV editorial, Gary Cummings said it this way to a New York/ New Jersey/Connecticut audience:

"Gradually over the years, tenure has become a barrier to quality education by making it nearly impossible for schools to fire weak or incompetent teachers. . . . Though tenure today is an article of faith in the teaching profession, there is increasing . . . talk of loosening the inflexible grip of tenure, so principals can demand excellence from teachers and remove them if they don't measure up. . . .

"There may have been a need for tenure 75 years ago. But today, with teachers' unions, with other job protections, the need may have expired. The need today is for high quality teaching, for first-rate educational management. Tenure for incompetents can inhibit or prohibit both of these goals."

It is in no one's interest to continue an incompetent teacher in the classroom. The cause of education is best served by eliminating such people as soon as is consistent with due process; the unions can be counted upon to see that due process is provided, either by statute or regulation, but they understand full well that a poor teacher is not a credit to their profession.

More educational "bang for the buck" is easier to shout about than to achieve—because in dealing with teachers, we are dealing with *people,* who cannot be shelved or discarded like excess inventory or obsolete merchandise. On the other hand, those who are paying for school services and those who are benefiting from them are people, too. Obviously, cost-effectiveness is a matter which requires understanding of the other person's needs and problems—and goals.

If there is one overriding principle which should be our guideline, it is this:

Cost-cutting which reduces the *quality* of educational services is false economy—eventually to be paid for in terms of generations of inadequately prepared young people.

MAINSTREAMING THE HANDICAPPED

One of the most recent developments in public education is the mainstreaming of handicapped children into regular classes. The federal government, with the states close behind, had ordered that these children, once purposely kept apart from their "normal" contemporaries, be given access to the public schools, where they will take their places in grades and classrooms appropriate to their age group. The rationale is very persuasive. First, it gives the handicapped child a chance to spend time with others like himself or herself in every way except for the handicap, to learn to live in concert with nonhandicapped people and to hold his or her own in that setting. Second, it gives the "normal" kids an opportunity to know and associate with and accept their handicapped peers. Third, it lifts a burden from the shoulders of many who are not equipped to pay the tremendous costs of maintaining handicapped children at private facilities.

On the other side of the ledger, we have already mentioned two seeming drawbacks of mainstreaming. If the handicapped children are to be properly instructed and cared for in public schools, the cost of so doing will increase school budgets significantly, with the U.S. authorities who mandated the mainstreaming still unready to provide the funding for it. At a moment when tax money is hard to come by, this is a real problem. We have also discussed the difficulties which might arise when a teacher must divert her attention from teaching her class to quiet a youngster whose handicap is nervous, autistic, or otherwise disruptive. The schooling of the class as a whole, including nondisruptive handicapped youngsters, suffers from such diversions.

Frankly, I think that mainstreaming of the handicapped deserves the best try we can give it. The process is still far too new and untested to call for a final verdict immediately. As with all experiments, there are bugs to be worked out. I am convinced that we should give mainstreaming a fair chance. Only experience will indicate where present arrangements may be altered in the best interest of the handicapped child and his normal colleagues. Let us put our hearts in it and our minds to it, and make it work if we can.

To be perfectly honest in expressing a personal observation, the worst enemies of mainstreaming are its most ardent supporters: the parents of handicapped children. Usually charming and persuasive as individuals or in small conversational groups, they become holy terrors when led en masse by a bullhorn-equipped firebrand. In all my years in education, I have not come into contact with groups of less reasonable, more intractable people. The term "nonnegotiable demand," which originated with the disruptive college students of the Vietnam era, has now become the property of the parents of the handicapped. They have one asset, public sympathy for kids generally and handicapped kids in particular, and they pump this emotional advantage for all it is worth. Whether they are picketing or invading public meetings or whatever, they refuse to observe procedural rules which apply to all, even the rules of order.

Examples? During my eleven years as Regent, I have only been picketed at my personal business office twice—on both occasions by parents and teachers of the handicapped. The first occasion, a relatively polite one, urged my help in changing a rule which was (in my view, as in theirs) not entirely equitable. The second was a media event, staged for the cameras and reporters, with shouting and horn-blowing and whatever else could attract public attention by disrupting the concentration of myself and my coworkers. That spectacle was followed by a picketing of the Education Building and the state Capitol at Albany, which the parents preferred rather than an offered opportunity to testify before a Regents' committee about their grievances. Another group from an expensive private school for the severely handicapped virtually took over two Regents' meetings at Albany with an angry invasion not only of the meetings but the press conferences which followed.

Their ardor is as understandable as their tactics are unacceptable. The present danger to education from their demands has been discussed earlier: With far more success than even minority groups have achieved, the protagonists of the handicapped have insisted not only upon equal opportunity but equal *results,* even when that would demean the entire educational system of credentials for successful achievement of given standards of performance.

Perhaps not every handicapped child can be or should be mainstreamed. Only time will tell, and trial-and-error. The criterion for mainstreaming should include not only the best interests of the handicapped child who is being brought "out of the attic" into a new educational life with his or her peers, but also the best interests of all the children in the schools they attend. One should not be helped at the expense of the other.

Further, we must be more precise as to our definitions of handicapped. We are getting there. Very few children enter school without some handicap, obvious or hidden. Perhaps it is physical: sight or hearing deficiency, inability to walk or use one's limbs, slurred speech. Perhaps it is psychological or mental: brain damage, phobias, hostility to other children, autistic disruptive tendencies. Perhaps it is experiential and social: linguistic problems, previous inadequate schooling, nonintellectual family surroundings, lack of home discipline, other family problems. The mainstreaming device is primarily intended to help those in the first (physical-psychological-mental) category; the others are in school already. But they all have handicaps which must somehow be overcome, and they all deserve special attention to overcome those handicaps. Most important, they must not be simply branded handicapped, handed a diploma or certificate, and tossed out of the educational system. To do so is to default on our obligation to *every* child.

Meanwhile, let's give mainstreaming the chance it deserves.

"CENSORSHIP" IN SCHOOL LIBRARIES

After more than thirty-five years in a career devoted to publishing books, I am a hard-and-fast enemy of censorship.

What's more, I know what it is.

And I am aware that much of what is called "censorship" is not censorship at all, but rather the exercise of responsibility for choice—a sometimes awkward exercise, perhaps, but hardly in the category of censorship.

Censorship is the action of keeping something from being published or performed or narrated. Censorship is Hitler's destruction of books by fire in Nazi Germany; censorship is the clipping-out of soldiers' letters home to prevent leaks of information dangerous to the war effort; censorship is the Regents' function (long since abandoned) of ruling whether a given film could be presented in the theaters of New York State.

The action of removing or excluding certain books from the library of a school is *not* censorship.

When a book is offered by its author for publication, editors in the employ of publishing houses may reject it. That is not censorship—although if *all* editors reject it, it may never see print. Publishing being a rather liberal pursuit, Senator Barry Goldwater's *Conscience of a Conserva-*

tive was turned down by so many trade publishing houses that the Senator finally had it published by a "vanity" house—one that will do a book subsidized by the author. (*Conscience of a Conservative* was so successful that a trade publisher gobbled it up on a later go-round, profits taking precedence over politics.) When a mystery novel is submitted to my book-club editors, they may accept or reject it—but they are not censors. Nor are the paperback publishers or motion-picture producers to whom it may be offered, should they choose not to accept it.

By the same token, those who select volumes for school libraries cannot (for budgetary reasons alone) buy every book that is published. They may be offered two books of striking similarity, but by purchasing A and not purchasing B, do they become censors? Of course not. They are exercising their responsibility to *select,* intelligently and conscientiously, books that are appropriate for the young readers who use the libraries.

Aha . . . but what of school authorities who *remove* books from school library shelves? Surely they are censors, aren't they?

No.

A board of education is responsible to the people of the community for all that happens within the schools, including the school libraries. Normally, they leave the question of book selection in the first instance to administrative management. But that does not abrogate their responsibility or right to have the final say about which books are to be available on the school library's shelves. If a book already there is challenged by irate parents or local citizens, and if the school board agrees that it is unsuitable for students of the ages served by the library (and should therefore not have been bought in the first place), they have a right to remove it because they, the board, are ultimately accountable for what takes place in the school.

In an ongoing dispute about the removal of some novels from a junior-high library in Island Trees, New York, the argument was advanced that some of the titles were Pulitzer Prize winners and long-time best sellers. That was certainly true, but such broad literary accolades do not necessarily make a given work appropriate for a young audience. The winners of the annual Cannes Film Festival may be great movies, but they may not constitute intellectual enhancement for my junior-high-schooler. The school library, designed to enhance the learning and intellectual development of the youthful readers it serves without impairing their morals, has a somewhat different purpose from the public library on Main Street, whose fare includes adult-oriented volumes and books intended primarily for relaxation and entertainment. A third "library," the local bookstore and the rack in the corner candy store, is even freer to purvey whatever the traffic wants, while mail-order catalogs help fill home library shelves. The absence of a given book from *one* of these certainly does not remove it from public availability.

It is passing strange that we will howl to high heaven about the removal of a book from a school library, but accept without a whimper the movie producers' rating system which is based upon the suitability of films for people of various ages . . . a process which in turn is grounded in the correct idea that not everything is right for everyone to see and hear. Add "read" to that, and you have the perfectly tenable rationale for selectivity on the shelves of school libraries.

As for questions of pornography, I seem to recall that the U.S. Supreme Court declined to attempt a definition of what was pornographic or obscene or appealing to prurient interest, saying that this was best left to community standards. Where the case of a questioned book involves judgments on such grounds, there is no more justifiable "community standard" than that set by those who've been chosen by the community to oversee the education of its children—the school board.

A forward-looking board will attempt to foreclose disputes by taking the community into the process of choosing school library books in the first instance. Textbooks must continue to be selected by teachers, but it is certainly possible to appoint and convene periodically a citizens' review committee to look over books which the administrative buyers would like to purchase for the school library. The committee should not have final say over which books are to be bought; that remains the prerogative of the board and of whomever it appoints to the job from among the staff. But prior review by community representatives (who will seldom agree among themselves about literary merit, but will agree more often than one might expect about acceptability) may forestall later demands for removals and all the furor which accompanies such squabbles.

EVOLUTION VERSUS CREATIONISM

For a half-century, the Darwinian idea that man evolved from a lower order of creatures has enjoyed a virtual monopoly in the biology curricula of virtually every school and college in the land, save those under the auspices of religious groups which hold to the Biblical account of creation as the correct explanation of the origins of the world and of mankind. The creationists, who once had reigned supreme while the evolutionists struggled to be heard, have been out in the cold.

But no more.

Now the creationists have come on fighting, demanding that both evolution and creationism be treated as theories, either of which could be correct. And the reigning evolutionists, now in control of most biology departments, are battling the creationists tooth and nail in every jurisdiction, insisting that the Biblical theory is not only untenable but also a religious notion that has no right to be mentioned in public schools.

In a few states, notably Arkansas and Louisiana, creationism has won the right to be included in biology courses, as a theory and not to the exclusion of evolution. In California, a judge has instructed that evolution is to be presented as theory and not as absolute fact. Some small gains have been posted elsewhere by the creationists, but the battle is far from over.

I have an open mind as to the merits of the contending theories. Certainly evolution appears to be the more "scientific" of the two, requiring acceptance as matters of belief a somewhat less spectacular succession of events than those described in the Bible. But that is not to say that creation *cannot* have occurred as the Bible said it did, and the creationists have advanced a sizable set of geological evidences that the process described by the evolutionists may not actually have occurred as they tell it. Darwin himself said that his views constituted a theory. I prefer to consider *both* views as theories, which is apparently all the creationists want.

What troubles me most is what the current controversy reveals about the American Civil Liberties Union. There was a time when the ACLU would have been right in there fighting for the right of *every* viewpoint to be heard. Certainly the cause of intellectual freedom would seem to be best served by the inclusion rather than the exclusion of competing theories in any area of human study; that point was made by one governor who signed a bill requiring the addition of creationism to school curricula as a theory.

But the ACLU of 1981 has moved to *suppress* the inclusion of creationist theory and thus to preserve the evolutionist monopoly in the schools. It will attempt to overturn new laws which include creationism in a state's educational offerings as a balance to evolution.

Because those who run the modern ACLU are so strongly convinced of the correctness of one theory (evolution) and the wrongness of the other (creationism), and so determined to keep out of public-school studies anything smacking of religion, even as a theory, they are willing to contract, rather than expand, the horizons of young people in the nation's schools, and to kill off the competition of ideas which has been our strength—and the ACLU's guiding principle—for so long.

The American Civil Liberties Union has come a far way since their founding more than fifty years ago. Unfortunately, they've come the *wrong* way, in this case at least.

THE GIFTED AND TALENTED

There's a lot of commotion these days about the fact that we are not paying enough attention to the education of those students who are especially gifted and especially talented in various subjects. Like every other special pleading, these complaints are coupled with demands for more state money to be exclusively spent for development of special talents.

There is absolutely nothing wrong with recognizing that certain children have been richly endowed with intellectual or physical capabilities which place them well ahead of their contemporaries. There have always been such stand-out kids, bordering on genius. When I was young, it was not uncommon for a particularly gifted young person to enter college at, say, fifteen, and to graduate at nineteen. The smarter ones in our schools were being "skipped" ahead all the time, if their parents were amenable.

I have noted earlier that the purpose of education, as defined lucidly by former New York Commissioner Joe Nyquist, is to enable every child to become all that he or she is capable of being. If that is true, and I concur in it, we should certainly be helping the talented kids to move along as fast as their talents permit. To keep them back, in classes which offer no challenge, is to subject them to a stifling intellectual environment and to cultivate poor study habits.

But that is exactly what we are doing. I mentioned earlier our seemingly unquestioning acceptance of the modernist "mixmaster" theory of class assignment, whereby slow learners, average achievers, and the specially gifted are tossed into class together *as a matter of policy* because to "track" children according to their ability to absorb education is an "elitist" practice which does not fit into integration philosophy.

Elitist or not, the idea of ability-tracking does follow the Nyquist formula; it does allow each child to learn at his or her own pace, and it allows the teacher to concentrate upon the special needs and challenges of his or her students, rather than having to try to reach each segment separately during the course of the school day.

Many mommies and daddies don't go for tracking, if their own child isn't in the advanced class. They see a lower-level achievement grouping as some sort of social brand, consigning Sonny to permanent inferior status and killing his initiative. What they don't realize is that Sonny will get the special, perhaps remedial attention he needs and can move into a higher-level group whenever he demonstrates ability to master the work at their rate of speed. Being dazzled all day by the whiz kids in a mixed class can be far more depressing than being a good student in the average segment.

The point is this: Which system will offer a child the opportunity to make the best of his or her own talents? My answer is that system which better enables the child to move ahead at his or her optimum pace and to receive as much teacher attention as is needed to do so. That system is ability-tracking.

The mixmaster theory has made us schizophrenic about our schools. On the one hand, we insist that all students, regardless of their needs or abilities, be thrown into a single pot, their classroom. Having done that, we then insist upon weeding them out again; learning-disadvantaged kids, mainstreamed handicapped kids, and now gifted and talented kids are to be supplied with special (and different) attention, aids, and assistance. Why not track them by ability and maximize the special help that can be applied to each student as he or she moves along apace with his or her classmates? It is a better use of taxpayers' money, and it is likely to be more effective. After all, it was effective when it was the regular order of assignment, before elitist became a dirty word.

Think about it.

TEACHING THOSE WHO DON'T SPEAK ENGLISH

It is bad enough that we in the United States do not insist that our native-born children learn at least one language in addition to English, but it would be a disaster if we did not make a maximum effort to teach English to all who come to reside here and do not know the national language.

Mastery of English was a foregone conclusion, a universal goal, for all those who reached our shores in the great waves of immigration during the 1800s and early 1900s.

Most of our immigrants were poor; they scrimped and struggled to save enough for steerage passage to America. The reasons for forsaking their native lands were varied: some left because of persecution or discrimination, some to escape military conscription; others fled economic misery. But most had one thing in common: when they left, they *left*. They were not transient visitors; they were determined to make the United States their permanent home, to learn the language, to become citizens, to find decent jobs at wages sufficient to support their families. Their intention to break with their homelands was strong; costs and travel conditions were such that they knew a long time would pass before they had an opportunity to return to the land of their birth—if indeed they ever returned.

That is not necessarily the case today. Take, for example, the large Puerto Rican population in the Northeast. They do not have to become U.S. citizens; they already are. They come from a land where both

Spanish and English are regularly spoken; they are not strangers to the tongue. And the cost of plane fare back to their native island is within the reach of most. Their break with their past is far less sharp, traumatic, or irreversible than that of those Europeans and Asians who came to our shores decades earlier, or those who come to us today as refugees from oppression somewhere in the world. And their impetus to learn English better than they already know it is not as strong. What is strong—as it was strong, despite the urge to Americanize, for the waves of immigrants of the Ellis Island era—is their understandable desire to maintain their ethnic heritage.

Show me an American of Irish descent—or Italian or German or Polish or Scandinavian or Chinese—who does not understand and sympathize with this desire, and I will show you a man who doesn't know the history of his own people in America. It is grossly unfair to criticize young people of Hispanic descent for not being as gung-ho about Americanization as the kids whose families stepped off the boats into the Land of Opportunity years ago. Our own native-born children are not nearly as well sold on the virtues of being an American as we were. Why should we expect others in our midst to react differently?

What is important is to teach English to those youngsters who are here in America and don't know the language.

We have always emphasized the need to learn English, and we still do. Now, however, we are fighting about how to do it best.

The old-fashioned way which prevailed during the mass immigrations was fairly simple; it could also be cruel and inadequate. Newly arrived students, most without any knowledge of English, were unceremoniously dumped into regular classes in all subjects, wherein they fended for themselves as best they could. The theory was that if these young people really wanted to become Americans (and they did!), they would undergo whatever sacrifices were needed, for as long as they were needed, to do so. Somehow, they made it.

The lot of today's non- or limited-English-speaking kids is much better. We now make a deliberate effort to enable them to learn English as quickly and thoroughly as possible.

Most such programs seem to be in the *bilingual* mode, which, as Fred Hechinger has defined it in the *New York Times*, ". . . holds that non-English-speaking children should be taught the regular academic subjects, such as reading, mathematics and social studies, in their own language, by teachers who master the children's native tongue as well as English, until they are ready to cope with English in regular classes."

Bilingual education's rival is a method whereby, as Hechinger reports, ". . . intensive English instruction [is] given to all non-English-speaking children together by specially trained teachers. Otherwise, they attend regular classes together with their English-speaking peers." This approach is called *ESL—English as a second language*—which is reasonably descriptive but almost certainly guarantees to rile the juices of those who recall the successes of the early immigrants and insist that in these United States, English is either the primary language or the only language—never, in any circumstances, the *second* language.

It is my observation that educators have an almost unerring instinct for pinning the wrong labels on things—names that are sure to provoke the greatest resistance. In the early 1970s, New York State organized an experimental program for use of closed-circuit television by classroom teachers; I've seen it in operation, and it appeared to work fairly well. However, although they could have called it Television as a Classroom Tool (TACT) or Instructional Video for Teaching (INVITE), or some equally accurate, more unabrasive title, they chose to dub it *Improving Cost Effectiveness* through Instructional Television (ICEIT), the first three words of which were immediately diagnosed by the organized teachers, whom it was designed to help, as a thinly veiled scheme to replace them with teaching machines. The result? Their protests "iced it," and I haven't heard about it since.

Bilingual education is perceived to have two major drawbacks. One is the tremendous additional cost of locating and hiring bilingual teachers able to speak in two languages to students from many different backgrounds. An ill-timed, ill-conceived decree from the U.S. Department of Education that would have required all school districts to provide native language instruction for every class of at least twenty-five pupils was scrapped by Secretary Bell, who estimated that (inasmuch as this was one of those programs that is ordered, but not financed, by the feds), the five-year start-up cost of $1 billion and the annual $150 million cost thereafter would be too onerous for the local school systems, which should be allowed to choose their own way of teaching English to non-English-speakers. The only mandate (of the courts as well as of the Department) is that the district must find *some* way to do it.

The second problem with the bilingual approach is educational rather than financial. Hechinger quotes one opinion that ". . . many non-English-speaking youngsters . . . come from homes where no English is spoken. In school, they attend most of their bilingual classes surrounded by other non-English-speaking children, while getting most of their instruction in their native tongue. After school, they return to a neighborhood where once again little if any English is spoken. The burden of teaching them English falls on a minute portion of their day. Since they are given to understand that bilingual instructions will keep them from falling behind in their academic subjects, there is little incentive for them to speed their mastery of English."

Further, a considerable body of agreement among modern language teachers holds that "immersion," that is, constant and virtually exclusive exposure to the language to be learned, is the best way for young people to become proficient in the language and its use. This, of course, is one of the justifications for the year of study abroad which so many colleges offer today.

My own experience tells me that this makes sense. While I took three years of French in high school and one in college, and no German at all, I found that everyday dealings with French, Belgian, and German civilians and military personnel during five Northern Europe campaigns in 1944–45 expanded my command of both languages to the point where I could carry on an intelligent discourse, albeit not on a high plane of vocabulary and not in the most polished grammar.

What's more, I've observed an excellent ESL program in action on Long Island, and it works.

While I doubt that all the results are in yet, except for a quite obvious cost-effectiveness advantage for ESL, and while I will therefore reserve my own final judgment as to which method does the job best, perhaps we should ponder the thoughts of Abigail M. Thernstrom, writing in *The Public Interest* in 1980:

"Bilingual education has spread to most corners of the nation. And judicial decisions make it especially difficult to uproot.

"Nor can its consequences be dismissed lightly. We once believed that the nation represented values to which immigrants could subscribe—values which transcended ethnic lines. And we believed in the role of schools in transmitting those values. The advent of bilingual education did not, of course, single-handedly strip us of our faith in American culture of sufficiently universal appeal to cross ethnic lines. But in promoting the notion that the process of Americanization was hopelessly ethnocentric, and in robbing the schools of their traditional integrative function, it has certainly played an important part."

12.

A New York Vignette

The Firing
of Joe Nyquist

I HAVE LIVED my entire life in New York State, first in New York City, and then in its suburbs. My experiences with education—as a student in the public schools, as a parent, and as the leader of the top state governing body—have all been in New York. For that reason, many of the observations and anecdotes in this book have their origins in the Empire State.

Lest you get the idea that this is a provincial book, however, let me add that I have learned a great deal about education in other states—from my reading, from more than a decade of close association with other state board members in the National Association of State Boards of Education (NASBE), and lately from my membership on a federal panel studying the financing of elementary and secondary education throughout the country.

New York is far from typical. *There is no such thing as a typical American state.* They're all different, and their different problems call for different solutions. That is at once the great strength of the American Union, and the reason why a single federal answer to a widespread problem may not be successfully applicable to every one of the fifty states.

Even so, there are certain truisms which do have validity across the board. One of these is that leadership, even in what is supposed to be the relatively tranquil world of education, is not a bowl of cherries or (to use a more current idiom) a piece of cake. Another is that our very necessary insistence upon excellence and quality sometimes points in more than

282

one direction, requiring a very difficult choice. Both of these truisms are illustrated in this chapter—the story of a decision which shocked the educational world.

No story is ever completely told. Even if it is only someone's fleeting recollection of a bit of action or a spoken phrase, even if it is an angle or a by-effect that has not been thought about or touched upon, there is always something more to every story. The vignette which follows is that "something more." I do not claim that it is the last word; it probably won't be. What I do say is that the story of the Regents' dismissal of Commissioner Joe Nyquist, a "red hot" news item while it was happening, is woefully incomplete and somewhat unbalanced so far. Having presided over the Regents' deliberations, in both public and executive sessions, I can amplify and add dimension to this segment of New York's educational history—from the point of view of one upon whose shoulders the burden of leadership did not always fall lightly.

On July 1, 1976, the fifteen men and women of the New York State Board of Regents paused during their public meeting to give a standing ovation to their Commissioner, Ewald B. "Joe" Nyquist, who was about to leave for Stockholm, where he would accept the honor of "Swedish-American of the Year" as part of our bicentennial celebration.

On November 19, 1976, the Regents fired him.

Here is what happened, and how it happened.

Ewald B. Nyquist (his charming and versatile wife, Jan, is the only human entitled to call him "Ewald") was raised in Rockford, Illinois, of Swedish stock. At the University of Chicago, he was blocking back for All-American Jay Berwanger in the mid-thirties; there he acquired the nickname "Swede," although by 1969, when I joined the Board, everyone called him "Joe."

To those who like him and whom he likes, Joe Nyquist is a warm, cheerful, personable, humorous, hospitable, talented, innovative man whose views on life and people are expressed frankly and spontaneously (a characteristic which I admire; not everyone does). Although we were occasionally at odds about this subject or that, my first four years as Regent, spent sitting next to Joe at the foot of the table, brought me to understand his essential humanity, which he sometimes offset (to his detriment) by his ill-concealed, almost fractious disdain of proposals he thought unworthy and of people with whom he simply could not establish a rapport. Joe was and is a straightforward man; if he likes you, you know it—and if he doesn't like you, you know it. What's more, he is the quintessential blocking back; those who stand in his way do so at their peril.

Happily, he and I hit it off from the word go. He was, and is, a friend.

It is for these and other reasons that my most frustrating failure as Regents' Chancellor was my inability to save him when the question of his continued employment as Commissioner was on the block in November of 1976.

Joe Becomes Commissioner of Education

My first meeting as a brand-new, wet-behind-the-ears Regent was Joe's first as Acting Commissioner, in May 1969. His predecessor, Jim Allen, had resigned in April to become Richard Nixon's U.S. Commissioner of Education (an odd-couple, liberal-conservative relationship which did not last overlong; shortly after he left government, Jim and Florence Allen died in a tragic small-plane crash). Having been Jim's Executive Deputy Commissioner, Joe was serving in May as Acting Commissioner until a permanent choice could be made from among a number of outstanding candidates, of which he was one.

Before I had a chance to become well acquainted with Joe, we had to make our choice. Other names were discussed and discarded; some of them (whose records impressed me) were vetoed as unacceptable to one or more Regents whose views were honored by the rest of us. It finally came down to Joe Nyquist: yes or no. A valid political truism being that you can't beat somebody with nobody, those on the Board who opposed Joe's designation (for a variety of reasons) came up short—but not by much. The vote was tight, but when it was over and Joe had won a majority, we closed ranks and made it unanimous. He was *our* Commissioner now.

Because I was new on the Board, I had been told a great deal by those on both sides of the argument. Rather than rehash these conversations, I will simply say that I was more persuaded by those who opposed Joe than by those who favored him, and I was thoroughly at odds with his stated position in support of busing for racial integration of the schools. I voted "no" on his appointment. Happily for the State of New York, I lost. My "no" vote was a mistake.

It was a mistake because Joe Nyquist was and is, in his own way, fully as dedicated to the promotion of excellence and quality in education and fully as conscious of the need for the highest standards of academic achievement as am I—or any other American who feels as I do. And he knew how to translate that dedication into practice. I was to learn this as the years of my Regents service and Joe's Commissionership went by.

A Fearless and Innovative Commissioner

New York's Commissioner of Education (while not a Regent) is not only the Regents' chief executive officer; he administers all education in the state, public and private, from nursery school to professional school, plus libraries and museums. Right from the start, Commissioner Joe Nyquist stepped out front as an educational leader and a man unafraid to take the initiative in developing new and effective ideas.

In his inaugural address at Saratoga Springs, he unveiled his idea for a Regents' External Degree program, whereby men and women, studying at home to pass examinations at college level prepared by college faculty, could earn associate's, and later bachelor's and master's degrees. When I left the Board in 1980, more than 10,000 of these home-study credentials had been awarded to Americans who would not otherwise have had a chance to qualify. The Middle States assessment team, which exercises stern control over quality in higher education, granted its hard-to-earn accreditation to the program in 1978, and other states have copied New York's pioneer effort, which was Joe Nyquist's.

When a task force of his own staff (of which he was usually fiercely protective) recommended termination of the more than a hundred-year-old Regents' examinations, Joe disagreed, recommending that the exams be retained, which they were—as I have discussed elsewhere in this book—as unique assurances of academic achievement proved on the basis of statewide standards.

Although the program was not finally polished and set into place by the Regents until after he had gone, it was Joe Nyquist who first initiated construction of a set of minimum-competency tests in the basic skills of reading and mathematics—a medium of accountability which has now become widespread in the U.S. in response to public restlessness about declining test scores and other evidences of inadequate preparation for existence in today's society. Credit for New York's program should be shared by Joe and by his successor, Gordon Ambach, for the success of this highly complex and strenuously resisted program ... which takes us a long way on the road back to effective standards of scholastic achievement.

One of the most controversial moves that Joe made in his quest for excellence was his decision, backed by the Regents, to place a moratorium upon authorization of new doctoral programs in New York State until existing programs could be reevaluated and steps taken to eliminate the weaker ones. This effort (which was quietly welcomed by college officials who would have been politically powerless to weed out the "duds" themselves and were happy that the state was doing it) was bucked only by State University, which took the Commissioner to court in an effort to prevent him from sacking any of their doctoral degree programs. They lost; Joe Nyquist—and standards of excellence—won.

There were many other instances of Joe's effective devotion to educational quality which I shall not mention here. Suffice it to say that his deeds, like his words, left no doubt in my mind that, despite our differences from time to time, Joe's devotion to excellence was just as strong and sincere as my own.

The Sore Spot: Busing for Racial Integration

As mentioned earlier, my outspoken views against forced transportation beyond normal distances for racial integration of the schools were published and well known before 1969, when the State Legislature elected me to the Board. Those views were directly at odds with Joe Nyquist's (and the sitting Regents') but squarely in line with the opinions of a substantial majority of New Yorkers (and Americans everywhere), as well as their legislators, whose uneasy frustration with the ongoing pro-busing stance taken by the Commissioner and the Regents (myself excepted) should have hinted at what was ahead.

For the first four years of my tenure, no other new members were elected to the Board; we had fifteen-year terms, one of which expired each year, with reelection being almost a foregone conclusion until the Regent reached seventy, after which the law we called "statutory senility" required retirement.

Suddenly, in 1973, the long tradition of automatic reelection was broken. Charlie Millard, a senior Regent whose support for busing placed him at loggerheads with the Republican majorities in the legislature, was denied renewal; his seat was awarded to Woody Genrich, an on-the-record opponent of busing. Steve Bailey of Syracuse, who supported the Board's policy, resigned later that year, to be replaced by Emlyn Griffith, another busing foe. Then Helen Power of Rochester and Joe King of Queens publicly joined me on the antibusing side of some votes; the Lone Regent had acquired four allies.

In 1974, the five opponents of busing became seven, one short of a majority, as Vice Chancellor Everett Penny of Westchester (no lover of busing, but a firm believer in unity behind the Board's majority) and Max Rubin of New York City retired, their seats being filled by Bill Jovanovich, whose spoken and written objections to busing were well known, and Ginny Klein, a peppery and vocal enemy of busing. I was unanimously elected Vice Chancellor in February of that year; although Jack Allan, who nominated me, and many of my colleagues still disagreed with my antibusing stance, they did not let that single issue color their evaluations of a fellow-Regent.

More Brickbats from the Legislature

Having tasted blood with their precedent-shattering rejection of Charlie Millard's reelection bid, and realizing that Nyquist served at the pleasure of the Regents without a contract, the legislative leadership redoubled its efforts to speed up changes in the Board's membership.

The fifteen-year term was cut to seven (the Assembly wanted five), doubling the turnover rate; a Senate bill which would have culled out two Regents per year (replacing the whole Board within eight years or sooner, considering retirements) was barely stopped before it became law. Jurisdiction over the administration of financial aid to students and colleges was yanked away from the Regents and handed to a new corporation. With great fanfare, the Office of Inspector-General for Education was created and manned by Dan Klepak, a tough-minded, veteran civil servant, charged with ferreting out suspected waste and extravagance in the educational system; finding none, he moved on to other things and the I.G. office did a Halley's Comet into history. In 1975, over the Regents' sensible but vain objections, the Legislature and Governor Carey transferred responsibility for the investigation and prosecution of medical-discipline cases from the State Education Department to the Department of Health—a change which had produced little if any improvement six years later.

And a measure was introduced into both houses which would have upset the long-standing independence of education by removing the power of the Commissioner, in his judicial capacity, to make decisions which were not subject to court review except on difficult-to-prove grounds that they were arbitrary and capricious. Actually, its passage would not have guaranteed protection against busing, because the whole subject was moving out of the hands of education authorities and elected officials into those of unelected federal judges. Indeed, shifting the onus of busing decisions from the Commissioner to the courts could have taken some of the heat off Joe Nyquist, but Joe was not an onus-shifter; he and the Regents (including me) opposed the bill.

It was not difficult to divine what the legislature was up to. They kept up the pressure on the Regents (and worked to speed changes in the Board's membership) for two reasons: to hasten abandonment of the Regents' probusing policy, and to hasten the dismissal of the Commissioner who was blamed for it.

Would the 1974 Electoral Upheaval Make a Difference?

Then came the 1974 elections. With the Republicans in disarray after Watergate, Democrat Hugh Carey ousted incumbent Governor Malcolm Wilson from the Executive Mansion and the Democrats piled up an Assembly majority large enough to assure them of the numerical strength needed to elect Regents in joint session.

What would this mean for racial-integration busing and for Joe Nyquist, busing's best-known champion in New York?

On paper, it looked good. Since 1969, all the Democrats who had served on the Board had gone along with its policy on busing. To those who habitually preferred labeling to thought, Democrat=liberal=pro-busing, while Republican=conservative=antibusing. And now it was the Democrats' turn to run the state.

This form chart had one fatal flaw: *many of the Democrats in the new legislature were not happy about busing at all.* Most of them came from urban areas where uprooting children for school assignments on a racial basis was a controversial hot potato. Rural Republicans from areas where few minority students lived were not subjected to anything like the antibusing pressures brought to bear on the city Democrats. The political scenario was not the sure thing that simplistic prognosticators claimed it would be.

Turmoil Inside the Board of Regents

Meanwhile, the busing issue continued to erode the unity of the Regents, which was so important to education in the state. A Regent's personal position on busing for racial integration began to govern his or her relationships with the other Regents—and that was bad news for a Board which relied for its success upon its members' ability to reach a consensus on many, many issues, of which busing was but one.

Chancellor Joe McGovern, who had for several years indicated a desire to step down, had no intention of leaving before this deteriorating internal situation was stopped; he had agreed, in 1974, that a new position paper on racial integration should be drafted in a sincere effort to reach a consensus once and for all. He assigned himself, Eddie Warburg, Frank McGinley, Bill Jovanovich, and me to the task of working up a presentable document. A series of misunderstandings, some quite bitter, required several tries before a final statement was adopted in February 1975.

For the first time, the Regents formally agreed upon a set of priorities which I had been urging upon them for years; they now were willing to state, as a matter of policy, that the health, safety, and well-being of children to be bused, and assurance of the quality of education at the end of their bus ride, were to take precedence over any other considerations. With some defections at both ends of the spectrum, we at last had agreement. Joe Nyquist announced that he could live with the new priorities, and directed school districts under busing orders to set up grievance procedures for parents contesting such orders.

With the busing question cooled (at least as far as the Regents were concerned), Joe McGovern announced his retirement, and (with Joe nominating and Ken Clark seconding), I was unanimously chosen the thirtieth Chancellor of the 191-year-old Board (and the first Chancellor from Long Island) on February 19, 1975, my son Walter's seventeenth birthday, to take office on April 1. Carl Pforzheimer of Westchester succeeded me as Vice Chancellor.

As I prepared to tackle what I knew to be one of the toughest jobs in American education—not only presiding over but *leading* the oldest continuing state educational governing body with the broadest policy-making jurisdiction and the greatest independent authority of any state in the Union—everything seemed to be rosy.

But everything was not what it seemed.

New Troubles Brewing

The first three Regents elected by the 1975 Democratic majority in the legislature took their seats with little fanfare (although a court fight was required before their election could be cleared). Mary Alice Kendall, Jorge Batista, and Lou Yavner settled in to become productive Regents; the busing issue having been shunted to the back burner by our February statement, their views on it were neither solicited nor manifested when they took office on April 1.

But new troubles were brewing for the Regents in the Capitol.

Every Governor of New York, as he takes his seat for the first time, learns to his disappointment that while he is responsible for including education money in his annual budget, he has no control whatsoever over the Regents or the State Education Department. The Commissioner, while technically a member of the Governor's cabinet, is an appointee of and responsible to the Regents, not the Governor. Governors have no built-in patronage in the Department, which employs more than 3,000 people. The independence of the educational system in New York may be a delight to the educational community—but not to the Governor. And Hugh Leo Carey was no exception.

Hugh Carey is (like me) a Brooklyn Irishman with an affinity for politics. Perhaps that's why we understand each other so well, and get along so well. Whatever the case, he quickly ascertained that the state's legislators (on both sides of the political aisle) harbored no great love for the probusing Regents—and even less for Commissioner Nyquist. What's more, he knew that the legislators, like the Governor, had no access to the fertile field of potential patronage that was the State Education Department. In his 1975 inaugural address, Governor Carey proclaimed the end of New York's "days of wine and roses" and began to wield a meat-ax on state jobs. Predictably, one of the hardest-hit areas was education; here the leaders of the legislature gleefully joined the Governor in lopping off some of the most valued top-level staffers in the Department. Of course, these weren't killed off by *name;* for example, an innocent-looking line in the budget eliminated "one Associate Commissioner for Legal Affairs." The trouble was that there was only *one* such Associate Commissioner: John Jehu, a remarkably learned public servant who had constantly aided legislators as well as educators with answers to their questions about the education law. When I stumbled through the snow to the capitol, asking for a reprieve for John and so many other hardworking and badly needed people, all I got was understanding smiles and no restorations of the cuts. If the Regents wouldn't give Joe Nyquist the sack, then the legislators would use their favorite weapon—money—to hack his top staff to pieces. It was a cruel time.

Simultaneously, the high-stakes players in the popular game of whittling away the Regents' authority started a new round.

Every incoming Governor of New York is treated to the same song-and-dance: take higher education away from the Regents and the Commissioner and set up a separate body (under *your* control, Governor) to be independently run; the Regents and the Department would thereafter have jurisdiction over elementary and secondary education only. To those who deal in power and empire-building within the power structure, it had a certain appeal. Although nobody in the higher-education community's nonpublic sector would touch it with an eleven-foot pole, Nelson Rockefeller went for it not only once, but twice; on the first round, his commission refused to go along, and on the second, the allegedly predigested report was not adopted by the legislature.

Malcolm Wilson, who knew a great deal about education and the importance of an integrated governance system for *all* education, was too smart to try it again. Hugh Carey, however, made the effort; his commission (the Wessel Commission) was set up to do the same job, and did it. There it was, just as we knew it would be: a collection of specious and invalid reasons why higher education should be separately dealt with under the Governor's control.

This time, however, we could no longer count upon as many good friends in high places in the legislature, although there were still some around, particularly Warren Anderson, majority leader of the State Senate. I was concerned that the antipathy which had long been brewing against the Regents and Joe Nyquist on the busing issue could just be strong enough to win the day for the Governor's plan in the legislature. To forestall any such happening, I set up Regents' task forces to convince key members on both sides of the aisle in both houses that the independence of education from *gubernatorial* politics must be preserved. We reminded the solons that, after all, our state constitution bestowed authority over education upon the legislature, not the governor.

It worked. I will always recall a particularly gratifying sight: grizzled Senator Ed Mason, a Republican farmer from upstate whose special devil was Joe Nyquist, urging his Senate colleagues to kill a sneak separation bill palmed in by the Governor's office toward the close of the session in 1976. Thanks to Ed and others (and specifically to "Andy" Anderson), the Regents'—and Joe Nyquist's—aegis over higher education was preserved.

Stirrings on the Board Again

While my attention was taken up with the defense of the Regents against attacks from outside, some members of the Board were growing increasingly restive about their Commissioner.

What touched off this latest rumbling was a decision by Joe Nyquist, in his judicial capacity, about an integration problem in New York City. It was claimed that he had not followed the February 1975 guidelines laid down as state policy by the Regents; Joe, in response, claimed that he had done so, and that his decision was in line with the responsibilities handed to him by the law. This did not satisfy the concerned Regents at all, even when the introduction of additional material by the city school board was the basis for a revised Nyquist opinion in the case.

There was, however, an important constitutional-legislative question to be resolved here. I had always been uncomfortable with that part of the law which gave the Commissioner, in his judicial capacity, plenipotentiary authority to decide cases within the educational community without either the courts or the Board of Regents being able to review such decisions. I felt (and said) that court review was not the answer, but I also felt that the Regents, the board of directors of the educational enterprise, should at least have the *right* to review (on their own initiative, not on appeal from contesting parties) whether their chief executive officer, the Commissioner, had acted in accordance with their stated policy. That is not only a right but a responsibility of any corporate board of directors in the country. *I did not challenge Joe Nyquist's ruling in the particular case at issue;* my observation was that he was within the guidelines of our February 1975 statement. I did, however, engage the voluntary services of an old friend, State Supreme Court Justice Howard Hogan, who studied my suggestion and agreed with me that the law deserved to be changed so that the Regents would have review power *on issues of policy only*. By a divided vote, the Regents proposed such a measure to the legislature.

This action was immediately misinterpreted as a slap in Joe Nyquist's face and a resurrection of the busing issue, although it was certainly not my intention to do either.

What was growing in the back of my mind was the chilling realization that, if dissatisfaction among the Regents about Joe Nyquist's interpretations and applications of their policies continued to gather momentum, and if the Regents still had no recourse to a review of his decisions on policy grounds, we would inevitably have to confront the ultimate issue that had for so long been urged upon the Board by Joe's enemies—*his dismissal.* The message was short and to the point:

"You Regents are his bosses. You—and only you—can hire or fire a Commissioner of Education. Either control him—or discharge him."

Because I was personally convinced that Joe was trying his best to act as the Regents directed (and as he had pledged to do on many occasions), and because I knew of all his contributions to the cause of educational excellence, I wanted to avoid such a debate at all costs. It could only destroy the unity I was struggling so hard to achieve on the Board; whether Joe was retained or fired, it could only damage his reputation as an educational leader of the first rank. If the legislature could be convinced to grant the Regents policy-review power, the confrontation could be forestalled and perhaps avoided entirely. Although I arranged for it to be introduced as a legislative bill, it died aborning—killed, I am afraid, by Joe Nyquist's friends and sympathizers, who did not understand its significance.

Battle Lines Are Drawn

I continued to hope, fervently, that the discontent with Joe Nyquist which I perceived on the part of some Regents would remain individual, internal, and unexpressed beyond the confines of the Regents' room. If the anti-Nyquist ferment became organized, it was sure to be leaked to the press and the public—and the die would be cast. The vote to dismiss or not to dismiss Joe Nyquist would then be inevitable. Not even the Regents' Chancellor could keep it from happening.

Late in 1976, I was asked to attend an informal gathering of Regents at the Fort Orange Club, across from the State Education Building at Albany, to participate in a discussion about Joe Nyquist. This was the first indication that I had of any collective movement on the issue, and I was very deeply concerned. At the meeting, I learned that it was not the first such get-together—only the first about which I was informed. My presence was now requested primarily but not entirely as a courtesy; the Regents present had no gripes with their Chancellor, and I had requested at the start of my tenure as their leader that they spring "no surprises" on me. They were now complying with that request.

The agenda for the meeting was simple. The Board members there wanted me to understand that after considerable discussion and debate among themselves, they had concluded that Joe Nyquist was not living up to his responsibilities as our chief executive officer, that he had become a liability not only to the Regents but also to the cause of education in the state, that he had made himself (by his attitudes as well as his words) persona non grata to certain Regents he obviously disliked as well as to important legislators, that a "bill of particulars" specifying several dozen complaints against him was being prepared—and that he should be asked to resign. I was informed that if Joe refused to leave, there were *ten* Regents, two-thirds of the Board, ready to vote for his dismissal.

The size of the anti-Nyquist group surprised me, as did the identity of some of its members (the full list was provided to me at my request). A Regent whom I had never known to speak unkindly of Joe had apparently been subjected to heavy constituent pressure (plenty of that was brought upon me, so I understood the problem). One Regent on the anti-Nyquist list had chided me in a 1975 circular letter to the Board for causing "discomfort" to the Commissioner by a speech I made on integration; now that Regent (probably also under pressure) was willing to administer the ultimate in "discomfort"—dismissal. And, contrary to predicted form, *four of the five new Democrats elected to the Board in 1975 and 1976* were said to be against Joe's continuing as Commissioner of Education. Two of these four later switched to his support, but the stretched-out equation, Democratic = liberal = probusing = pro-Nyquist, proved to be an oversimplification.

What troubled me most about all this was the argument advanced by the group of Regents, all of whom I numbered as friends and still do, *that the retention of Joe Nyquist as Commissioner of Education jeopardized the future of my Chancellorship and the effectiveness of the Board.*

Chapter and verse were cited, including the items recounted earlier, indicating the unhappiness of many legislators with the Commissioner personally, with the way he handled his office, and with the Regents' continuing support of him. I was reminded how the hostility of the lawmakers had negatively affected the Regents and the Department. The Governor's office was not neglected in the summary presented to me; one of his more vocal cabinet commissioners, John Dyson, had repeatedly attacked Joe Nyquist as a "king" inflated by his own power (acquired through his continuing endorsement by the Regents). While Governor

Carey disclaimed sponsorship of Dyson's widely publicized swipes at Joe, he did not disavow them. Joe was a member of the Governor's cabinet, and I was given to understand that his attitude there was not appreciated by the Governor.

My initial reaction was that neither the Governor nor the legislature had any responsibility for or authority over the way the Regents and their Commissioner ran the educational system of the state; the group's response hit a note of realism. While the independence of education was certified in theory, the Governor was responsible for the education budget and various related matters (e.g., the power to set aside the Regents' quadrennial Master Plan for higher education, which Governor Carey actually did in reacting to our 1976 Plan). Further, I was reminded that the legislature, in addition to its budgetary power, has virtually complete authority over the Regents, per Article XI of the State Constitution, which specifies in clear language that the Board of Regents "shall be governed, and its corporate powers . . . may be increased, modified or diminished by the legislature. . . ." The point was well taken.

The message which my fellow-Regents were trying to convey to me was unmistakable: *Everything I was trying to do to recapture unity among the Regents and to restore the Board to its traditionally respected position of authority in New York's educational community was endangered by the retention of Joe Nyquist as Commissioner.*

If I accepted that premise, the conclusion to which it led was equally unmistakable: *It would be in my interest, as well as education's, for me to join, perhaps to lead, the action whereby Commissioner Nyquist would remove himself—or be removed.*

And if I demurred? It was made very, very plain: The movement to unseat Joe Nyquist would be carried through to its conclusion, however bitter and divisive the process might be. *And they had the votes to do it.*

Man in the Middle

It had been a long day. I was not only physically and mentally exhausted but stunned by the realization that what I had believed to be the individual, personal antagonism of some Regents against Joe Nyquist was broader and deeper than I knew, and that it had now jelled into a concerted, determined movement by what appeared to be a majority of Regents to oust him, one way or another.

As happens so often to those who accept leadership roles in public life, I found myself squarely in the middle of a battle *I could not win.*

If Joe survived, the internal animosity of Regents against the Commissioner and against each other because of the Commissioner would persist, as would the outside pressure upon the Board, to our detriment.

If Joe lost out, a conscientious public servant of long experience whose professional leadership was acknowledged by the educational community of the nation would, as I saw it, be unduly punished for his candor and his support of generally unpopular positions.

I needed time—time to organize my thoughts and decide upon the best course of action for me, as Chancellor, to take. Before leaving the meeting, I made several points clear to my colleagues:

First, I would not make any commitment to join, much less lead, the drive to oust Joe. I conceded that their arguments were food for thought, but cautioned them not to count on me as an ally.

Second, I intended to check personally with every Regent not present who had been named as one of the ten-member group pledged to the removal of the Commissioner; I was frankly skeptical about a few of those names, and said so. They had no objection.

Third, as Chancellor, at their request and in the interest of fairness to Joe, I would meet with Joe privately to inform him of what was in the wind and convey to him the group's hope that he would step down voluntarily. We all knew, I think, that although he was sixty-two and recovering from a recent bout with cardiovascular surgery, Joe Nyquist would in all likelihood reject such a suggestion; quitting was not in his character, especially quitting under fire. Nor would I urge him to quit. I would simply convey the wishes of the group of Regents to him and carry his response back to them; however, because of the seriousness of this very personal matter and his known heart condition, I would do this when I felt the moment was appropriate, albeit without undue delay. (My concern for Joe's heart problem was real; at one executive session, I had taken the unprecedented step of excusing him, because I had been informed that his resignation would be demanded then and there. Happily, it was not; cooler heads prevailed and the showdown was deferred.)

Finally, I wanted it understood that none of us would "go public" with even a hint of what was transpiring. If these Regents were sincere in hoping that Joe Nyquist might step down of his own accord, they would not foreclose that possibility by telling the world that he had been told to quit or be fired. The man's professional reputation—his career livelihood—was at stake; he *must* be given a fair chance to save face if he chose to do so. What's more, public knowledge of the move to unseat him would harden the positions of all involved, excite the passions of the educational community (already troubled by unsquelched rumors that the Governor and the legislative leaders were out to "get" Joe Nyquist), triple the already mounting pressure on the individual members of the Board, and generate all sorts of unwarranted and inaccurate speculation that could only hurt the Regents, the State Education Department—and Joe Nyquist himself.

When I left the Fort Orange Club and returned to my motel for an uneasy night's sleep, I *thought* that I had the unanimous agreement of all present that our discussions and their possible action against Joe would not be revealed to *anyone* except our fellow-Regents and (through me) Joe himself.

I was wrong.

Somebody Spills the Beans

Before I had a chance to sit down with Joe and explain the situation and the options to him, Leonard Buder of the *New York Times* called me. Len said flatly that he knew all about the Albany meeting and the move to oust Joe; he was even able to give me (correctly) details, including the names of the ten Regents who had been identified to me as anti-Nyquist votes. Obviously, he had been fully briefed by a Regent who had been at the Fort Orange Club meeting. No one else knew the precise details that Len repeated to me. Was I prepared to deny the story, which he would run in the next morning's edition of the *Times?*

I was furious. Pulling the cork on this extremely touchy matter was damnably unfair, not only to Commissioner Nyquist but to me as Chancellor and to the Board itself, just recovered from the busing fracas and hardly ready to face yet another controversy, another crisis of public confidence. All the work we had put in to restore consensus, unity, and calm to the Board seemed about to slip away because of a broken promise.

But I was not about to lie to Len Buder. He had the truth, and he was determined to tell it. Once before, by committee agreement rather than personal choice, I told less than the truth to a *Times* reporter, Gene Maeroff, only to be embarrassed by the facts within minutes. So I confirmed the accuracy of Len's story, indicated that the issue was by no means certain, and let him know (as he reported later) that I was very unhappy with the "leak."

Who leaked the story to Len Buder? I am 99 percent sure that I know. But as long as that one percent of doubt exists, I will not speculate in public print. We will have to await that Regent's posthumously published autobiography for confirmation—and that Regent is still a good friend whose posthumous autobiography I hope I never see.

When I hung up the phone with Len Buder, I knew what I must do, and it wasn't easy. Joe Nyquist *had* to know about the move to oust him, and he had to know it from me—before some newshawk collared him and before he read the next day's *New York Times*. I called him, told him the whole story, and arranged to meet with him at our earliest possible convenient moment. As I anticipated, he would not resign voluntarily, not in any event, but certainly not now, under public fire. And I could not blame him.

The die was cast.

Proceeding to Judgment

The rest of the story has been pretty well told and retold, but not completely.

Once the cat was out of the bag, I no longer enjoyed the luxury of remaining uncommitted in the hope that my neutrality would enable me, as Chancellor, to do *something* which would avoid the rancor and bitterness of a final confrontation.

When the anti-Nyquist Regents argued that Commissioner Nyquist's departure would eventually lead to an improved atmosphere not only among the Regents but toward the Regents, their point was not lost on me. They were very likely right—and it had been my stated hope and promise to restore the high standing of the Board of Regents.

Because I had worked so closely and cordially with Joe, as Regent, Vice Chancellor, and now Chancellor, I was aware of some of the factors that bothered many people who did not know his good points as well as I did.

It was quite evident, for example, that he thoroughly disliked two of the Regents, whom I will not name here, just as it was evident that they wasted no love on him. Once, when he extended to Barbara and me a typically hospitable invitation to stay as his and Jan's house guests when all the Regents and their spouses were there for an outdoor dinner, I asked him quite bluntly if he would be willing to extend the same overnight invitation to every member of the Board. With equal bluntness, he replied that he could not do so, without being hypocritical, to the two whom I shall not identify. I thanked him for his frankness, and I know he understood why I could not accept his hospitality if *all* of my Regents colleagues would not be welcomed on an equal basis. It is not difficult for men of principle to understand each other.

Like any good chief of staff, Joe was protective of his professional colleagues in the Department—sometimes with complete justification, sometimes *too* protective. I was not always sure that he understood and accepted the changing nature of the Board; the Regents of not much earlier times were inclined to accept the staff's recommendations without much question, but the new breed (of which I was one) were "from Missouri," requiring thorough proof that staff recommendations were justifiable. For example, when I was designated by Chancellor McGovern as chairman of the Regents' Committee on Higher and Professional Education in 1973, I insisted (with the Chancellor's backing) that colleges and universities be warned against offering, in their catalogs and brochures, degree programs *which the Regents had not yet approved.* Until then, it was almost a foregone conclusion that staff okays would be rubber-stamped by the Regents, but that was not my notion of how the interests of New York students should be protected by the Regents, as charged by law. In 1973 and thereafter, the Regents examined each application and staff recommendation carefully before voting formal approval or rejecting a request. Joe Nyquist made no bones about his belief that his staff's original recommendations should have been accepted. That was typical Joe—he picked his staff, and they did their jobs properly; he saw no point in any further questions. If the Regents declined to accept staff recommendations pro forma, he considered that an adverse criticism of them, and him. If, as sometimes happened, a Regent was overacid in contesting the findings of a staff member, Joe took it as a personal affront and reacted accordingly. It is not difficult to understand how a record of small clashes began to build and to be held against Joe by those with whom he tangled—even when he was right.

Half of the public-school students in New York State attend the schools of New York City, which is a subdivision of the state. Although the State Constitution assigns to the Regents and the state government responsibility for "the maintenance and support of a system of free common schools, wherein *all* the children of this state may be educated" (emphasis supplied), the Regents and their Commissioners at Albany had traditionally allowed the city's Board of Education and Chancellor to operate their own fiefdom with a minimum of state intervention. Only on urgent petition did we act on city matters like the school decentralization of 1969. There was no constitutional support for this "benign neglect"; it was just the way things were. And the Regents were happy to leave them that way. So was Joe Nyquist.

I was not. The nationwide and statewide deterioration in the quality of educational services was particularly evident in New York City's schools, some of which, according to some accounts, were virtually out of control. Although I recognized that the largest metropolis in the land was a giant, complex machine, difficult to manage and subject to constant political maneuvering, the kids in the city's public schools were still included among "all the children of the state," responsibility for whose education was given by the constitution to the Board of Regents, over which I presided. After 1975, when Lou Yavner and other Regents initiated a project to bring together all elements of the city's educational and social community to study and recommend action to help the schools, I backed the idea heartily. Joe Nyquist, on the other hand, did not think very much of it. He felt, I am sure, that we were stepping into a morass from which there would be no educational gain and no escape with dignity should we fail. His reluctance was another cause for discontent on the Board. As of this writing, we still do not know whether he was right or wrong; to the best of my knowledge, the project continues.

These were some of the sore points which had gradually alienated Joe from certain members of the body he served as chief executive officer—a body which could fire him at will, and which was considering doing just that. We will never know all of the personal reasons why those Regents unhappy with Joe finally came to the point of opposing his retention as Commissioner, but we do know that they were many. Some observers dismissed the case as a one-issue hatchet job—Joe Nyquist's downfall was all because of his hard-line stance in favor of busing. *Not so.* Busing was *one* of the reasons and a concern of *some* of the Regents, but it was only one, and it did not, by itself, tip the scales against Joe.

My own course of action was clear.

Joe Nyquist and I had differed on many issues and proposals, but our differences were honest, and we honored each other's right to his own opinion. Some felt that he had not acted in accordance with Regents' policy; I disagreed. Most important, I *knew* Joe Nyquist, and why he did what he did in the way he did. To cut off the brilliant career of an educational leader of national stature, a man whose record of accomplishment was acknowledged by his peers everywhere, was excessive punishment—and for what? Stubbornness? Abrasiveness? Lack of diplomacy and tact? Small sins, possibly, but hardly enough to justify such a final verdict.

Putting aside my concerns about the future problems which the Board and I might face if Joe stayed on (and I will confess that those concerns were serious), I set about the uphill task of saving his job for him.

A Familiar Political Phenomenon Takes Shape

The fall of 1976 wore on, as I worked strenuously with Regents Jack Allan, Ken Clark, Harold Newcomb, many of our retired Regents, and others, to garner support for Joe. We did win back two of the ten originally claimed as anti-Nyquist votes, but our best efforts still left us one short of a majority. Moreover, the unwillingness of some good friends on the Board even to talk with me about the question told me how hardened and immutable their positions had become—a bad sign.

And I saw a developing scenario much like that which had killed off the proposed new State Constitution produced by the 1967 Convention to which I had been a delegate. It shapes up this way:

When the resolution of many broad questions must come down to a single yes-or-no decision on one combined proposal into which they are all incorporated, those who may approve some elements of the proposal but hold strong convictions against other parts of it are likely to vote "no" in the final showdown.

That was what was happening in the Nyquist case. With my proposal for Regents' review of the Commissioner's policy decisions down the drain, there was but one question to be decided: keep Joe Nyquist or fire him. I could see the negative combination building, and it did not bode well for Joe.

November 19, 1976 — the Ax Falls

The Regents' November meeting is traditionally held in the undersized offices maintained by the State Education Department in New York City—a tradition which I unsuccessfully tried to scrap for reasons of efficiency, but which my colleagues upheld as a "showing of the flag" in our biggest urban center. So it was that in November 1976, New York City was the site of the final chapter of the Joe Nyquist story.

A long, bitter debate in executive session took up most of the preliminary day, November 18th. I have never presided over a more acrimonious proceeding. Regents were so emotionally involved that they stood and shouted and pointed fingers and waved fists; had not the windows been closed against the November winds, we could have been heard for blocks up and down Madison Avenue.

Traditionally, Chancellors have kept order among their orderly colleagues by tapping gently with a tiny gavel on a small square of identical wood. A silver panel adorns the handle of the gavel; it reads: "Olive wood from the Holy Land, presented to the Regents of the University of the State of New York by Jacob L. Holtzmann, Regent 1949–1958." Although it had survived for almost two decades, my savage pounding for order during the Nyquist debate split the wooden block sharply in two, for which I have silently apologized to the late, respected Regent Holtzmann many times.

Joe was excused during the heat of argument, but it was agreed that he be presented with the "bill of particulars," with enough time to organize his responses and present them to the Regents in another executive session. He did so, more calmly than I might have done under similar circumstances, and he was politely received by all the Regents present, but it was easy to see that not one mind had been changed, either way.

He came up one vote shy. After the talking was finished and Joe was excused, the thing was nailed down: eight for dismissal, seven against. On the brink of tears, I called a recess and told Joe of the verdict, apologizing for not having been able to change the one vote that would have made the difference. He had expected the bad news and received it without emotion.

The formal vote would be taken at the open, public meeting on the following day, November 19. Some of the profiring Regents asked that I consider avoiding a roll-call vote by simply announcing that the Regents, in executive session on a personnel matter, had decided to terminate Joe's service as Commissioner. I would not hear of it—anything less than a roll-call vote would be branded by the media as a star-chamber proceeding, and we were being portrayed in a bad enough light without that. What's more, a man about to be deprived of a career is entitled to know who is responsible. I had no intention of permitting a rehash of the debate; although I knew I would be criticized for the decision (and I was), the public airing of charges against Joe would have been rubbing salt into already-too-painful wounds. The Regents were told that they could file statements for the printed record of the meeting.

The morning of November 19, 1976, one of the most difficult days of my life, found the cramped Regents' Room filled with press, radio and TV people, staff, friends of Joe and Jan who had been quietly told what was about to happen, and spectators—including a fidgety throng of Westchester County mothers accompanied by wide-eyed little kids festooned with placards pleading SAVE OUR SCHOOL! who stumbled into the jammed room over wires and tripods and feet, determined to focus attention upon the feared closing of an elementary school building in their local district—a matter with which the Regents were powerless to deal. I summoned help from Tom Sheldon, Deputy Commissioner for Elementary and Secondary Education (who was to resign publicly later that day, after the Nyquist dismissal); he led the Westchester contingent into another room and explained the facts to them, while I prepared for the voting on Joe. It had to be the next order of business, as the media would not leave until it was done, and the prospect of accomplishing anything else in the prevailing confusion was remote.

Having established a semblance of order, I recognized, by prearrangement, Vice Chancellor Carl Pforzheimer, who rose to offer (in a voice filled with emotion) the resolution: The Regents thanked Commissioner Nyquist for his many contributions to education in New York State and terminated his employment as Commissioner, effective on June 30, 1977. Several seconds were heard, and capable Bill Carr, Secretary of the Board, was directed to call the roll. A "yes" vote was to dismiss Joe; a "no" vote was to retain him. By tradition, the Vice Chancellor voted first and the Chancellor last. Bill began his ritual:

Vice Chancellor Pforzheimer: Yes.

Regent Allan: No. [One apiece.]

Regent Indelicato: Yes.

Regent Clark: No. [Tied at two each.]

Regent Newcomb: No. [For a brief moment, Joe was ahead.]

Regent Genrich: Yes. [Tied again.]

Regent Griffith: Yes.

Regent Klein: Yes.

Regent Jovanovich: Yes.

Regent Kendall: Yes. [That made it seven against Joe— with one more "yes" needed to dismiss him.]

Regent Batista: No.

Regent Yavner: Yes.

That did it. The reporters could count; the decibel level in the room rose sharply, the cameras started whirring, and there was a mad rush for the few available phones. Through the din, Bill Carr continued with his roll call, although the outcome was already certain: Joe Nyquist had been fired.

Regent Chodos: No.

Regent Barell: No.

Chancellor Black [I summoned what remaining voice I had]: NO.

But who cared? Eight-to-seven or whatever—what difference did it make? I announced the count: eight in favor of the resolution, seven opposed; the resolution carried. Joe Nyquist had been fired.

And that's the story.

At least, that is as much of the story as I care to recall a half-decade-plus after the event. Perhaps some of the other participants will tell us of their personal recollections; until such time, the narrative you have just read is all that I can offer.

There was an awkward, embarrassing press conference later, after the furor had subsided a bit. What do you intend to do now, Commissioner? (I will continue to serve until June 30 of next year, and will then move on to whatever is next for me.) What will the Regents do now, Chancellor? (Begin looking for a new Commissioner.) How do you plan to do that? (We will organize a search for a successor; obviously, plans have not been made for it as yet.) On and on the empty, painful questions went—until I said "Thank you" and the conference was over.

Later, I issued a statement which was intended to placate the educational community, already in a ferment over the course of events. Because their main cause for concern was the widely held belief that the Governor and the legislative leadership had pressured the Regents to fire Joe Nyquist, I thanked the Governor and the legislative leadership for *not* intervening. That was what I said, and I had no evidence upon which to base any other conclusion. But to this day, I am not really certain that the Governor and the legislators played no role in the matter.

In retrospect, I find it difficult to assign any other reason than pressure as an explanation for a few of the anti-Nyquist votes. But I have no proof and I make no charges.

Joe Nyquist served out his term and departed without fanfare on June 30, 1977. He and Jan left Albany and moved further upstate to the lake country; at this writing, he is a commuting vice-president of Pace University with an office at Pace's Westchester campus.

After a long search, the Regents chose Joe's former Executive Deputy Commissioner, Gordon M. Ambach, from among a large number of highly qualified candidates for the job of Commissioner. Gordon worked well with me during the last three years of my tenure as Chancellor and continues to do a fine job for New York.

And the relationship between the Regents and the State Education Department on the one hand and the Governor and legislative leaders on the other was restored to its fruitful effectiveness of earlier years. In that respect at least, the opponents of Joe Nyquist can cite practical results in support of their arguments.

But excellence is excellence—and if I had to do it again today, I'd still vote to keep Joe Nyquist as Commissioner. When I've made up my mind, I can be stubborn, too.

Conclusion

THERE it is, at least for now.

Much more remains to be said, and to be done.

Some readers may be disappointed not to find references to such important educational matters as the control of proprietary schools (profit-making specialty institutions), the importance of libraries and museums to our national education effort, the need for a unitary approach to the education, examination, certification, and disciplining of teaching professionals, the persistent problem of phony diploma mills, the ominous significance of declining abilities in reading and math to national defense, the value of in-prison education in reducing recidivism, and many, many other subjects. Perhaps next time . . .

Some of my friends and associates will, I know, wonder why there has been no chapter on "values" and "values education," inasmuch as my concern for standards of excellence pervades the whole fabric of this book. An explanation of its absence is in order.

For several years, the Regents struggled to produce a position paper on values, as the next in a series of such papers we issued in the 1960s and early 1970s. Despite all the time and effort and work put in by Regent Frank McGinley and his colleagues, the Board could not arrive at a statement upon which we all were prepared to agree, and which said something of . . . well, something of value, something that had meaning above and beyond a collection of pious hopes and shopworn platitudes, something that would be a ringing call for action.

I think that the Regents' failure to settle on a "values" statement stems from the nation's overlong immersion in the theory that if a proposition isn't agreeable to *everyone,* without dissent or exception, the schools should not promulgate it as a positive value. The rationale for this retreat from values seems false to me. It is suggested that no dissenter should ever be embarrassed, and that such embarrassment would be an unconscionable suppression of his right to differ. Indeed, we appear to have discovered yet one more new right as a result—a right to escape the consequences of one's beliefs, words, and actions. Whatever the case, the complete-unanimity requirement makes teachable "values" hard to come by.

The problem is not traceable entirely to the U.S. Supreme Court's *Engel* ban against prayers in the public schools, although that is part of the problem, most values being essentially the fruit of moral judgments. Morality is built on sandy soil indeed if our highest moral authority is not a Supreme Being but a majority of the humans in some lawmaking body. But that is not all.

The problem also turns up when we think of patriotism, which is not a religious matter. Yes, the flag salute and the Pledge of Allegiance are still practiced in the public schools, but that seems to be it. The Regents of Teddy Roosevelt's time published a fat blue volume with the U.S. flag on the cover, entitled *Patriotism* and packed with curriculum guidelines and reference materials for teachers to use in their classrooms. What would happen if we were to reprint that book today? There would be roars of outrage from the liberal-modernists, and we would hear, ad nauseam, Samuel Johnson's remark about patriotism being the last refuge of a scoundrel. (Those who have read James Boswell know that Johnson was not alluding to love of country but to patriotic pretense as a cloak for self-interest.) Yet the National Education Association in 1981 suggested that its million-plus teacher-members inform their students that all of American society is inherently racist and that virtually no progress has been made by blacks—two charges that are highly controversial but are to be presented to the children as factual. In rebuttal, Albert Shanker posed a very pertinent question: "Should students leave the classroom filled with shame about what America once was—and without any sense of pride about what it is now and is trying to be?" Unasserted values wilt for lack of support. We continue to stifle our own reaffirmation of those elements which make our country great, while its critics continue to pound away at perceived national shortcomings past and present, risking almost no challenge within the educational community.

Our mistake has been, and is, substituting the requirement of *unanimity* for that of *consensus,* and limply assenting to the notion that if we speak affirmatively about values that are generally accepted, we are "imposing our views upon others."

We will have no hope of restoring values to the public schools until we are willing to say (and are permitted by the courts to say): "Most Americans believe that X is a positive value. Those who do not so believe have a perfect right to differ, and we will listen to what they have to say. *But we will not be silent* about Value X, we will not ignore it, simply because some people don't consider it a value."

But wait a minute . . .

Here I am, jaw set, eyes glinting, mounting my white charger and leveling my lance again, ready for yet one more battle.

That battle must wait for another time, perhaps another book. This one is finished. Or it will be finished, after this final word: *Don't give up on American education, especially on American public schools.*

We once had a fine system, probably the finest in the world—so we know it can be the finest again. We've let things slip in recent years, and we admit it; the evidence is there, and we cannot deny it. But we know, also, what must be done to bring our schools and colleges back to their former glory, and beyond. . . .

If you close this book with the realization that our unswerving, irreversible commitment to our nation's future generations must be a commitment to *excellence in education for all children*—a goal from which we must not be diverted by political, social, egalitarian, or even typically American compassionate considerations—then writing it will have been worthwhile . . . for that commitment to excellence, to quality, to standards, is the *one* sure way to restore American education's preeminence in the world.

Thanks for listening.